Disclaimer And Copyright Information

Copyright 2011 Ben Settle

No part of this publication may be reproduced in whole or in part, or transmitted in any form or by any means, electronic or mechanical, including photocopying, recording, or by any information storage and retrieval system, without permission in writing from the publisher.

Published by:
Settle, LLC
PO Box 866
Long Beach, WA 98631
ISBN: 978-0-9795786-3-2

While all attempts have been made to provide accurate and verifiable information in this publication, neither the Author nor the Publisher assumes any responsibility for errors, inaccuracies or omissions. Any slights of people or organizations are unintentional. This publication is not intended for use as a source of legal or accounting advice. Both the Author and Publisher want to stress that the information contained herein may be subject to varying federal, state and local laws and regulations. All users are advised to retain competent legal counsel to determine what federal, state and local laws or regulations may apply to the user's particular business. The Publisher and Author make no promise or representation that you will make a certain amount of money, or any money, or not lose money, as a result of using our products and services. The use of this publication should be based on your own due diligence and you agree that the Publisher or Author are not liable for your success or failure.

NOTE FROM THE AUTHOR:

Before you read, please note the following "disclaimers":

First, while this book is blatantly marketed towards Christian entrepreneurs, non-Christians will still get a tremendous amount of value from it. The principles inside can be used by anyone, for any business category, selling any kind of product (assuming you're not breaking the law or selling anything unethical or illegal).

Two, I purposely edited out as much of the doctrinal content as possible (more or less). There really wasn't that much, anyway. But the last thing I wanted was for anyone getting so distracted by a doctrine they vehemently disagree with that they miss all the great business lessons inside.

And finally, as far as any Christian ideas or Biblical quotes go... always, Always, ALWAYS see what the Bible says for yourself before believing what you read here. We're only human, after all, and none of us are beyond correction or learning.

Oh, and one more thing.

You do not have to read this book in any specific order. It is designed so you can open it to any page, at any time, and find a powerful business building tip you can apply to your business at will. Just go through the table of contents or flip through the pages and read whatever stands out. Enjoy!

      -Ben Settle
      www.BenSettle.com

Introduction

I've known Ben Settle for almost a decade. By "known," it has been solely a long-distance relationship because I've never met Ben. Still, I know Ben better than many people I see in person several times a month. Ben Settle is uniquely qualified to produce a book such as this. His combination of being a world-class advertising copywriter, his salvation, his tell-it-as-it-is attitude, and his realistic views of the way people and business work, put him at the Captain's helm for a book like this.

This is a fantastic book. The fact I am one chapter's subject has nothing to do with my saying that. As a matter of fact if anything, it makes me hesitant to write this… But I'll say without hesitation the rest of the book is fantastic and leave the judging of my chapter to you where it belongs.

The impact Christians had on the world for centuries was obvious. All the hospitals were built by Christians. All the schools were built and run by Christians. Even Harvard started out as a training place for the clergy. (How things change; it now solely equips enemies of the clergy.) Somehow we gave up the initiative and decided that government can do a better job. Things have gone downhill ever since. The government runs the healthcare. The government now runs the schools. We even let the government begin dictating how funerals and burials were to be administered and where. 100 years ago, the strongest witness we had in our arsenal was pointing out the church window to the graveyard in the churchyard: everybody's destination. Without that visual reality, the death of the unsaved is a minor annoyance at worst and certainly not something many churches these days seem to worry about much.

The one place I can see where Christians have fought the good fight to get something back that we willingly gave up is in the realm of home-education. Christians are leading the fight. As the number of home-educated students increase, the government schools have a harder time competing. The government tries to put legal bindings on home-education but so far their attempt has been futile. A band of strong-willed, Godly believers, especially in the late 1970s, began fighting for the right to home-educate their own children. Their battle turned into graduates who are today's most productive, happiest, intelligent, and trustworthy adults.

Why can't we fight to regain other territory?

The most important territory we can fight for, in my opinion, is America's business. We see what happens when a business is run by Christians in the way it should be run. The business often thrives (e.g., Chik-Fil-A), the employees are happy, and the customers are even happier. The highest earthly calling we have is to serve others. Only a Christian understands what that means. Business will be successful when business serves others. A business that does its utmost to do just that should be the winning business in its sector. A business that serves its customers should experience profitable growth and runaway word-of-mouth advertising.

Christian Business Secrets gets the ball rolling. Here are interviews by Christian leaders in several fields, leaders who excel at what they do: serving others. Here they open their hearts and mouths for us. They tell us what they did wrong and what they learned along the way. They tell us how being a Christian business owner differs, what is possible, and perhaps most important: what is expected from Christian businesses. For to whomsoever much is given, of him shall be much required, a wonderful exhortation by Luke (popularly paraphrased in 1962 as, With great power comes great responsibility).

If you have a business your business will benefit from all you read here. Everything you implement should bring results, both short-term and long-term, both on earth and in Heaven. Because when you serve others in a true, Godly way, and understand that a profit is required to continue serving others, you will have a formula for success. Having read this entire book that you hold in your hands, let me assure you that if anything, there is simply too much great information here for you to apply in one week, a month, or even a year. That is fine. Just begin applying what you can. Tell others about it. Buy copies for your employees. Expect from them what you expect from yourself. They will value you for that.

In 5 years, businesses owned or run by Christians all across the nation will blossom if they follow the advice here. Who knows, in 10 years somebody might notice how successful the home-education was, and how Christian business owners achieve runaway success that others don't, and perhaps somebody might want to try to get healthcare back where it belongs: in the hands of private groups of Christians who love life. In 15 years perhaps the intrusive nature of the United States government will finally be pushed aside and run by George Washington-like leaders who understand that freedom breeds success.

Christian Business Secrets can be a first step towards nation changing. I do believe that is possible. It is my hope and prayer that you do too before you are done.

                Yours because of Him,
                Greg Perry
                March, 2011

Table Of Contents

1. Businessman Abducted By Aliens And Rescued By God.....7

2. Selling For Souls On eBay.....66

3. How To Have "Supernatural" Success In Business.....136

4. Ancient Business Secrets Of The Bible.....171

5. Survival Of The Wisest.....221

6. The Business Of Forgiveness.....271

7. Secrets Of A Marketplace Minister.....333

Businessman Abducted By Aliens And Rescued By God

Interview with Guy Malone
www.AlienResistance.com

BEN SETTLE: How did you get started in your ministry and business, and what were some of the challenges you faced along the way?

GUY MALONE: It was the Heaven's Gate cult suicide that got my attention and kind of called me into public speaking or ministry or writing (really writing at first) about this topic.

As you know, background wise, I was a childhood experiencer of this phenomenon. I grew up having visitor experiences, I believe, in my house before I was a Christian. I was under the impression or delusion that I was an alien abductee, because I had all the memories and stuff that people were reporting on in books and television, but I kept it to myself for the most part because the couple times I shared it with girlfriends or something like that, they'd dump me right off the bat. So I learned real quickly to keep my mouth shut about this. After I became a Christian, I snapped and realized this is not truly alien, this is demonic deception. The first church I went to taught heavily on spiritual warfare and the unseen realm, so I got a crash course right at the beginning of my Christian walk and I felt personally set free from it. So that's one element. But even as an adult Christian I still didn't want to tell people about my past or what I believed, because I'd already learned the lesson, the rejection, that happens when you do. So I kept quiet and I was just living my happy little life. I was in sales and selling oil drilling investments at $10,000 a pop, commission only, and had a nice place to live. But when the Heavens Gate cult suicide became public, that these people killed themselves based on what they believed aliens were saying about the Bible, I personally felt somehow responsible.

I always felt called to write a book on this explaining my views, but I was personally waiting until my parents died because I didn't want to embarrass them. But when this happened, it seemed like a sin of omission in that if I had shared this information that I have, this understanding, maybe one, maybe none, maybe all 39 of those people might not have killed themselves. They might not have believed the deceptive doctrine. I had the information that I could have shared to help those people make a better decision and I wouldn't do it. I was selfish and didn't want to be publicly embarrassed. I didn't want to embarrass my family. After that happened, I was moved to act. I don't really feel responsible because I didn't do anything, but I failed to act in time and I didn't want to see it happen again. I just realized this end times' deception is becoming so prominent now. This is the same year that Phoenix sighting happened. It was on the front page of *USA Today*, *UFOs Over Phoenix*. My own older brother, who somehow contacted me after the Phoenix sighting, said, "The truth is getting out now," because he was a big believer in UFOs. We both were kind of growing up. That hit very close to home when he contacted me. My own brother is falling for this deception. He could be the next Heaven's Gate cult suicide.

Finally, the way I phrased it back then, I got to know a couple of my geek friends a little better and got help with FrontPage and making the first website. I wrote down both my personal experiences as well as my New Testament theology on what I felt was behind all of this. Then we put it out there on the Internet for people to find. The dynamic I ran into early on was I could have written *Come Sail Away* without revealing anything personal. I didn't have to tell my story that I was an experiencer or anything like that, but I realized that I needed to early on because I knew people weren't going to like what I was saying. "It's not really aliens. It's all demonic." Nobody wants that information. That's not what they're generally looking for or wanting to hear. The dynamic that I got feedback on immediately was because I shared the graphic details and the private hell of my own life, some people were like, "I don't agree or I don't like what you're saying, but you of all people have definitely earned the right to say it and to have an opinion on this subject. You had the motivation to do the research and find out what's going on."

So I had to share them both at the same time, both my ideas and my experiences. The funny thing is that was back when the Internet was still pretty new, late 90s, '97-'98. If you had a cool web page and you emailed Art Bell, they'd link to you. I went from getting 20 hits a day to 600 overnight.

BEN SETTLE: Do they still link to you from there?

GUY MALONE: No, now it's www.CoastToCoastAM.com, but it used to be www.ArtBell.com. Interestingly enough, the webmaster was a Christian. He was also the webmaster for his Church, wherever he lived, so you could email him directly and request the link and he would post it. They posted them chronologically, the link of the day. For a while I was there at ArtBell.com and at the very top, the first thing you saw was *Come Sail Away: UFO Phenomenon & the Bible*, www.SeekYe1.com. That's the day that overnight I got 600 hits and a load of email. Then chronologically, I began moving down further and further on the links list. Now I don't even know if ArtBell.com is his. But within a month your link was gone. You just got a ton of exposure for that month. Back in the Internet that long ago, the people that were looking at the site also began linking to it because – oddly, and this was done very intentionally – it looks like a new age site and it still kind of does. It had a black background and that just wasn't done by Christians back then.

BEN SETTLE: That's really brilliant actually. And you did that on purpose?

GUY MALONE: Yes, definitely on purpose. I didn't want it to look like a Christian website. I wanted to suck people in, give them a little bit of my story up front, and then they were getting the Gospel presented to them before they even knew what they'd gotten themselves into.

BEN SETTLE: That's interesting. You're not pitching them anything up front. You're just trying to get a hearing.

GUY MALONE: Exactly. The major thing was all these new age cult websites started linking to it left and right, and they would only look at the Home page and they'd be like, "Oh, UFOs and the Bible! This is cool!" but they wouldn't take the time to read it. They'd just link to it. At the same time, in the late 90s, I would e-mail or submit the site to the major Christian search engines or link directories, and every one of them rejected me because they wouldn't look past my Home page for the content. I remember I used to get in email arguments with these webmasters. "It is a Christian thing. I will fax you a letter from my church, endorsing this view." They just couldn't get past the topic, and I ran into that in Roswell as well, as the dynamic repeated itself.

What were some of the challenges I faced along the way? One of the biggest parts of the story is bouncing back from rejection and continuing on with what I thought God was leading me to do. It was really the foundation of everything this ministry's been about, because when I got the calling and the affirmation from my church in Nashville to move to Roswell, to do this as a missionary type kind of thing, I had no plans of opening a store front. I had no plans of ever holding conferences or public speaking. I simply had a book in hand now. It was online for free to read, but now I had it in hard copy. The biggest vision I had for moving to Roswell was to get that book placed in all the tourism hotspots and then set up reorder procedures for the places that would carry it if it sold, then move back to Nashville in six or nine months. That was 1999.

BEN SETTLE: You ended up staying quite a bit longer.

GUY MALONE: Yeah, but it's Roswell's own fault. That's what I loved pointing out to them. The UFO Museum you see when you visit Roswell, that lady that runs it… Well, I've got a top 10 list – jokingly, I don't really – but I've got my top 10 reasons this person hates Guy Malone. I've earned quite a few of them. I did say in a public interview that was published right here in the local monthly free newspaper that came out. They did an interview with me and I told them that story about what happened when I got here. The UFO Museum would not carry the book because it dealt with religion, they said. Then the Christian bookstore, the big one on Main Street, wouldn't carry the book either because it dealt with UFOs. I was completely stunned. I moved here with a vision and a plan to get my book placed where I thought it would be most effective and the demand would be. I was under the delusion that the church of Roswell was going to welcome me with open arms. You know, "Oh, wow, finally a Christian view on UFOs." Well, that didn't happen either. It was just rejection after rejection and I was stymied. I had to get a job waiting tables and sat around for six months kind of depressed, rejected, and not knowing what the heck to do next. I said in I think the 2005 lecture that I was obviously between a rock and a hard place, the intersection of Rock and Hard Place Avenue. That is my address. It must have been God. I hooked up with Joe and Chris and started working on the www.AlienResistance.org site within like a month or two after moving here. Locally the rejection thing was big. At least we were creating this Internet presence that was getting linked to us being accepted worldwide both by Christians and non.

I finally just got the idea, I realized it's not just me, there are other Christian books on this subject. I opened that ministry storefront downtown as a bookstore offering Biblical perspectives on UFOs and aliens to the tourists that would come here. Again, it's Roswell's fault. The UFO Museum, if they'd just carried my book, I'd have left probably. If the Christian bookstore there would have just carried my book, I'd probably have left because I would have felt, "Okay, mission accomplished. They've got my address. I'll ship them more if they sell." It was the rejection factor that meant, "Well, I'm here. Now what are you going to do?"

BEN SETTLE: I know it's not an exact analogy, but it reminds me of that scripture where the prophet is never respected in their own country. You're actually trying to do God's work and the Christian bookstores are not letting you or the churches or anything.

GUY MALONE: Right. In both cases, I understood where they were coming from. They didn't want to deal with the controversy and the flack they would receive from their customers and people walking through there. The UFO Museum had already experienced a history of getting yelled at by religious people and the local Christian church that what they were doing was demonic. The funny thing is I'm standing in their bookstore and they're saying, "We don't carry books that deal with religion." I pointed to three and I said, "Yes, you do." She goes, "Well, those are old and we're not reordering them." The thing is they were receiving so much flack from local Christians, I sympathized. I know how mean-spirited Christians can be sometimes about stuff. I sympathized.

The same thing with the Christian bookstore owner. I know how his customers might react if they saw this new age looking book sitting on the shelf up there. I did understand. I sympathized with both points of view. I was the one putting them in a hard place. I understood perfectly why the UFO Museum wouldn't carry it because they didn't want the flack from Christians. I understood exactly why the Christian bookstore wouldn't carry it because he didn't want to hear the flack from Christians.

BEN SETTLE: If you could go back, would you try to make two different versions of the book – one that would have maybe more of a Christian cover and maybe the beginning is different, just to kind of set them up because they're Christians and talk to them? Do you think that would have worked had you done something like that?

GUY MALONE: It might have. That might have been a wiser approach, but it wasn't necessarily the book. The book cover, he told me, was the reason he rejected it. He specifically said because it dealt with UFOs. They didn't carry Chuck Missler's book either, the *Alien Encounters*. It was already published by the time I got here. I looked around. There were no Christian books on UFOs in the Christian bookstore in Roswell, New Mexico, oddly enough. You would think that would be the biggest market of any city. You would think the ability to make sales would override having to deal with angry people that just don't get it. But no, I don't think it would have worked. At least not at that store in that city, because they already had a standing policy apparently.

BEN SETTLE: Makes you wonder why they were in Roswell.

GUY MALONE: Well, they live there. They were born there. They grew up there.

BEN SETTLE: Maybe they should have gone to Las Cruces or something then.

GUY MALONE: I didn't picture the demand was there. That was the rationale for coming to Roswell and for opening the storefront. This is the one place in the world people are coming to day in and day out year round, because they want the truth about UFOs and aliens. I believed I had it, so I just plopped myself down and made myself available and offered this Biblical perspective on UFOs and aliens to people that were coming to Roswell. That's a funny thing, man. They're coming here, they're paying money to travel, they're like, "Please, I'll pay you if can just tell me the truth. What do you have?" It's all over town.

BEN SETTLE: You're in front of that moving parade. That's the ideal way to sell anything is to get in front of the moving parade and not have to chase the parade but be in front of it. That's exactly the best way to do it.

GUY MALONE: That's more or less how it started. The challenge was the constant rejection and the closed doors. That had to be measured against I guess the calm, the fact that God did send me here. Of that much I was sure. I'm supposed to be doing this, but I just had to get through the six months of depression and seek God for, "What am I supposed to do now?" Because everything I had planned, everything I envisioned, fell flat basically the first week I was here, and I'm like, "Uh-oh, now what?"

BEN SETTLE: How does that saying go? "If you want to make God laugh, just tell Him your plans?"

GUY MALONE: I've never heard that before.

BEN SETTLE: I don't know who told me that, but it seems to be true in every case I've ever seen. Fast forwarding to today, how'd the event go this year? Pretty good?

GUY MALONE: The lectures this year? They went well beyond what I expected. They were very well received and a lot of people seemed pretty convinced by my Roswell explanation. If I'm doing a manmade view of Roswell, telling people it's not really aliens during the UFO Festival, I've already said I was just happy to get out of there with my life and without anybody yelling at me and hurting my feelings. [laughing] Both Friday and Saturday mornings, two rooms of people, I would estimate at least a 75% conversion rate, if not 90%–95%. Nobody argued with me. Nobody brought up, "Well, yeah, but . . ." Nothing. I got lots of good feedback on that. It's funny, it was the spiritual views talk, the Christian view, "Are aliens demons?" – that one I had three different people walk out on me during. It could have been just based on time. I'm not sure if it was content or they just had to be somewhere. I just said, "Thanks for coming," as they were walking out. And the first person didn't even leave until almost an hour into the lecture.

BEN SETTLE: When you showed me the rough notes or outline of what you were going to talk about, it's not surprising that it did well, because you have this contrast theory working in your favor.

GUY MALONE: Yeah. Contrasting what they already believe, you mean?

BEN SETTLE: Yeah. I'm trying to think of the best way to explain it. In marketing we call it selling against type. Even if someone doesn't necessarily agree with it going in, it's the fact that it's just so completely opposite. They have no choice, they have to at least hear you out, and that's half the battle.

GUY MALONE: Yeah, they're outraged. Selling against type, I've heard of that.

BEN SETTLE: We do this in sales letters all the time. You start with saying something that is so completely off the wall different that it just goes against so much of what they thought. They have to at least hear it out, even if they just want to think of what reasons to tell you why you're wrong. They have to hear it out.

GUY MALONE: We get a little bit of that, too. But as long as it's convincing, I'll tend to sort of shut them up. I came with that intent.

BEN SETTLE: You must have a pretty thick skin.

GUY MALONE: I really don't actually. My feelings get hurt easily. I used to wrestle with all kinds of acceptance and security issues and fear of man and all that stuff. It's developed by the grace of God, to toughen up. As long as I know it's God – it's like that Moses thing – "If you're not going to go with me, I don't want to go."

BEN SETTLE: That kind of leads me into the next thing I wanted to ask you about. Your ministry is very interesting, because you're actually out there fighting the battle. You're not just sitting behind a desk or whatever. You're actually out there in the thick of it, really in the trenches. Your ministry definitely has a business side to it, with the DVD's and the conferences and that sort of thing. How has spiritual warfare affected this as far as the business side of your ministry?

GUY MALONE: That is an interesting question that I don't really know how to answer. I'm sure that it has, but I don't have the words to elaborate on that one, honestly. It's just there, I'm sure there are opposing forces. The main thing is really just trusting that, "Okay, God sent me here. Okay, this is the next thing God has shown me to do." I'm not a huge spiritual warfare prayer person. I don't spend most of my mornings rebuking and binding and loosening stuff like that. However, even before I came here and developed what we now call a mailing list, I would let the people know that do have intercessory callings and who have even volunteered themselves to be available. Those are the people I've turned to and shared my plans with.

Part of my mailing list used to be, if I was going to a UFO conference, a secular one – "I'm leaving at this time on Friday. Please pray for travel and the times of the event are from here to here." I would always use the phrase "for those so inclined," because I knew I had secular people on the mailing list. "For those so inclined, please pray during this time." It might be a cop out, but in a sense you might say that I have graciously received the benefit of letting other people do that for me. The main thing is knowing that people do have intercessory callings, and if they're willing, enlisting them, and allowing them to do what they're gifted at and called to, while you do what you're called to. I guess the point I'm making is "one body, many parts" – there are no "one man shows" in Christ.

Before I even moved here from Nashville, this guy in the ministry training I had, it was a Master's Commission for 18 months, and what he told me was you need four people to cover you in prayer while you are doing this Master's Commission. That was the assignment every one of us MC students were assigned. Find four intercessors and share your life with them. The funny thing that he told me is, "You may not know it yet, but your four intercessors are already praying for you, because God has already put it on their hearts. All you have to do is look around, and you probably know who at least two of them are. It's those weird ladies that come up to you, and they smile and they tell you they've been praying for you. They may come up to you occasionally and tell you they've got a word for you, or they'll ask you how you're doing." He said just stop and think, and as soon as he said it, I pictured two of them. I went to them and asked, "I'm going through this MC program. Would you be willing to pray for me?" They were like, "Oh yeah, I already am praying for you." I'm thinking, "I'll be darned." Now I have to find two more.

As far as what you're doing in the book, anything dealing with spiritual warfare or any area of ministry, you first have to either identify or solicit your intercessors, the people who are going to be praying for you and who are going to be hearing from God. If you're not already, and even if you are, you need the type of people who can get woken up at three in the morning with a prayer burden, and will get out of bed and go to their knees and start praying for you or whatever God lays on their hearts. That's the people you need in any type of ministry – especially though, like you said, in the trenches, etc.

Just learning that lesson from the Master's Commission, I started out that way with this thing before I even left Nashville. I knew who my prayer people were. I would communicate with them regularly via email. I let the inner circle, so to speak, of prayer warriors know my plans, or at least what I think are God's plans for me. I'd update and apprise them of what, where, when, why I was doing anything. That aspect of it, the way the mailing list has grown now, is it's sort of a ball I'd say I've dropped. I used to have my mailing list divided into three different categories. The general mailing list was everybody that wanted to know UFO news stories, conferences, links, and new articles, but I had two other mailing lists. One was regular givers, like donation people, which was the smallest list of all, of course, and also intercessors. I would actually say in the mailing list, "I'm compiling a separate mailing list. If you are an intercessor, or if you will commit to pray, I'll be sending you stuff that may come more regularly and it will contain details that probably not everybody on this mailing list wants to know."

Again, I did that for a couple of years for sure, but the way I did it was internet based. I don't know who's responding to this. I don't know if it's some secret cabal or someone who's against me who would sign up for that mailing list as just another plan. So I would say my practical advice is to keep it among the people you know. Identify who God already has. I love this old quote – I think it's Brother Andrew – that says, "God does nothing in the earth except in response to prayer." That's not entirely true. I'm more of a God is sovereign type person. He does what He wants to. But He does move in response to prayer for sure. I think it's just logical, with that as a backdrop, if God is calling you into ministry, he is at the same time or even before you knew that you were called into ministry, He is raising up the people to be prayer warriors for your ministry, because we are a body. It's not a Lone Ranger or one man show. Every portion of the body has to be functioning to get God's will done on the earth. We just have different roles. But intercessors and prayer warriors is a gifting, and whether your church has a ladies meeting every

Wednesday morning, or a men's Saturday prayer breakfast or whatever, all you have to do is look around. There are people that are intercessors. They are called to prayer, and they will do it if you ask them.

BEN SETTLE: When you mentioned the old ladies, one of the people later in this book, his name is Matt Gillogly, had a very similar experience. He just knew God was telling him to do something, and he said it would come from the weirdest places. He mentioned some lady in church just kind of came up to him and mentioned the exact scripture he was praying over and said, "I'm praying for you."

GUY MALONE: Yep, that's how God sometimes does things. I've experienced it in other realms as well. I'm glad you got a second witness for this as far as people reading your book, if they're thinking about getting into some crazy ministry or business opportunity or whatever, point blank it's good that you've got that from me and at least one other person.

BEN SETTLE: Yeah, the second witness, definitely. One thing I wanted to ask you a little bit earlier, actually you mentioned two things. You kind of didn't want to delve into this while your parents were still alive, and then you also mentioned your brother was very into the UFO stuff too. My first question is what did your parents think when you went into this? What was the reaction?

GUY MALONE: With hindsight, I found out that the phrase "Nothing to fear but fear itself" applied. I had let this fear paralyze me for years from doing what I thought God wanted me to do. But much to my surprise, it turned out that my dad bought extra copies of the book and sent it to his relatives! They weren't the least bit embarrassed about the content of it, especially when the context is it's not even really aliens. All of that stigma is gone. It's just Christian stuff. You know, "Guy experienced some demonic visitations when he was a kid, and now he's found the secret to set him free…" My dad is not oriented towards the content. He's just, "Hey, my son wrote a book. Have a copy. Hey, my son is on TV. Go watch it." He's not even caring or discerning what's being said. He just saw my passion, and is glad for my successes. That's the funny part. Nothing to fear but fear itself.

My mom was raised a Christian. We didn't grow up as a church family, but she also got overall that this is a real ministry thing and realized that my church was affirming it. They were completely accepting without asking too many questions, or without being critical, or without being embarrassed. That shocked me. I was actually glad to move, but the thing is there was almost two years between when I started writing the web page and book in 1997, after the Phoenix sighting and after the Heavens Gate suicide. That was the summer of '97 and I didn't move until the summer of '99.

So for one thing, I spend all these months writing the book and then I've got a web page, and then I finally go through the print on demand, or what used to be called vanity publishing. I found somewhere locally that would print a hard copy at an affordable price, but I'd already spent a year doing this on the internet before I had it in hard copy to give to my parents. I remember my dad saying one thing. He was not into computers. All he knew was I've flitted around my entire life. I had really no goals, no ambitions. I dropped out of college. I was a partier, then I became a Christian and I was at church all of the time, and just working odd jobs at whatever I had to do – working for UPS, mowing grass, waiting tables, whatever – without that sense of direction that a parent wants to see in their child. Before he ever read the book, all he could say was, "Well, I can see this definitely has your passion, and you're putting your all into it." Therefore, he was already okay with it. It didn't matter what it was. It centered me, it grounded me, it gave me a direction and I was acting and moving on it. That's all he saw. At least they read it start to finish. If they read only the beginning… "My son's telling people he's an alien abductee? Oh my God." You know, that could have been embarrassing. But it's a short read. It's not that big of a book.

BEN SETTLE: How did they react when they found out you were an experiencer, and they didn't even know? What was their reaction to that?

GUY MALONE: There hasn't been one yet. [laughing] I'm still waiting for their reaction. They've never said anything good or bad about it.

BEN SETTLE: You think they'd be like, "That was going on and we didn't even know about it?" Maybe they are still in shock or something, because it would be shocking to hear something like that.

GUY MALONE: Well, part of the book was the FAQ on generational curses, and how a lot of this stuff comes generationally.

BEN SETTLE: Yeah, I understand.

GUY MALONE: I guess the book said all it could say and it answered everything that could be answered well enough to where they didn't feel they had to react or comment on it. To them it was pretty much, "Okay, you have a book. We're proud of you, and you're doing this and we'll support you." That's just the type of people they are.

BEN SETTLE: Didn't you have a grandparent or an uncle or something who worked at the air base in Roswell?

GUY MALONE: Not at the air base. It was my mom's father, and he did work for the Army. When he retired he went to work for an entity called Army Map Company. That was just their business name. He was a cartographer, and he is credited as the inventor of the relief map. He flew in planes around the world and made maps for the Army, and then for books afterwards. My mom remembers when the first thing came out in Roswell 1947, and all he said were the words, "Believe it." He had an office in Washington, DC. My mom described to me that they had a basement apartment within walking distance to the White House when she was very young. That's how close they were. All he said was, "Believe it." He never spoke of it again.

BEN SETTLE: That's kind of chilling, isn't it?

GUY MALONE: Yeah. The thing is, without my mom or my dad knowing of my interest in this stuff, I remember being told that story by my mom as a small child. So again, my interest level from not being a Christian is, "OMG, this is true. This stuff is real. I'm an alien abductee. Aliens are real, and they've chosen me to pick on."

BEN SETTLE: You know what's interesting? This is just from a purely marketing or persuasion perspective for someone who's just in business in some way, is how you, through no fault of your own and some ways on purpose, you've positioned yourself to be very credible in this area. You lived in Roswell, you had experiences, your mom's father said something. If I wrote a book on this, it would have nowhere near the impact because I don't have any of this going for me. But you have all this going for you.

GUY MALONE: Credentials built in.

BEN SETTLE: Absolutely, and there's actually a lot of power in that when somebody is selling something. You build your product around your proof and credibility, and it makes it far more likely that people are going to want to buy it. I just find that very interesting.

GUY MALONE: Neat. I've learned that whenever I was not in Roswell – like you said, in your own hometown – but if I went to a conference, I set up a table. I learned this early on, years ago, and it was just me. I'd just pack up the pickup truck and drive to these conferences. I'd set up a table. I'd have all my stuff out. I'd have my signs, my free flier handouts that had the web address and they were topical articles. I had a few books. I didn't have a lot of money. I didn't have a lot of products, just my book and a couple others. This is way before DVD's were even in the mix. People would just be walking along, the way they do at all trade shows. They don't want to be sold. They don't want you talking to, or soliciting them so much. But if you let them stare at your table long enough and don't force it, they'll maybe pick up a freebie or want to buy something. But… the moment that someone said, "Where are you from?" and I said, "Roswell", I heard back, "New Mexico? You're from Roswell, New Mexico?!?" And it was "game on" from there! Instant interest. It's better than having Ph.D. at the end of my name.

BEN SETTLE: Yeah, it really is. That's amazing.

GUY MALONE: Like you're saying, credibility and qualification-wise, when you're anywhere but Roswell, being from Roswell, people just assume you know something they don't – like "inside information" which as you know is always a great selling point.

BEN SETTLE: The only way you could get more credibility is if you were from Mars or something. [laughing]

GUY MALONE: Men are from Mars.

BEN SETTLE: This actually leads into the next question. You spend a lot of time going to these secular events with I'm just going to assume in some cases pretty hostile people, bound up in new age demonic doctrines and all of that, and that seems like one of the most hostile places you could probably be going to with the gospel. How do you go about persuading them to take a look at what you have to offer? I mean besides the Roswell thing, which definitely helps, but what tips do you have on selling your ideas to them so they hear you out?

GUY MALONE: This is the angle I think I could most help with in speaking and the book you're working on. Not a lot of people do it, go into hostile environments and share the gospel, but several things came to mind. As you were saying, you have to look at it from their point of view, for starters. I thought it would be a hostile environment. I went braced for battle, or braced for verbal abuse. But it turns out that that factor was minimal. It's very, very minimal. What I found was whether it's the Roswell Festival or any other UFO conference, these are people who are taking time off of work in many cases, they're traveling, they're paying money to attend this conference and hear all these speakers – they want to know the truth. They want someone to tell them. The thing is, in many cases they are experiencers themselves and they're looking for answers. In other cases, they just have a strong intellectual curiosity. But the point is, they came to the event, and to some extent they're coming to you because they want to know. They want to hear it all. They want to hear every possible answer.

So my answer about persuading them is that as long as you are not aggressive, fanatical, dogmatic, or a Bible thumper so to speak, if you're just simply presenting to them from your point of view and your research, keeping in mind that they came up to your table, you detach yourself from the outcome and let them walk away with a free flyer with your URL for more, because 99% of the time you're not going to get to dump your whole spiel on any one person. The main thing I had was the satisfaction of, "Here's a card, here's a flyer." It would be up to them and the Holy Spirit what happened from there, but the main thing is keeping in mind that from their point of view that, they want to know. Don't present yourself as fanatical and dogmatic, argumentative or insistent – just available. Just be calm, cool, collected and somewhat detached from whether they buy or not.

That was one of the first things I noticed was effective, and I got the most distribution of literature and information and cards when I took that approach.

BEN SETTLE: That is extremely helpful. Anyone who sells anything for a living should take what you just said and memorize it, because it's exactly how it is no matter what you are selling.

GUY MALONE: I just didn't realize. Like you, I thought it would be an extremely hostile environment. It wasn't until after I did it a couple of times that I realized, "Wait a minute. They're coming to us, the vendors, and the speakers. They want to know. They have a need to know."

Here's the other thing that's kind of cool. I call the way I run my tables, and even the store when I had it here, the Salvation Army approach. Eat this up by the way. Include it in the book without anybody's copyright. "Giving people what they think they want, creates the opportunity to give them what you think they need."

BEN SETTLE: You sell them what they want, and you give them what they need.

GUY MALONE: Yeah, and for some reason that snapped. That's what Salvation Army does, and that's why they're effective. When I say that, I should throw in the caveat as long as it's not illegal or immoral or sinful. But they're coming to you with a need, so meet that need. In my case it's information. They just want information. They don't want to be sold. They don't want to be pushed. As soon as you give off that vibe going that your sentence is about to end with, "…buy my book," that's when they start walking fast. But if you say, "Here, this is free. This is my website. You can take your time and learn more whenever you want to. I'm here for the rest of the weekend if you want to come back and talk."

BEN SETTLE: It's so biblical, too. That's how Jesus went around. He went to the people who were suffering. They wanted relief. It's really what selling is all about. It's not just pushing people and pressuring them and, like you were saying, pounding the table. "You need this! You've got to have this!" Spend your time with the people who are sick, not the people who are healthy. You know what? I can even break that down to a more basic thing. If someone has a headache, they're ready to buy the aspirin. But they're not going to buy the aspirin if they don't have a headache no matter how great a sales person you are.

GUY MALONE: Yeah. I'm looking at the text here. How do you go about persuading them to take a look at what you have to offer? A technique I've found is very effective, especially if I'm the only person manning the table, in persuading them to take a look at what you have to offer, is I would often leave the table. I'd walk away and look like I was just another person perusing the other vendor tables. I'd kind of get a relationship or conversation going with the two or three people nearest me. I'll get into that part in a minute. But I'd go over to someone else's table, talk with them, maybe buy something, but I would just keep an eye on my table. What I found in my many experiences is more often than not my table was busier when no one was at it than when it was being manned. Again, in this niche field, these are people that want the information but they don't want to be sold or have anything pushed on them, especially if it's religion.

Now as soon as I saw someone was standing at the table, especially if it was for several minutes going by, then ding, ding, ding that's a prospect, whether it's a sale or a conversion, however you look at it. I might chime in and be like, "I'll be right back over there if you need any help," or "This is my table. I'm Guy. If you have any questions just let me know," and then turn around. The funny thing was, I found half the time that that broke whatever mode they were in. As soon as I'm a voice that I'm available, they might leave. It was half and half.

BEN SETTLE: It's kind of like when you are at the store and you do need help, but the guy asks you if you need any help and you say, "No, I'm just looking."

GUY MALONE: Yeah, your wall goes up immediately. "No, I don't need any help," even though you want it. The other thing I wanted to say as far as tips for people that are doing especially Christian outreaches at secular events, I've learned that the other vendors around you, if you're not careful, are going to be hostile to what you have and to why you're there. They're going to overhear a lot of your conversations, and they are going to be sick to death of you by the time the weekend is over if you're not extremely careful. This is a tip that I found very effective, but really it's two or three things.

So the first thing is – and again, I only learned this from experiences – look at stuff from the other person's point of view. When you're a conference organizer, you've got a thousand things on your mind. Five minutes from now you're going to have another thousand things on your mind, and they are having to deal with stuff left and right. The people that sold you the vendor table, they are in the thick of what is probably the busiest weekend of their life, and they're stressing. My advice is "DO NOT ADD TO THAT PERSON'S STRESS LEVEL BY BEING NEEDY!!!" In fact, be the opposite. Be the solution to their problems. I take stuff with me to work conferences that I know I'm not going to need. I take an extra extension cord. I take duct tape, clear tape, masking tape. If you have the ability to do it, a printer would be great, if a person can actually travel with a printer, and your laptop to print your own signs, then you can also be helpful to others that need to print something on the fly.

The thing is, I don't go up to the conference organizers asking them for tape and stickpins, and for ink pens, or for change. Take your own bank of $100 in fives and ones, plus whatever else. That way the other vendors around you who forgot to bring something important, you are the answer to their problems all of a sudden. Be the one who can say "Hey, I got extra pens" or "…

an extension cord you can borrow…" Or if you hear someone at their table and they are trying to break a bill or a hundred, you just chime in, "You need ones? Yeah, here you go man." It's very Jesus Christ oriented to be a servant to those around you. You can help them. You win immediate favor when you help someone out in their time of need. If you actually have a staff or a crew or whatever, we've done this when there are two or three or four of us at times, we actually go up and say something along the lines of, "You know what? It really only takes one person to man our table, and we've got three with us. Do you need someone at the door, or do you need someone that can help move stuff around?" Usually they do. Most events are run on some paid staff, but a lot of them are just volunteers – with varying levels of competence, honestly. If you actually have a body, a person – they need bodies, if for nothing else than just to stand at the door and make sure that everybody that walks in has a name tag or the admission or whatever. Some of these events have two or three things happening at the same time and they don't have enough bodies to cover every need. This gives you a chance to meet that need, and offer to be that body. I've done that many times.

One of the funniest things happened at a UFO conference once. They weren't even advertising that they were selling tables. This was their first time doing it. I wrote them, "Can I buy a vendor table at this event? I noticed you don't have them listed." They said, "Sure, it's $100." Well, I was the only one, and they put me right next to the registration table because it was a very small area. It was very bottlenecked getting from the hotel lobby or wherever it was into the conference room itself where the speaking was going on. So without planning it – it was completely God – but with hindsight, I can look back and tell you how to do it, but I only experienced it and watched it happen.

The first time, I became an extension of the check-in table. All my literature was right there. People were just walking down the line, getting their badge, getting their whatever, being pointed in the right direction, and then the next thing they ran into was my table with all these free flyers. They started picking them up. I'm like, "Do you want a stapler for that?" Yes, I brought a stapler. I was handing out flyers all the time, so I got in the habit of bringing a stapler. I also realized that people didn't all have bags. They've got more crap than they can carry. If you've got a bunch of loose sheets of paper, boom, here's a stapler. They were stapling their conference letter with their instructions and schedule and itinerary to my material and carrying it around with them all weekend. They'd come back and realize it, and sometimes have all kinds of questions for me. But the thing is, with this particular conference I wasn't just siphoning off of them by saddling up next to the registration table. That's where they put me to begin with, but I was offering help. I was like, "Do you need a bathroom break?" I'd heard their spiel enough times to be able to say it for them.

Sometimes their table would get too crowded, and people were asking questions. Just by being next to the conference organizers all weekend, I knew the answers to the questions that people were coming up with, so I would just start taking the second or third person in line. "Yeah, the bathroom is this way," "No, this doesn't start until 3:00." As long as it's genuine, as long as you are a genuine individual in your heart to serve and to help people – both the attendees to the event and the conference organizers – before long you will blend in and you will seem as if you are one of them. Once, at a very large New Age conference, I was actually given a pass to the event's "invitation-only VIP after-party" just because I'd served them so much while also working my table that they considered me staff! Think about that – there I am, presenting blatantly Christian material that completely debunks and counters what most of the conference speakers are there to present, yet because of a serving attitude am favored enough to get invited to an unpublished event in the top floor of the hotel, where only event staff, speakers, close friends and staff were gathering. Perks aside, the ministry and making of friends and contacts continued even after the event was officially over. They will receive you because you are actually being quite useful and helpful, and they've got more work to do than they can ever get done. If you start answering people's questions about where the bathroom is and when the next thing starts and here's the schedule of events, you are taking headaches off of their hands. You're taking people with needs off of their hands.

So that's my hugest advice is go prepared and take more stuff than you need – like I said, extension cords, all kinds of things, extra pens, a huge bank of fives and ones, and whatever else you can, if you have enough money to do so. Then look for opportunities to serve the people that are there, that are running the event, and it opens so many doors for your faith and ministry. They get to where they appreciate you. I heard – after a couple years of doing this – of being back at a conference for the second or third time at events that are held annually.

Maybe they don't like what I am saying, but me as an individual, they figure they do kind of like actually. That's the difference, is if you're not hostile and if you're not abrasive. It's what people say about the Gospel all the time. Our message is quite offensive, but we don't have to be.

BEN SETTLE: That whole story has so many interesting nuggets in it – just the way you were positioned right in front of the moving parade we were talking about, and you did something very interesting. You got the unofficial endorsement of the conference organizer. It's like you said, you became like one of them. They couldn't distinguish between you and the organizers.

GUY MALONE: Right, and I didn't plan it. It was a completely God thing. It's just the way it worked out, and all of a sudden I'm in the middle of that dynamic. Seeing God's genius in it, I learned my lesson and found out it is reproducible. You can do that anywhere. You become the help that they need, and you're right, you do kind of gain the unspoken endorsement from a person of authority.

BEN SETTLE: It's very similar to when people run magazine ads or TV ads, or if you're listening to talk radio where the ad looks like it's an actual article written by the newspaper.

GUY MALONE: Yes, they have to put up in small letters at the top or bottom, "Paid advertisement."

BEN SETTLE: They do, and there's a way around that I heard where you put that in the headline if someone is doing some kind of a magazine or a newspaper thing. It says "For readers of the ____ whatever magazine," and then it feels like it's coming from the publication.

GUY MALONE: Then they don't stick you with that "Paid advertisement"?

BEN SETTLE: They do, but usually that's in smaller type so it kind of almost gets ignored. Again, it's just to get a reading. It's not like you're trying to manipulate anyone, but it's just that wall that you were talking about that goes up. There are people who are going to read this book, I think, who are doing conferences. Maybe they are not doing ministry type conferences or anything like that.

GUY MALONE: But they're going to events.

BEN SETTLE: Yeah, absolutely.

GUY MALONE: Be helpful, that's all I can say. Be the answer to someone else's problem by being way over prepared in the stuff that you carry. If you have a staff or a crew with you, turn them loose to go help the conference organizers, or whoever's in charge of the vending or seating or whatever.

BEN SETTLE: That is just really, really good advice. That could be a game-changer, quite frankly, for people who are going to events and that sort of thing. Very interesting.

GUY MALONE: Like I said, the other vendors around you, especially if you're doing ministry as opposed to just a product, they're going to be overhearing your conversations. They're going to begin to hate you. What I was saying earlier is you form relationships with the people around you at the tables very easily, good or bad. It happens quickly. But in a lot of cases I've found, and what I was saying about having the stuff that they need if they forgot something, just keep your eyes and ears open when they are setting up, if they forgot tape or whatever. The one thing that does is, if you weren't there to give that assistance to them, they were probably going to go to the conference organizer or the vendor chairperson or whatever it is. What I've seen happen is pretty soon the organizers snap to the fact that by people coming to you for stuff they're not coming to them, and that's one less headache they have to deal with in the moment. You and the vendors around you all have the same goal. You want to make sales. You also all have the same needs, and this is what I would advise that you pay attention to. At a weekend event, everyone is going to need to go eat, everyone is going to need to go to the bathroom etc. If it's a friendly and not a competition oriented type of thing, you can actually be the person to initiate that. "We're here for you. I'll watch your table if you need to go to the bathroom." Take the step of introducing yourself and telling people, "I've got stuff if you need it," and that kind of thing, especially if you think you're going to be in a hostile environment. Show yourself friendly is what the Bible says. Just show yourself friendly and able to help them.

Just remember, you've got the same needs and you've got the same goals. If you can help them with their goals or their needs, they're much less likely to be offensive. They're much less likely to be working against you, or just staring you down. You know, you can feel that hate vibe. You can just feel it. It's powerful sometimes from someone that's listening to your conversation. The position I find myself in is I am there, they're going from one table to another, and I'm saying the exact opposite of what they just heard. I am dismantling sometimes what the guy next to me just told them. In a matter of speaking, I'm telling them why this person is wrong.

BEN SETTLE: Yeah, I can see how that would be hostile.

GUY MALONE: Yeah, so if you've initiated to somehow find any way to make a good impression or to help out the people around you from the get go, that at least helps settle the hateful vibe.

BEN SETTLE: There's a story, and I don't know which airline it was, but they were having problems and everybody was stuck in the airplanes for four hours. They couldn't go to the bathroom and all that, right? It was just total misery for everyone and they were hating the airline. So what the airline did is they gave everybody free ice cream and all was good again. The moral of the story is you can't hate somebody that's giving you free ice cream. It sounds like that's kind of what you were doing. You were being that person, and it's interesting because, really, technically they probably wouldn't have done that for anyone else. You're the Christian there anyway, it is normal for us to see that. But for other people I think it's probably like, "Wow, what is he doing?"

GUY MALONE: Exactly. I've felt that a lot, but it's consistency more than anything. Another thing I've noticed about the UFO community, if you will – it becomes its own family or its own culture or whatever. After a while you realize that people have different views on this topic, but you don't have to be hostile to each other. People that are into UFO's specifically are already on the lunatic fringe of society. They don't get to talk about this stuff every day at work, or to their family members. So once they are in an environment where that goes, you're already kind of one of them. Whether you'll have a successful relationship depends on you, and how you handle yourself from there. But the consistency of showing up year after year and being at the same events, it's just like, "Oh, there's the Christian guy. I hate his views, but he's one of the family."

BEN SETTLE: You're like the crazy old uncle in the corner no one trusts, but all the kids like to hear stories from.

GUY MALONE: Yeah, he takes the dollar out of his pocket. He has a shiny dollar, and they say, "Oh, let's go see uncle. He gives us money every time." My grandfather did that when I was a kid. We loved him, because we knew as soon as he walked in the door he was going to hand us a dollar.

BEN SETTLE: Even if all the other grown-ups can't really stand the guy, everyone else likes him. You mentioned the word fringe, which is kind of interesting because it leads into the next question. Even within the UFO community, I'm just going to go on the assumption that the Christian view is considered fringe within the fringe UFO culture.

GUY MALONE: It is.

BEN SETTLE: Weren't you the conference organizer for the entire city of Roswell in 2007?

GUY MALONE: Yes.

BEN SETTLE: How did that happen if you are the crazy old uncle?

GUY MALONE: It's kind of a continuation of a previous question, of meeting someone's needs. I'll add to it. It's expertise. That would be the one word answer. When the city first got involved, they're not UFO people, generally speaking – for example, the City Planner, the guy you have to go to to get your permits, and the PR officer, the woman who's supposed to promote the city of Roswell.

I saw in the newspaper that the new mayor had said that they were going to begin working on the UFO festival for the first time. This was August 2006. I don't remember how I heard it, but I heard that they were going to a certain UFO conference that I'd been to twice, basically to learn how UFO events are done. I knew off the top of my head, that is one of the more new aged-leaning events in ufology. They were going to make contacts, and they were going to be inviting speakers, and all this stuff. The city paid for them to go to this thing in California. They were just there to promote Roswell and make contacts and learn how to do stuff. But I knew, "Oh no, these are the freakiest new age cult people" at this one particular expo. So I wrote them a letter and I said, "Hey, I know you're going to this event. I've been there twice myself." I sort of gave them a paragraph by paragraph review of many of the speakers that they were going to run into there. I was like, "This guy is highly entertaining, and he's funny and he draws huge crowds. But he's also been sued for faking his bio. His bio is entirely fake. He's not credible. If you invite him to the city of Roswell, you will make The City of Roswell look bad to the UFO community. And now, this guy is actually a UFO cult recruiter. Here's his website if you want to know more. His presentation focuses on this, but that's just to get you hooked in. So if you go to his lecture and if you bring him to Roswell, you're going to wind up opening the door for UFO cults. Now this guy is excellent. Government records, sheer science, sheer documents. He gives a fine presentation, and he would be a good person to have. You should get a relationship with him."

I gave them the lowdown on like six different speakers that I was familiar with, good or bad for review. They went to the event, and apparently they found out I was spot on in everything I said about everybody. All I know was this guy that I've never met before comes to where I work, he hands me a card and says, "Hi, I'm Zach Montgomery. I'm the City Planner and I'm on the UFO Festival Committee. On behalf of the UFO Festival Committee, the mayor and I would like to invite you to be our conference organizer this year."

Expertise, that's all it was. They recognized I had an expertise in this field that they did not, and that's how it happened. But I made myself available. I served them. I wasn't asking for the position. I wouldn't have dreamed it was possible, for that matter. I had the goal of keeping the UFO cult stuff out of the city event. I knew if they went there with no knowledge, they'd be impressed, they'd be hoodwinked, and they would invite an element into Roswell that – both as a Christian minister and as a UFO researcher – I didn't think would be good. Then the city itself would receive the backlash for it. In a way, I was being protective as well. I didn't want them to invite stuff into Roswell that was going to make them look bad and receive all kinds of backlash. But they could have easily been hoodwinked into doing so without knowing better, so I shared my expertise. That might be the best answer to how that one happened. I shared my expertise, they recognized it, and then put me in the position of authority.

Of course, you know how I work in this. I invited enough credible secular people who didn't have a new age message attached to what they were doing to share and draw the numbers, and of course, I mixed in a few Christian speakers. There were 30 presentations that weekend, and five of the speakers were Christians. Only one of them did I include – well, myself and Mike Heiser. He did his talk, "Could Christianity accommodate a genuine ET reality if it's proven to be true?" The city basically paid for one Christian point of view out of a dozen, which is pretty innocuous. You're not going to get that whole church and state backlash from just that, and he wasn't doing a particularly religious talk anyway. It was theological, but at the end of it there was no altar call. But because we had workshops and we had rooms and all that stuff, I was going to be saying yes or no to who was going to come and speak in Roswell, beyond what the city was paying for, and I early on gave a heads-up to some Christians in this field. "Dude, I'm the organizer. Do you want to talk? Okay, the budget's already spent. The city won't pay your expenses, but if you want to tell me you're going to come, I'll give you the slot now before it becomes common knowledge that it's open."

BEN SETTLE: The way that was structured like that, it's sort of that concept that if you have a lot full of white cars, the red car will stand out. You had all those secular speakers giving the science probably and all the credible stuff, and then you have the theological point of view, which probably just stood out like crazy, like a beacon.

GUY MALONE: Yes, but to the point that it could be ignored by people who knew they didn't want that. That didn't mean that they came to those talks, but my view then was if you put five Christians scattered across the convention center and with their lectures on the schedule, that's enough room for God to move. I don't have to be in control of it. I don't have to orchestrate it. That's where I can trust the Holy Spirit to draw who He will to the right people. They say 90% of life is showing up. Just take the field and see what God does from there.

BEN SETTLE: That's the best way anyway. You open the feed sack and let Him actually rip it across the top so it's all neat and everything and doesn't spill out all over the place like what happens when we try by ourselves. There's another question I wanted to ask you. When you do these conferences and when you do the events and you're setting your tables up and all that, on average do you find that a lot of them are open to hearing the Gospel and that sometimes they even become Christians? Does that happen a lot?

GUY MALONE: To use the words "a lot" would probably be a little inaccurate, but the early part of the question, are they open? Yeah, they came because they want to know, as long as you're not offensive. It has to be again like the Salvation Army. It has to be tailored in a way that you're actually answering the question or the need that they have, and then presenting that the solution is actually Jesus Christ or it's found in the gospel. It's not a dogmatic, "Here's what we want you to believe." It's, "Here's what our research shows," and you're giving them the information to draw their own conclusion whether this is a correct point of view or not. Yes, we have prayed with people. We have had people email us afterwards. I've had people contact me two years after an event, and email me. "I didn't agree with you, but I kept your flyer. I've been on your website. I've read your book. I've watched this, and after two years I'm convinced."

BEN SETTLE: I can only imagine what would happen if you had an organized email system going for you there, and you were just emailing a regular newsletter about what you're up to. I remember when I was on your Christian Symposium site and I'm like, "Where can I opt-in at? I want to hear more of this."

GUY MALONE: I forgot to do that. I heard you say that. That's the one. My other site does have, "Click here for future conference information."

BEN SETTLE: I just wondered if you were constantly in contact with people just via email on a regular basis – I don't know, it's all hypothetical, but if you're having that kind of effect when you go there and God's working that way, man!

GUY MALONE: That's a good encouragement. That's something we need to consider. The tail end of your question was, "And most recently your speech in 2010," – this is a case where the keyword would be flexibility. I was available and I had this new good lecture I wanted to do on, "Are aliens demons? What's the evidences from the spiritual view of it?"

When The City of Roswell was putting together the 2010 conference I contacted them very early, and the one thing I have going for me is there's no travel expenses if they use me as a speaker. I asked and I offered. "I've got this talk and it's really good. Do you want me to do it?" They emailed me back that they would like me as a speaker, but the conference they were putting together, it turned out every talk was themed to Roswell. I didn't get to do the talk that I wanted to do, but I gave them the talk abstract about my manmade view of The 1947 Roswell Incident. So I had to tailor what I was doing to meet their need, and they responded positively. Looking at that e-mail reply, their exact words were "Thank you. Great title, & a provocative abstract. Go for it."

Basically, kind of like Bob Dole, I'm a resume candidate at this point because I've worked with the city and I'm local and I have whatever level of prominence I do. Agree or disagree with the view, this person is a resume candidate at this point because of expertise, because of years of service, because of notoriety, etc. I didn't get to go in there with my agenda to do my, "Are aliens really demons?" talk that I offered. Basically they said no, but they left the door open by saying, "Here's the theme of this year's conference," so I had to propose something tailored to what their needs were.

I love the way God worked. It pushed me into writing a lecture that I never would have done, at least as a lecture. I've always sort of half-way wanted to, but heck, I've got the website and it's all up there, but I had to do a lot of new research so that my lecture would not just be me reading the website, because why come to the lecture if that's all it is? But I was told over and over again afterwards how persuasive it was, and I've since seen it open doors and relationships with people who wouldn't necessarily be otherwise interested in my religious views, but do consider me credible nonetheless as a result of this happening. I just wanted to answer that last part of the question, most recently in 2010. It boils down to making myself available, and starting back in 2006 with a genuine desire to serve the city, and make sure they didn't look bad based on uninformed choices. From there, a genuine relationship formed. Afterwards, I was a resume candidate, and I had to be flexible and tailor what I was going to do to meet their needs.

BEN SETTLE: All of that can be applied to any type of marketing or persuasive selling.

GUY MALONE: That's why I tried to frame it that way for you.

BEN SETTLE: I appreciate it, because that's really going to help people. Again, a lot of people reading this book probably come in with that pre-conceived notion. Unfortunately, a lot of Christians have a hard time being in business because they think it's dirty and they don't want to sell. They think they're manipulating and all that. Well, if they're doing what everybody else is doing they are, but if they do things the right way there's no problem. It's in perfect harmony with everything.

GUY MALONE: It can be done morally and in integrity. Just don't push.

BEN SETTLE: There's a guy named Bernard Baruch who was considered the most persuasive man of the 20th century. He used to advise presidents and Wall Street brokers. He could walk into a room with all these conflicting egos and he'd walk out and everyone would say, "Well, we came to an agreement." Somehow this guy did that. Before he died they asked him, "What is your big secret to being able to do that?" and he said, "I simply find out what people want and I show them how to get it."

GUY MALONE: I think I've heard that before.

BEN SETTLE: It's very simple, and everything you've been talking about here is just that. They want to know more, they want the truth, and you're presenting it in a way that it's very easy to listen to at least, and let them make their own decision. It's just great. It's in perfect harmony with good marketing.

GUY MALONE: I think the most effective sales technique I have, and it's based on my personality and the way God made me, is I'm more customer-service oriented than I am sales. You've heard the phrase "take aways" and all this stuff with sales. I genuinely come across as detached from the outcome. I'm here to share. I'm here to answer your questions. You're free to spit in my face and walk away and it won't rile me. I got interviewed on one radio program, and it turned out their whole point in inviting me on was to make fun of me, and I never got mad. I just kept sharing the information, or I kind of laughed with them or at them or turned something around in a couple cases so the joke was on them. But the thing is, they were two college kids, they were trying to get my goat and I recognized it. They had a perceived need that conflicted with my goal of sharing information.

BEN SETTLE: What happened in that show?

GUY MALONE: They ended the interview early. It was scheduled for an hour and we did about 25 minutes. Then I just listened online to the rest of their program. They were like, "Man, he wasn't going for it!" That's exactly what they said. That's another thing that people say. There are people that are going to come up to you, people that are there to sell their point of view. Even though they don't have a vendor booth, they're there to argue and convince you of what they believe is true. There are people that are going to want to argue with you right there at the table, and you cannot let them get your goat. You cannot match their level of hostility or their desire to argue.

Again, part of it is remaining detached from the outcome. What I've found is very effective to do in that situation, when a trouble maker comes and wants to argue, they'll get loud and they'll try to make you be loud, so hand them something for free and just point blank tell them and make them realize they're being an ass, more or less. Say, "I understand what your point of view is, and it's obvious we disagree. It's pretty pointless for us to have an argument right here in front of everybody. Here, let me give you this free DVD and then email me with your thoughts after you've watched it," and send them on their way and walk away from the argument. I've found that very effective in diffusing those occasional hostile things where they're just coming up to argue. Point out that you're not here to argue, give them something free, and make sure they walk away.

Sometimes at a crowded event where there's a lot of people, that person wants to argue with you and you're itching to rebut all their points too. You could spend 20 minutes with that person while 20 people walk by your table and you don't have the opportunity to wait on them. You have to be quick to diffuse that argumentative person. Give them something free and walk away. What I've done lots of times is say, "Here, watch this for free. It's an hour lecture, and obviously we don't have time to do it right now. You can have it for free. Here's my card. Email me your thoughts afterwards and we'll continue this conversation. Or if you decide you like it, you can mail me $5 for it later. You can send it back for free or you can throw it in the trash when you get home."

BEN SETTLE: Do you ever get a 10-page email dissertation on why you're wrong afterwards?

GUY MALONE: No, not really actually. That hasn't happened. I don't know if they watch it or not, but I've found in that case they're not asking you for information. They're not there because they're there to learn. They're there to push something and they're there to argue, so that is not your target audience. My pastor used to say this in Nashville all the time "The fields are ripe for harvest. Pray therefore the Lord of the harvest will send out workers," but he said, "Here's the way most Christians go about it. Would you stand there at a tree full of green apples and yell at them to be ripe? That's the way most Christians go about things." Jesus said, "The harvest is ripe. Go out and work it." Most Christians spend a lot of their time on fields that are not ripe for harvest. You can't argue a green apple into becoming a red apple. You've got to be sensitive to the Holy Spirit and find out when the apple is turning, and that's where we come in as Christians to present our information and guide people through the process and present Christ. That's what you run into at these events. There are some very argumentative people who are there simply to argue and to share their point of view. They're not coming to learn. They don't want what you have. Don't let yourself waste too much time on them.

BEN SETTLE: Casting pearls before swine basically?

GUY MALONE: They will devour your time if you let them, and you will be less effective and you'll share less information and make less sales, whatever your goal is, if you spend your time letting those people do that to you. They're just generally looking for someone to attack to so they can argue and have a good time doing it, and they know they're going to walk away not convinced about your point of view.

BEN SETTLE: That happens even if you're just selling books or anything. If you have a customer who says, "This book sucked. It's the worst thing ever. I wasted my money on this," you're real tempted to email them back and say, "No one says that to me!" or you can just delete it and be done with it.

GUY MALONE: My ministry partner Joe Jordan is a lot better at that than I. He always says, "You know what, I've got this little key on my keyboard and I'm not afraid to use it. It's called the delete key."

BEN SETTLE: Doesn't he get a ton of hostile responses?

GUY MALONE: Yup, he does too. It's like when you're at a restaurant and a waiter is telling you about the special, or showing you the desert tray. It can be either a really enjoyable experience, or it can be really annoying, depending mostly upon your needs and his motivations. Is he doing it because he'll be in trouble if he doesn't? Or to make a sale or to win a contest? Or is he doing it because he genuinely believes he has something great to tell you about that you might be really interested in if you just give him a minute to share? I've done enough restaurant work and ministry both to know that, to a lot of people, I think the motivating factor shines through as much or more perhaps, than what you're actually saying. But what I mean by "detached from the outcome" is that I really think I have something that meets your need and I just want to provide you with all the information you need to make the decision that's right for you. And once I've shared the information, I feel a sense of genuine satisfaction. I'm done, and can walk away feeling good about whatever decision you make – so long as I've done my job of telling you... ALL you need to know about Jesus, UFOs and abductions, or the chocolate cream pie for that matter. By feeling satisfied that I've adequately done my job, I'm just not pushy about what you decide from there. In a way, it also boils down to respect I think – respecting the other person's needs, and their right to make a decision that may or may not be what you think is right, or that meets your agenda.

The thing is, there is a very subtle but persuasive power if you can walk away from the encounter detached from the outcome. They may not have bought what you were selling then... but... the seed was planted. And that's a very biblical concept. Okay, they were too full to buy your desert in that particular moment.. or they just needed to leave quickly. Whatever. It didn't meet their need, at that moment. But the fact that you shared the information you genuinely thought they'd be interested in often means that they may come back some other time to buy what you were selling. And Christian ministry or general sales-wise – they'll remember you as the person who respected them and was genuine in the effort to meet their need. Like I said, I've gotten e-mails and phone calls from people over 2 years after meeting them in person.

BEN SETTLE: When you had your Christian bookstore in Roswell, what were some good lessons you learned just in business in general doing that?

GUY MALONE: The first thing is keep your day job. In my unique case I was offering a product that people didn't really want. The thing I did learn was real quickly was that you may need to offer them something they do want, just to get them in. I didn't sell a whole lot of books, not enough books to keep a store open by any stretch of means, and I lived there to be able to afford to pay the rent on the business ministry location. I actually lived inside of it. Books and coffee do tend to go together, so I bought some Starbucks coffee off the shelf at Wal-Mart or Albertson's, and I was offering Starbucks coffee. That's something people wanted and they came in for. That whole little Second and Main downtown area in Roswell, there was nowhere to get a cup of coffee. And people were there at 9 in the morning waiting for the UFO museum to open. Meanwhile, across the street, I had coffee, so some of those waiting would come to see me.

The other thing was part of what actually helped pay and fund it is you've got to go back in time to like the 2002-2006 era when there wasn't even cell phone service in Roswell for most carriers. Now there is and now people have internet in their hands. I was offering internet access just through donations and a helpful guide, Jody Harris, who was sympathetic and wanted to help with my ministry. He really needed some coffee, so he'd come in all the time and drink all the coffee he could without really having to pay for it. He worked on computers for me, where I was able to offer internet access for $2 minimum, $6/hour, something like that, because for people who were traveling, that's what one of their main needs was. They needed to be able to go in and check their email, delete their spam, and at that time internet did not come standard in any hotel in Roswell. The advice that I learned that applies to this question is you have to be kind of cutting edge and anticipating the needs of what people do want, just like the guy who said, "Find out what they need and show them how to get it." I had people coming in for coffee and coming in for internet, and they were paying my rent – well, I was too. I always operated at a loss, but the bills were getting paid on something that I wasn't even there to do, and it helped keep it open.

Occasionally someone that came in for coffee only or someone that came in for internet access only would start looking around, would start asking questions, and then it was on. By meeting those needs I was able to share a lot of the information that I wanted to, and sometimes pray with people and see a salvation or two. It's not because they were interested in UFOs. They weren't interested in aliens. They were interested in coffee or internet access. But going back to the Salvation Army approach I mentioned earlier – if you can meet their perceived need, it often opens the door to present the answer to what you think their real need is.

BEN SETTLE: It keeps going back to that thing if nobody wants it, no one's going to buy it. It's a good lesson, because a lot of people do want to sell products that nobody wants.

GUY MALONE: I guess to pay the bills or to keep it afloat or just to attract people you do have to offer, like you're saying, what they did want. You have to anticipate the need. I saw that need all the time. People started asking me, "Is there anywhere around here I can get internet access?" That situation doesn't apply anymore because now there's internet in every hotel. People have laptops and they have it on their telephone, but the lesson to be learned is there is something, if you just listen to the people that are walking in your door. What are they asking? What need are they expressing? I knew the internet thing as a business plan was a thing of the past, even when I opened it. It's just that Roswell hadn't caught up with the rest of the world. They didn't have high-speed internet access in Roswell until about 2004. I was on three different mailing lists – EarthLink, Quest, and cable. I was like one of the first ten people in town to have high-speed internet, especially at a business location.

The other thing is the customers or prospects are going to express a need. It may not be the one you're there to fill, but if you hear it more than twice, you ought to start thinking, "Huh, maybe I should meet that need, and then more people will be coming to me," and then there's the opportunity to present the rest of your stuff naturally or organically.

BEN SETTLE: There's a lot of wisdom in that simple lesson. I bet you a lot of people go to the store and they wonder, "Why don't they carry this?" and they'll ask the manager, "Why don't you carry this?"

"Well, we just don't."

You're thinking, "Maybe you should."

There's a guy I study a lot in internet marketing named Ken McCarthy. He has this book called *The System Club Letters,* and he talks about when he lived in San Francisco he watched a couple Korean immigrants who came over and started a convenience store in his neighborhood. At first it didn't look like they were going to make it, but what they started doing is just asking everyone who came in, "What would you like us to carry?" and within a couple years they were just booming and thriving, giving people what they want.

GUY MALONE: I'm on his mailing list. I delete it most of the time when it comes. Maybe I got on it from yours actually. Are you familiar with getpaidforwhoyouare.com?

BEN SETTLE: No, I'm not.

GUY MALONE: I like his approach. He has a book on introducing you to MailChimp.com, whatever your area of expertise is. Maybe you've survived a divorce or loss. Because the internet is so big, there's plenty of people out there who want and are searching for and are willing to pay for whatever your life experience is. He just takes you through this whole how-to process. The book is for sale, but it's a free download as well, the same as you were saying, just enter your email address. I've got it in hard copy. I haven't read it all the way through, but I've read some of it on PDF before it came.

BEN SETTLE: I've never heard of David Wood. I'm opting in to his list right now actually.

GUY MALONE: I've always meant to ask you if you're aware of this guy and what do you think of him?

BEN SETTLE: Believe me, there's many people I don't know who I should know of. I'm always happy to find the legitimate people out there to take a look at, because most stuff online you can't trust.

GUY MALONE: He's very genuine, very interactive and all that stuff. You'll like getting his emails. Honestly, yours are better than most of his now, because the sales pitch is there more hardcore than yours is.

BEN SETTLE: For me email is just talk radio on glass. That's all it is. It's more of a show than it is a sales pitch. Like you say, you're giving people what they want. They want entertainment and fun first. They're not opening an email because they want to buy something.

GUY MALONE: Yeah, and you use a lot of touchstones too, I've noticed, and that's awesome.

BEN SETTLE: It's really not even a very complicated system. You'll see that it's actually very easy. Believe me, your personality will go perfect with email, it really will. Some people really have a hard time doing this. Eventually it comes around to them, but some people are more natural at it.

GUY MALONE: My problem is being too verbose to write short emails like you do and still get a point across. That's going to be a skill that I'll have to refine.

BEN SETTLE: You know what it is? It starts out harder to write shorter stuff. I want to get mine under 300 words and it's just hard. It's just one of those things that the more you do it, the easier it gets. I've got to give you credit for something. I was watching one of your old videos and you introduced somebody and you had this saying that I haven't forgotten since, and I've shamelessly used it and I need to give you credit for when I use it: "Keep it like a woman's skirt – short enough to get attention, and long enough to cover the details." That's perfect and that's exactly how email should be, or any type of written thing.

GUY MALONE: One thing I would like to add is one of the most successful events I had was the 2004 conference that mixed the secular and the Christian. Really the first thing I have to say about this is when the 2003 conference was over, I was done. I had no plans whatsoever to do this again. I wasn't about to put myself through it. People were asking me, "Are you going to do this again next year?" and the first thing out of my mouth was, "Yeah, if God is punishing me." But the thing is, after it was all over, that Monday morning I woke up with this huge plan and vision in my head of who to invite and what to do. I'm like, "God, that's going to cost $10,000. I don't have it," but I didn't say, "I can't do it or I won't do it." I just realized this is totally from God, so I started sending out the emails inviting the speakers and so forth.

I think a key to all this is you have to have a vision from God. You have to be doing His business. You have to be doing something that comes from Him, and then He can bless it. Just as a practical lesson – and this goes right along with meeting people's needs of what they want – is there were seven Christian speakers and seven non-Christian speakers. The ones I invited were not the new-agey ones that would be doing objectionable material. They were the strait-laced people like John Greenwald and Rich Dolan, people that did have good information. At the end of that panel discussion, Joe Jordan thanked them both for being there, because the church, the audience he was going after at the time, doesn't even realize there's a problem or that there's anything to this UFO stuff. If we're saying, "Here's what the Bible says about UFOs," if they don't believe in UFOs or there's anything to it, then they don't care what the Bible does or doesn't say about something that they don't even believe is real in the first place. Having these people give such convincing presentations that this is real, it opens their minds and opens the door up to, "Okay, now I'm convinced." You might say that I was able to channel other people's expertise to actually help create the market for what I wanted to share.

The interesting thing about that event was people came in one sense because it was Roswell and they'd never been there. That 2004 event was the most pre-sales I've ever had on anything – maybe not 2007, actually. In 2007 I capped it when we got to 100 because of the size of the room. I paid all those air fares and spent like $14,000 that weekend. Most of it was based on pre-registration sales. People were coming because of the celebrity status for the good information of the non-Christian invitees. The rest of us were almost complete unknowns to the people who had paid to come to it, but their following came to our event. They came to hear John Greenwald or Rich Dolan, but while they were there and they paid for it, they also heard Guy Malone, David Flynn, Mike Heiser, and they walked away thinking, "These Christians have got something." But they wouldn't have come if it was just us, I don't think. 2003 had like 10 pre-registrations.

BEN SETTLE: That's a really good point. When people are trying to create products, like this book – I'm not writing this, you guys are.

GUY MALONE: You're doing the same thing. You're riding on other people's expertise to create your market. I'm not knocking that.

BEN SETTLE: Believe me, I'm learning more from this book probably than the people who are reading it, so maybe there's a little bit of that in it too. But still, it's very true. I've created many products like that, where you find – and I hate to use this term – but you find the "rock stars" and you get their help, then their credibility rubs off on you.

GUY MALONE: Yes! It's true, it does by association. For years afterwards I could be somewhere else at another conference, California or D.C., and people would sometimes go, "That's Guy Malone. He put on that really cool conference in Roswell." Also I went from being, "There's Guy Malone, that Christian guy saying aliens are bad. Keep away from him" – to being, in the terms we're using, meeting a need that people had. I provided something they actually wanted, and then that became my reputation after 2004.

BEN SETTLE: If I was in the UFO community and if I was a secular guy, I would be trying to get you to contribute to my conferences and books. Now that you've spoken at Roswell and you ran the conference, you have a lot of credibility in that area. Maybe they do, and they should, and then that would give you a platform obviously to teach what you have to say. I wish they were smart enough to ask you.

GUY MALONE: I think it's coming more now. After this Roswell 1947 talk I did, there was a conference organizer there who came right up to me and started talking and saying that she works with this and that, and would I be able or willing to reproduce it elsewhere, and I'm like, "Absolutely." This should tie in to what we were talking about giving people what they want and need, or the Salvation Army approach of ministry. What God has graced me with in this particular Roswell talk is – you remember the movie – and the way you write your emails I know you'll like this example – the movie *The Rock* with Sean Connery.

BEN SETTLE: Oh yeah, I love that movie.

GUY MALONE: You know how it ended? They're driving off in the car with the microfilm going, "You want to know what really happened in Roswell?"

BEN SETTLE: Yeah, and the Kennedy assassination.

GUY MALONE: Bill Clinton speaking in Ireland responds allegedly to a young kid's question, "I don't know what happened in Roswell, but I really do want to know." That's the treasure I'd say God has given me with this particular lecture. People all over the world don't care about UFOs and the Bible, don't care about demons, but they do want to know what happened at Roswell though. If I can provide them at least a credible answer to that, it's the Salvation Army. It opens the door for everything else. I think that's the biggest theme that you and I keep hitting on, is you have to find out what they need and what they want. Offer it and then find a creative way to attach what you want them to have as well.

BEN SETTLE: That's a very powerful concept. There was this copywriter, long deceased now, named Eugene Schwartz. He wrote this book called *Breakthrough Advertising,* and it's almost like a textbook. It's kind of hard to get through, but he talks about the concept of gradualization, where you start with what someone already believes, and then you gradually move toward the stuff that they wouldn't normally accept otherwise. It sounds like exactly what you've been doing.

GUY MALONE: I think so, accidentally, but the trial and error of learning.

BEN SETTLE: From what I've noticed, you surround yourself with a lot of strong Christians and smart people. How does this help with the business side of your ministry, or does it? I don't know if it affects it either way.

GUY MALONE: It doesn't really apply too much, because we just run it from our computers here at the house. But for one, that's scriptural. When going into battle, get a multitude of counselors. I was made aware of that before I ever moved to Roswell. I know it is biblical advice. There's victory in a multitude of counselors, and I'll have to look them up and send them to you exactly. It's funny, I operate by them but I can't quote them. One thing is that is biblical advice, and when you do so, you get a lot of free advice. You surround yourself with people who are smarter than you or are gifted in areas that you're not, if they're willing to help and willing to offer. You can't be disingenuous about it. You've got to be real and have real relationships with people, and they've got to be sorta kinda called to help you, but it is a good position to put yourself in, to be around people who are smarter than you are and to be around people that have gifting and expertise or Ph.D.s or skills that you don't have. I'm sure you're aware of this guy David D'Angelo.

BEN SETTLE: Yeah.

GUY MALONE: I used to be on all that stuff years ago. He advised guys that were wanting to pick up girls, that you had to have a circle of friends that were better-looking than you, because by association you become one of them – better-looking, smarter, richer, better at this stuff, whatever like that. This is the same dynamic. In one sense it rubs off. In one sense they'll help you if you're doing a godly thing and you're not only profit-oriented or only using-them-oriented. If they're a little bit called to help, it's just sound biblical advice to surround yourself with a multitude of counselors. People often use *Star Trek: The Next Generation* as the perfect example of how to run a business or ministry or anything. You've got Captain Picard, they meet around the table and he listens to input from people that have expertise in areas that he does not, before making any decision.

BEN SETTLE: I never thought of that before. That's a very good analogy.

GUY MALONE: I've seen Christians use that as the perfect leadership model.

BEN SETTLE: Okay, now I have to ask you this. Let's face it, we'd be letting everyone down if we did not address it. What really did happen at Roswell and why should a Christian care?

GUY MALONE: I really like that question. All the pictures, all the documents, and all the links that I used as sources are at www.RoswellUFOCrash.com, where I argue it was a manmade event created partly by scientists that the United States imported from Nazi Germany, who were working on exotic aircraft at the end of the war. They never got them into mass production, but they had some amazing flying machines, and there are several books and documents now that can prove and show you the photos and the schematics of what they were doing. We brought them over here and put them to work secretly in White Sands, New Mexico and Ft. Bliss, Texas and Wright Field, Ohio. It's an easy jump when you see the photos of what they were working on in Germany and what they were designing, to realize that what happened in Roswell – just a couple hundred miles away from where they were stationed and doing experiments two years after they got here – was a manmade event.

The second half, why should Christians care – the angle I took on this is an extra on the DVD. To me, what I used to have written up on the website is that the Roswell incident is to belief in life on other planets pretty much what Paul is to Christianity and what Bill Gates is to computers. Computers used to exist and they were big and took up a whole room, and the only people who knew how to operate them wore white coats who had pocket protectors. Bill Gates and Microsoft may be ripping off Apple for that matter, but with a graphic user interface they popularized computers and made them mainstream and got it down to desktop. While it's true that Jesus had risen from the dead, everybody that was hearing that message was a Jew and was in Jerusalem. Paul is the one that took it to the Gentiles and to the world and popularized or at least informed the world about the resurrection of Christ from the dead. I think the Roswell incident very similarly is considered by many people to be the proof text that there is life on other planets. I don't think that's a biblical view, though. I honestly don't think there is life on other planets. That's part of the whole other lecture I did this year.

But when it comes down to why people should care, it's that if it is indeed an unbiblical world view, we are given the command to cast down vain imaginations that exalt themselves against the knowledge of God. That's kind of how dismantling this belief in aliens – or whether there's life on other planets or not, I should say – is that belief in aliens in Roswell opens the door to all kinds of occult and new-age belief systems for people. I go over that in the other lecture. The fruit of it is awful. It leads people to believing in reincarnation. They're inviting spirits into their lives without knowing they're spirits. They really believe they are aliens. Roswell, again and again and again, becomes the proof text for it. The polls from the 1940's and 50's show that not one in ten people believed in life on other planets, much less whether it was happening here or that it was coming here. Now two-thirds to three-quarters believe in it. I think popular belief in Roswell is the main game changer in those statistics. There's been Hollywood, there's been Steven Spielberg etc. It was going to happen anyway, just like computers existed anyway, but Roswell has been key in popularizing it and making it mainstream. If it can be dismantled or if it can be disproved, all the sudden the door is closed for many people for occult belief systems and inviting these spirits into their lives.

BEN SETTLE: Very, very good. Where can people go to get more info about you? Do you have a website you'd like to share?

GUY MALONE: www.AlienStranger.com links to all of my websites in this field. Our ministry site is www.AlienResistance.com.

To learn about the Roswell crash, go to www.RoswellUFOCrash.com. To learn about the spiritual side of alien contact and the religious messages that aliens are allegedly imparting to people, based on all the studies and interviews and Harvard and MIT type of studies, the newest lecture that is also on video online for previewing is www.AreAliensDemons.com.

The newest conference website with all of the DVDs for lectures – the two that I've mentioned, plus Joe Jordan and Mike Tatar – is www.TheInvisibleBattle.com. They can all be watched for free online, and they can also be purchased if someone is so inclined. For that matter, they can support us. Even if they don't want to order the DVD but they want to watch it for free and feel like they should donate something, there's a button up for that too.

BEN SETTLE: Finally, what advice do you have for someone reading this book who wants to know more about being a Christian and if it's really the answer for them?

GUY MALONE: If they're wondering if this stuff is real, if Christianity really is the answer, if Jesus is true, I can only give the advice that I myself did when I was like 21 years old. I was kind of at my wit's end and I just prayed out loud. "Jesus Christ of the Bible" – I specified, because I was pretty sure there might be tricksters or fake spirits also named Jesus – I said, "Jesus Christ of the Bible, if You're real and if You're really God, then I invite you to show Yourself and prove Yourself to me. If You're not, then You can't even hear what I'm saying anyway so it doesn't matter," or something like that.

I just called out and said the name of Jesus Christ. I didn't invite Him to be my Lord and Savior. This was not a conversion type of prayer, but I invited Him to prove Himself to me if it was really true, and He did.

BEN SETTLE: That seems to be the case when people are atheists. If they seek Him out they find Him, but if they don't and they just close their mind to it, they don't and continue to disbelieve. I like your way of doing it. You're again taking the pressure off.

Guy, thanks, I really appreciate you doing it. If there's anything I can ever do for you, just let me know.

GUY MALONE: You've done much already. Thanks!

Christian Business Bonus Tip #1

Following is a Bible-themed article written to my website newsletter subscribers. To join my free mailing list and access 700+ pages of advanced web marketing tips, go to:

www.BenSettle.com

The Guidebook To Supernatural Marketing

Lately I've been reading a lot of Biblical prophesy.

It's always been a big interest of mine. And one of my favorite Bible prophesy researchers is a guy named Lynn Marzulli whose stuff is always a meaty read.

Anyway, here's why I bring it up:

Lynn is VERY good at getting on radio.

I ain't just talking about "Christian" radio shows, either.

But also on secular shows with huge audiences — like "Coast 2 Coast" with George Noory, for example. And every time he gets on these shows, he does something anyone in business can use to get more response, more sales and more customers.

What does he do?

He makes the "ordinary" fascinating to the mainstream.

In other words, he makes ideas that normally only excite Christians appealing and intriguing to non-Christians (who he's always trying to reach out to).

Example?

The big one is when he talks about the Bible.

He doesn't call it The Bible.

That terminology has very little appeal to non-Christians. And judging by how few Christians read their own Bibles these days, it's probably not all that exciting to them, either. So instead Lynn calls it something else:

"The Guidebook To The Supernatural"

Booyah!

How cool is that?

Just by <u>reframing</u> the name of The Bible, he captures the interest of those who'd normally have no interest in it at all (or who may even be hostile to it.)

This gives him a fair hearing every time.

Opens minds that are normally closed to such ideas.

And takes what might seem dry, dusty and boring to some people, and makes it fresh, exciting and, yes, cool.

Again, you can do the same thing.

Take your ideas and product titles and inject energy into them.

Make them interesting.

Make them unique.

And make them hard for even your hardcore *skeptics* to ignore.

Yep, it's work.

(Thinking often is hard work, after all.)

But it's always well worth the effort.

Ben Settle

For over 700 pages of advanced web marketing tips and secrets, go to www.BenSettle.com

Selling For Souls On eBay

Interview with Greg Perry
www.BidMentor.com

BEN SETTLE: How did you first get started in business, and what were some of the challenges that you faced along the way?

GREG PERRY: Well, I do several things. Even though I do own a business – Greg Perry & Company – and it's incorporated and everything, I really consider myself an entrepreneur and I just do a lot of things. I don't really think of myself as being in business. I just do a lot of business, and psychologically there's a difference, even if technically there's really not. I've been an author of several books on various subjects, and I do major selling on eBay and all kinds of things, generally other things that include often just buying items when I can get some low prices on some electronics that are unusual, and I resell those mostly on eBay, but some other places as well. I kind of do a little bit of everything. I do a lot of affiliate work.

You asked how did I first get started. I used to work for other people in more traditional jobs, but Ben, I am really lazy. I'm just a lazy guy, so I never really cared for that. I traded the 40-hour work week away, since I'm too lazy to work for a business, and now I work about 90 hours a week for myself, if that makes sense. Anybody who owns his or her own business or is an entrepreneur, such as yourself, will completely understand what it's like to just be too lazy to work other people, so you overwork on your own. It's all about risk and reward. I think it's wonderful that people are different. I really like the different business people. I admire them. I completely admire people who prefer to work for other people, because that's what most people do. I wish that I were more structured and could do that – I really do. There are times that I wish I could do that.

From the beginning I always kind of was on my own. When I was about 7 years old my father brought home a big bucket of brand new combs. I don't know where he got them, but there were probably 250 combs, and they were all wrapped up and new and nice, and he said I could have them. So I went out the next day and went all over our neighborhood door-to-door selling those combs. I just thought this was a great business. I don't know if I remember saying this or if my parents have said it so much since, but what I would tell people who would answer the door, which usually was the lady of the house, because it was summer and they were home back then – I said, "These combs are brand new and they're 10 cents apiece, or you can get three for 30 cents." I seriously had no idea why people thought that was funny. I just thought that's the way they do it, so I've kind of had an entrepreneur attitude without trying. It just comes naturally to me.

In school I always did real lousy, all through junior high and high school. I was a very mediocre student. I never understood anything that was going on in history and math. I didn't know what was going on. I never did any homework. I never understood what they were saying. I always felt like I missed three years of something, but I played the trombone. I'm kind of musical, so I was in as many band classes as I could to keep my average up. But something funny happened in college, because it turned out that when you go to college you can choose your own field of study. You can pick your own classes and learn basically whatever you want to learn. I just thought that was a racket! My second semester of college I got a 4.0 straight A average, and I graduated close to that four years later with a 3.7. Then I got my Master's degree. I think that says a lot about me, that when I control my own direction I seem to do better. A lot of people aren't wired that way, and that's fine.

A little preview of what I hope we can get into later, but basically if you don't like a lot of risk – and most people are risk-adverse; they don't care for risk too much and they want to work for someone else, and that's fantastic and they're probably way smarter than I am. Even though I might make more than that traditional person in one day or one month, I might not make anything the next day or the next month. You know what that's like, but I don't mind that risk and I think most people do. I guess that it's the risk taker in me that enjoys this sort of entrepreneurial thing, being in business for myself. I don't know. You've heard of Dan Kennedy and you know about Dan quite a bit. I'm really impressed by what Dan has to say much of the time. Dan says everybody has a boss, and your boss and my boss, Ben, are our customer base. In a way, you have to know your boss better than most people who work for other people, because you spend all day writing ads that have to sing to your buyers. I spend all day writing books and eBay ads that have to sing to my readers and my bidders. If you and I fail to understand our boss's needs, we will fail very quickly. That is the big downside with what we do. We always have to keep that in mind.

BEN SETTLE: The interesting thing when you talked about risk there, I've thought about that too. I think it's more risky for people to be working at a job right now. I see people and they're devastated. They lose that job, they have nothing to fall back on.

GREG PERRY: That is true. That's a good point. We might see that more than they do because of what we do. You and I live with the fact that if we fail, then our wives don't eat, our families don't eat, our dogs don't eat, we don't eat, and things are really bad if we fail and don't do our job. I think that on a day-to-day basis, you and I get better feedback than someone working for someone else. The harder we work, we almost immediately see that in a payment of some kind. Other people don't have that instant feedback, so I don't think they realize the risk that they are under also. In a way it is more standardized across the board, in that in general day-to-day, they don't have the risk of their income fluctuating as we do, but they do have the devastating risk, some people, if they lose their job, that's really going to put them in a problem, especially with the economy the way that it is today and possibly the way that it's going to get much worse before it gets better.

BEN SETTLE: You said there was a difference between the psychology of doing business and actually just doing business. What does that mean exactly? I think I know what you're talking about, but I want to hear what you have to say about that.

GREG PERRY: I have a formal business structure that has all of the usual business things. It has a corporation tax return and a checking account that's just for the business and a Federal tax ID number, and I have an incorporated business that produces an income and has expenses. I find a way to get around to recording all those expenses whenever I think of it. It is a structured formal business. When you first asked am I in business for myself, I should have said, "Oh sure, I'm in business for myself," but I don't think in those terms psychologically. I'm more task-oriented than business structure-oriented. If I were to buy a business, such as a used bookstore or a car wash or something, I don't know that I could really run that business, because it has to be extremely structured also and that's not the type of person I am. I'm unstructured. I'm task-oriented. I would be worrying more about getting the car cleaned if I owned a car wash than recording all of my expenses properly, and that would be a big problem for me because you have to be able to keep a good set of books whenever you own a business like that.

I psychologically still think of myself constantly as an entrepreneur and I've got to do this job, then this job, and I've got these tasks to do, and this is the income I might see if I do A, B and C; whereas, from a business standpoint, it's really a very structured business. Where that corporation is might surprise you, but my corporation is actually for my books, for being an author. I've written a lot of books, as you've mentioned. I have all of my royalty statements going to my sub-chapter S corporation, and all of my writing related expenses come out of the corporation. I find that that works better from a tax standpoint for several reasons, many of which I've even forgotten, but our eBay and all of that is more of just a standard Schedule C on a business form, just a little on the side type of business, even though it's grown to be a giant income, expense, and sometimes headache, even though we like it. It's not really a formal business. It's more of a hobby business. I view all of that the same. If I've got a book to write, "Well, I've got to write my book." I don't think of it as, "Well, my business, my corporation needs to show income." I don't really think in those terms. That's why I think in a structured, physical business I would be more of a failure.

BEN SETTLE: There are those of us like you and me who are on the production side, but we really avoid the administrative side. You need both.

GREG PERRY: You're absolutely right. I don't know, maybe you have a bookkeeper. I don't. I was talking to Jayne, my wife, yesterday that I think maybe in January I'm going to have to get one, because I'm not good at that and I'm not consistent, and I think a bookkeeper would make me be more consistent. I think

I'm accurate when it comes to taxes and all of that, but I don't do it in a structured way that allows me to integrate that part of the business into what I do very well. It's more of a chore, and I think if it were more structured by a bookkeeper or something that showed me a better way to do it, I think I would be more successful in that as well.

BEN SETTLE: How many books have you written? Not just published books, but also e-books and self-published. Overall, how many books have you written?

GREG PERRY: I don't think people believe me when I say this, but I really don't know for sure. I think I've written about 80-something books that have been published by major publishers. We're talking about McGraw Hill and those types of publishers, all non-fiction. I wrote one for Thomas Nelson and Prentice-Hall, and about 85 or so titles have been published, and then maybe 15 or 20 e-books and self-published books that I've done since then.

BEN SETTLE: The published ones, they're mostly computer-related?

GREG PERRY: The majority of them have been computer-related. I don't know in the future that they will be. They might be as far as eBay topics or something. I started off writing programming books on the C programming language and Basic and Visual Basic and all of the languages that were in the 80s and 90s. Then I started writing more about applications such as Windows and Office and Open Office, and I've written several books like, *Making Movies with a PC* and all of that. I moved to the applications side and found out these are a lot easier to write, and they sell a whole lot more books. I haven't written a programming book since. That's sad, because I've lost some of my skills. I have not kept up with programming as well as I should, but it allowed me to write a lot of books and see some fairly decent sales.

The largest computer book publisher is called Pearson Education. They own Q and they do the, *Teach Yourself Something in 24 Hour* series. They sell the most computer books, or at least they did in the '80s and '90s when I primarily worked with them. I had their #1 and #2 top-selling books of the summer, which is pretty amazing. I was shocked to hear that. One was a Windows book and one was an Office book. That turned out to be a good move for me, to move from the programming side to the application.

BEN SETTLE: You're writing a book called *Selling on eBay the Christian Way*. Where did that idea come from?

GREG PERRY: Jayne, my wife, helps me a lot with our eBay business. I buy a lot of things and resell them, and also we have a lot of people that bring us things to sell for them, although we've had difficulty the last three months getting to the rooms full of things we have to sell for other people. We do run an eBay consignment business. We charge 20% of the final selling price for our fee to do that. That's on the low side. If you go to a retail store and leave your items at an eBay selling store, they'll charge 25% to 35%, sometimes 40%, and we just charge 20%. Although I don't do a lot very well, Ben, I do eBay very well. I leave copywriting to experts such as you, but I do understand copywriting principles and I understand eBay and I can write an eBay listing that sells. I was telling a friend a year or so ago, he wanted me to sell some things for him. He had bought a few things on eBay, but I said, "Look, I can get often more than 20% for what you're trying to sell, depending on the item, but if you sell it, you're not very good at it and you don't know how to write ads." Our forte is selling rare books, and I think he had a bunch of rare books. He didn't know how to tell if it was a first edition or anything. I often tell clients that I can usually get 20% or more selling their items over what they could sell them for, so they might as well let us do it. They don't have to do the work and they get basically the same amount of income.

I was telling a friend that I pull more bids and final selling prices for many items than others that sell the very same thing, and he said something like, "Wow, you must exaggerate a lot when you write listings." That really stunned me. That really bothered me. I don't exaggerate. When I write an eBay description, it's the same way I write books. This is basically how I write an auction – What would I want to know about this item if I were thinking about buying it? What do I need to know about it? I just answer my own question, and that's what I do and it works. In a way it's the Golden Rule from Scripture. I not only want to write listings that I'd want to see, but I want to treat our buyers the way that we want to be treated whenever we buy something. We buy a lot on eBay. Anytime we need anything that's not immediately perishable, that can be shipped in the mail, I always check eBay for it. It can be anything. It can be potato chips or something. I can't think right now of what it might be. We buy toothpaste and everything on eBay. I know what it's like to be on both sides of eBay in a major way. I got to thinking, I want to teach people how to do this the right way, because someone can't be successful on eBay if they do exaggerate. They can be successful for a short time, but their buyers are going to get angry and leave low feedback for them. They're not going to come back to them and they're not going to last very long. Whenever you complain to eBay about sellers – I don't really like this, I don't really think it's fair – but eBay almost always take the buyer's side by default. It's up to the seller to prove the buyer wrong, and that's sometimes difficult to do. That's the rule of the game.

That's fine. As long as I know the rules, I can work with that. Sellers that are not honest, that did not do the right thing, that don't understand also simple copywriting and selling principles, they're not going to do very well.

About four years we sold a book. It was about a $50.00 book. It was a semi-rare first printing book. After we sold it to this guy, he paid and I sent an email telling him we wrapped the book well and we shipped it, and then I sent him the tracking information and I left feedback for him on eBay. I always leave feedback. On eBay, buyers leave feedback for sellers to tell how good of a job the seller did, and the sellers leave feedback for buyers that say what the buyers like. I left feedback immediately upon receiving a payment, because he did his job. If I don't ship the item he still did his job, so I leave feedback as soon as they pay. A week later, UPS rapped on our front door with this huge box of cookies, breads, and candies from this bakery in Chicago. It turned out that this guy that bought this book owned and ran this bakery, and the note inside said he was so impressed with us as sellers that he wanted to return the favor. He and his wife sent all of these goodies. We had no idea anything like this was even in the works. Then a year later at Christmas, we got another massive box from them with even more breads and cookies and all this stuff that his wife makes at this bakery they own, and the note said, "We just wanted to follow up and make sure you two were doing well." Is that something or what?

BEN SETTLE: That takes the whole feedback thing to the next level.

GREG PERRY: I know. We just thought seriously, not being falsely humble, we truly look at each other, Jayne and I sometimes – by the way, they are not the only ones that have sent us stuff like that – and we think, "What on earth is the reason these people are impressed with us? We sell on eBay. That's all we do." I don't know. I really hope we can get into this a little bit later, but anybody in business should do one and only one thing if they want to be successful. I truly mean this. To be successful, she or he should be in business to serve others. That's it. If you truly serve others, you will be successful. If you don't, you'll fail. You may not fail right away but you will fail. If you serve others, that means you're meeting their needs. If you're meeting the needs of others and you're successful, that means one thing. It means you're serving others very well. Instead of being embarrassed at being successful from serving others, you should be proud of a job that you're doing. Pride is not something that we seek after, but to be proud of a son who does well in some sport, you might be proud of your son. That's not a bad pride. If you are proud of a job that you worked hard and did well because you served someone and made them happy, you should be proud of that job.

All of this came together. I'm a Christian and I thought, "I want to write a book that targets the Christian market." I want to show Christians that if they're serving the needs of their customers and they're not exaggerating, which is what that guy accused me of, and if they're not doing anything wrong, quite the opposite, I find it extremely simple to support with lots of Scripture the serving of others. As a matter of fact, one could say serving others is maybe one of the three great things of the Bible. It's real high up there. I want to excite other believers who want to sell on eBay, and I want them to feel joy, not guilt, at being highly successful, and so I want to teach them how to be successful. I really don't like what the world has done. In a way, the world has bruised the body of Christ with guilt. As you know, God tells us through Paul, there's no condemnation for those who are in Christ Jesus. We shouldn't be feeling guilt all the time, but that's what we take on. It's just silly, wrong, and evil, and the world tells us we should be ashamed if we're Christians and we succeed. They're telling us if we serve others, we should be ashamed. Heaven forbid. I think we should feel joy when we succeed. Freedom is a godly concept. Bondage is an evil concept, and I want to excite Christians and show them that freedom and selling and serving others and being successful, if you do it the right way, is a godly concept.

I actually have another sub-Christian market in mind. What I really hope takes a hold of my book is the home-schooled market. Most home-schooling families are Christians – not all, but most are. Some families are not Christians and they just don't like the destruction that the government schools do to their kids. Most home-schooled families are Christians. eBay is a wonderful place to teach home-schooling kids about math, business, buying low and selling high, serving others, responding quickly to questions that people might have for you, and about using proper grammar and proper spelling when you're writing listings, because if you don't, it's going to look sloppy and they're going to think you're a sloppy seller. It's like a business that you walk into and it's dirty. An eBay listing with a lot of mistakes is sloppy. It just doesn't bode well for your business. I think there are a bunch of concepts that home-schooled families can use. If you know any home-schooled families, they have like 932 kids. They always can use the extra money anyway. I think it's a win/win/win situation. I am trying to put a lot of tips for home-schooling families in this book as well. I considered writing a separate one called, *eBay for Home-Schooled Families,* but I don't know at this moment. I'm still combining them in the same book. That's the whole emphasis, the whole genesis for the book that I'm in the middle of right now, trying to get finished.

BEN SETTLE: I was just thinking, maybe even especially for non-home-schooled Christians, it would be even more important because these kids are being torn in all these different directions that are not good for them, and how difficult is it for someone to have a little eBay business while they're still in high school? They're going to come home and be checking their stats and serving people and being responsible, instead of going out and messing around with their friends and getting into trouble.

GREG PERRY: That's a real good point. It really is. It's a great point. Of course they are, and they're going to be developing skills that will help them immediately when they graduate. They're going to be far more ready to enter whatever business they decide to go into or whoever they decide to work for. They have already experienced interactions with customers on an extremely personal level. eBay's extremely personal. You get to know your buyers pretty well sometimes. That's a good point. I may steal that and put it in my book.

BEN SETTLE: Please do. I'm just thinking, at that age, how easy it would be for maybe a 15-16-year old if they had guidance and everything. All their friends have video games and all this stuff and books they're not reading and games they're not playing anymore and clothes they're not wearing anymore, because styles come and go, and they have a built-in inventory there they don't even have to pay for. It's all profit.

GREG PERRY: You're absolutely correct. I think that's brilliant. That's a great insight.

BEN SETTLE: The reason I thought of that was because there was this book called, *Rich Dad, Poor Dad*. Have you ever read that?

GREG PERRY: Yeah, I've read it.

BEN SETTLE: He told a story in there, or maybe it was *Cashflow Quadrant*. It was one of those two books. He was telling the story about how one of his friends had a 16-year-old kid and the kid wanted a new car. He said, "I'm not going to teach him anything by just buying him a new car." What he did was took $1,600 cash and he invested it in the stock market and said, "Here, make it grow." That kid would come home every day and, instead of messing around doing whatever, hanging out, he's coming home and checking his stocks and learning about stocks. He's really learning real skills. I don't know what happened, but I wouldn't be surprised if he actually earned the money doing it that way.

GREG PERRY: I wouldn't be surprised either. It's been several years, but that seems familiar. In a way, the kid had a lot better video game than all his friends. He was learning and earning at the same time.

BEN SETTLE: That's exciting, even when you're an adult.

GREG PERRY: It is. Every day, you're absolutely right.

BEN SETTLE: I want to touch on something real quick that you mentioned. I wasn't intending to ask you about this, but it's such a hot button for Christian entrepreneurs that I've talked to, this issue of guilt. Why do you think they feel so guilty? Are they misinterpreting certain Scriptures, or is it just something they're being told? What do you think about that?

GREG PERRY: They are believing myths that are not in the Bible, first of all. You said are they misinterpreting Scripture? I'm going to make some generalizations in answering, and you can tell me to shut up and you want to move on to a different topic if you want, because I'll probably step on toes. They're not misinterpreting Scripture, because a lot of Christians have no idea what the Bible says. They don't know. They don't read it. They read books about the Bible sometimes. If they're really good Christians, they read books about the Bible. They always go to church and listen to the sermon and to Sunday School, but they don't know what's in the Bible. They don't know what God says about basic issues. I used to guest host a national television show that was a talk show, and we would talk about Christian topics a lot. You could ask someone a real basic question out of Scripture like, "What does God say should be done to young adults who aren't married and they have sex?" Most of the time people will say, "They should be stoned to death." That's crazy. Why would God say kill them over that? God's punishment is they should get married. That's punishment for them. I say that tongue and cheek, but He says, "They should get married." That's a very small example of a real basic truth in Scripture that hardly anyone knows. We've listened to Hilary Clinton's favorite verse, which is, "Love the sinner, hate the sin." That's not in the Bible. The Bible doesn't say that ever. The Bible doesn't say we can just separate the sin from the sinner and just let everyone go to heaven. That's exactly the opposite of what the Bible says. There's going to be a lot of elbow room in heaven, because most people aren't going to be there. Narrow is the way, not wide, to get to heaven. It's very easy to get there, but most people won't be there, I'm sad to report.

Here's another one, "All sins are equal." The Bible doesn't say that. The Bible actually says exactly the opposite over and over. The Bible has all sorts of varying degrees of punishment for various crimes and for various sins, various ways that you face consequences and pay and repent for certain things that you do. Someone at a little church that we were visiting once was really adamant about this all sins are equal thing. I said, "Jesus doesn't say that."

He says, "Yes, he does."

I said, "Show me." He couldn't. He said, "It's in there. It's implied."

I said, "Let me ask you a question. Frank, is one sin unpardonable in the Bible and no other sin is unpardonable? Is there one that's not pardonable?"

He says, "Yes," He starts looking at his shoes, "Yes."

"Well, then that sin's not equal with all the others, right?"

"Well, yeah but that's the exception."

"Well, okay then all sins aren't equal. You don't ever want to say that again, because you're lying to people." I said, "What about Jesus when He said, 'Which of you has the greater sin?'" And then Jesus answers his own question. He was talking about Pontius Pilate for washing his hands of it and letting Jesus go on ultimately to his death, or the disciple that betrayed Jesus – "Which one has the greatest sin?" Jesus then answers that.

The concept of all things are equal is totally not biblical. It goes on and on with things like that, that people don't know what the Bible has to say about everyday matters. They think it's this Holy Book that is not approachable unless you're a pastor or a Sunday school teacher. The Bible was written for you and me. It was written for us. It was written for the lay people, especially Paul talking to the body of Christ, which is what we are right now. We are in the Body of Christ. Paul was really down to earth and he'd say, "Don't sin. Here's what you have to do if you do sin. Here's what you do if you're in a church and someone comes in and doesn't do right. Here's exactly what you do. Here is exactly how you give to the poor." What do we have? We have churches that have soup lines a mile long, completely violating everything Paul said. Paul said, "Don't give people food like that. Don't give people money like that. Don't do it. You're going to ruin them." We ignore what Scripture has to say and we believe the world. Then when we fail, which we will, we have all this guilt. "Oh, we were trying to do the right thing." All we do is just have guilt, and the world loves to pile guilt on Christians. If we had just known what was in the Bible to begin with and read God's simple words – 95–98% of the Bible is very simple to understand. I know there are a very small percentage of things that are hard to understand, very small, but not right and wrong issues. We're talking about eschatology things, end times, really advanced stuff. We're not talking about right and wrong, and we're not talking about guilt and joy and all of those real simple things. I think guilt comes from a complete lack of opening that big, thick, dusty book on most people's bookshelves.

BEN SETTLE: You said something a couple of months ago on Facebook. It was the best quote I'd ever heard. I don't know if I've ever told you this. You said something about how most Christians aren't even getting milk. They're lactose intolerant.

GREG PERRY: Oh, yeah. That was actually not mine. That was an acquaintance of mine up in Denver who said that. Paul talks about the Christians of his day, the Corinthians and all those guys. He says, "You guys can't handle the meat of Scripture. You need milk." In other words, you're just little babies. They just can't handle meat. They're not old enough to chew it. They're not old enough to digest it. You have to give babies milk. He said, "You're like babies. We've got to give you milk."

What we see today is today's believers are lactose intolerant. They can't even handle the milk.

BEN SETTLE: I thought that was a great analogy. This is on the side, but it's interesting. You mention the mile-long soup lines at some of the churches, basically doling it out for nothing and not really giving people an incentive to even try. I was interviewing Terry Dean for this book and he talked about that. He knows a pastor. He said that line went down really quick when he started saying, "Okay, no problem, but you're going to have to sweep the floor first." In other words, you're going to have to earn it.

GREG PERRY: Yeah, right, and then it just goes away. I understand. It's like the guys on the street corner. If you actually offer them a job, they will not take it.

BEN SETTLE: I used to live in Illinois and sometimes I'd go to Chicago. I never enjoyed big cities, but I remember some of those guys out there making pretty good money just begging.

GREG PERRY: Yeah, it's a big racket.

BEN SETTLE: People don't even realize. You have the sob sisters. It's obvious. You just watch them. You watch them go, and they're actually dressed pretty nicely and you maybe see one of them get into a pretty nice car.

GREG PERRY: Oh, definitely. There was a local story in Tulsa, which is close to where I live, and they followed all four of them and did hidden cameras and stuff. Several of them on one major street corner all had a room at a nice hotel right across the street and they would take turns. Three of them would be in the hotel room doing whatever they do, and then one at a time they would take turns going out to the street corner to make their money. It's really a racket. I think a lot of dumb Christians will give them money, but also a lot of liberals will give them money. I don't really mind that redistribution of wealth. Liberals are being stolen from. It's like, "Oh, it's okay."

BEN SETTLE: Better that way than have the government force it out of us at gunpoint, I guess. We will get into the politics in a little bit, because I will have to ask you about that. I want to get back to your book for a few minutes. What are some of the tips that are going to be in that book or that you've already written that someone listening to this could maybe use if they wanted to go on eBay and start selling?

GREG PERRY: I think it's really important that people respond quickly to others who might be potential customers. I think that builds business real quickly. It engenders trust among bidders and buyers. eBay is a little bit different from Amazon or BestBuy.com in that they don't know their seller. eBay doesn't sell anything. eBay simply brings buyers and sellers together. Your buyers don't know you. They don't know me, and if you're selling something, there has to be indications of trust on the seller's part before someone will spend a lot of money with you. One way that they get trust is to give a fast response to questions and concerns. I think that if we see a need, we should jump to help that need and we should do it in a proper way. If we see a good desire, we should seek to help fulfill that desire. eBay is such a huge one-on-one universe. An auction is up for about seven days on the average, and we often answer 10 to 20 emails about an item over that seven days. We get to know our buyers. We answer questions quickly. We ship quickly. We pack well. All of those things are being good stewards of the abilities that we have. I believe that eBayers, people who are new to eBay, might fall short on some of those things. I want to encourage them not to.

You and I spend a lot of time at the computer, and I know that you do because I'll ask you a question and you'll answer within a minute. It might be 11:00 pm or 8:30 am or something. I know that you and I spend a lot of time on the computer. If I get a question on eBay, I really enjoy immediately answering it. The first thing I'll say is, "Sorry to take so long to respond but..." then I'll answer the question. They'll always write back and say, "What do you mean sorry to take so long? I've never had a question answered that fast." It's fun to do that, and they laugh at it too.

I want people to write honest descriptions. All these things are just standard Christian stuff, and yet it's incumbent upon us to do this stuff to sell our items and to engender trust. Even better, how does Scripture sell things? Scripture sells itself by offering truth, right? Not exaggeration. Sometimes exciting language is used. God is exciting, so the Word of God is exciting. It uses exciting language. I like to call it fantastical language. The Word of God offers truth. It doesn't just offer truth, it is truth. God is not a God of truth. He is truth. He, by definition, is truth. Unlike some religions whose so called "Holy Book" changes over time – changes a lot actually – and unlike the Humanist Manifesto that's now entering its third major revision if I have my facts straight, the Bible doesn't have to come in a three-ring binder so we can add and take out pages and change it. It doesn't change, because the character of God doesn't change. Our first lesson as business people from scripture should be to tell the truth.

How else does scripture sell itself? It tells stories. Jesus once said that everything Moses wrote is true. Every single dotted "i" and crossed "t" that Moses wrote is true. Those are historically true and accurate stories. Often it tells stories that are not true. They teach truths, like the parables. You've written about this before. Those parables are thinly-veiled avenues to teach truth. Through parables, which are not always literally true, they do teach 100% truth, and those stories get people's attention. We need to tell stories when we sell something. That helps us sell items whenever we tell a story about it. It might just be a two-sentence line about how we acquired it, and yet people find that interesting. It humanizes it. We're not just some unknown seller. The buyer begins to feel as though she or he knows us, and that helps business.

How else does Scripture sell itself? It uses descriptive comparisons like, "It's easier for a camel to go through an eye of the needle than for a rich man to enter the kingdom of God." By the way, I think a lot of Christians, through guilt, would run from that verse, so I like to use it a lot because I think it's a good verse. We know from many verses about money that it's the love of money, not the possession of money or the making of money, that's the sin. You always have to look at the context whenever you see a scripture verse. Jesus was telling his disciples that all earthly things are going to pass away. It's sort of like the missionary, Jim Elliot. You may have heard of him. He said, "He is no fool who gives away what he cannot keep, to gain what he cannot lose." A person is not a fool who gives away what he can't keep, to gain what he can't lose. That's a marvelous statement about being in the body of Christ. Jesus was teaching his disciples the importance of following Him at that point in Matthew. As freedom lovers and business people, we shouldn't shy away from those verses just because at first glance we don't like the wording. If anything, we should run to them to help others understand their meaning. Let's say we're selling something for gardens and we say, "Your garden's produce will rise like a spaceship at NASA when you use our soft rock phosphate for your calcium in your garden." Or, "Your sales will skyrocket when you read Ben Settle's book and start implementing his sales techniques." We know that comparisons paint pictures. We see that in Scripture. Jesus painted pictures in our minds with His stories, and so do the writers of scriptures whom he inspired, like David in the Psalms. David wrote, "As the deer pants for water, my soul pants for you, oh God." Actually, that might be a Psalm. I'm not sure David wrote that specific Psalm, but he wrote most of it. He may have written that one. It paints a wondrous picture that this deer is out in the wilderness running and he's panting for some water and looks for a creek, and the writer of Psalms, his soul pants for God. It's the longing, that desire. It's a great word picture.

A lot of my suggestions revolve around how to respond to buyers, how to write descriptions, and how to paint pictures in our buyer's mind to explain the truth. I actually want to say one other thing that I'm going to talk about in this book. I haven't written this section yet. There were times we refused to sell things for other people, depending on the item. We'll tell a friend, "Yeah, we'll sell whatever. Just bring over what you have and we'll try to sell it." Some things aren't worth selling and we'll just give them back to them and won't even try it, because it just isn't worth it for them or for us, or it just wouldn't sell and be a waste of time. At the same time, there are certainly some items I just wouldn't sell. If someone brought me over a Satanic Bible, I wouldn't sell that. Someone brought over a Koran one time to sell, and I refused to sell that. You have to use discernment and you have to use wisdom. One friend of ours has a huge library of books at her home and she brought several books over about evolution. Her husband, who passed away and owned this library of books, had a lot of books on creationism and evolution. They covered both sides. I often like to list those books on evolution, and between the lines if I sell that book, I'll talk about all the problems that the evolutionist faces in dealing with truth and how they've been exposed. I don't know if you've heard of the *Finding Named Lucy* subject of falsehood and such a farce, but then they try again. I like to sometimes sell items that other Christians might be hesitant about. If I think I can somehow witness inside that listing, I find that a challenge and I often will do that.

Also, be ready to admit to your shortcomings also. That's so important. Christians should know that better than anyone. I wrote a report called *Three Powerful Words that Turn Angry Buyers into Happy, Repeat Customers*. I'll tell you what those three words are, "Please forgive me." I don't know why, but hardly anybody uses those exact words anymore for some reason, and yet that forgiveness is ultra supreme. By the way, in Scripture we're taught that it's a sin to forgive somebody who refuses to repent. God certainly never, ever forgives someone who refuses to repent. If we're fully clothed in His righteousness, then we're wrong to forgive those who are not repentant, but when I make a mistake on eBay – perhaps I ship the wrong item to somebody – I truly, truly am sorry. I did not want it to happen. It makes me angry at myself. It makes me feel terrible for my buyer, and I truly want that buyer's forgiveness. So I just ask for it. I say, "Please forgive me." My repentance is more than words. It has to be. It has to be demonstrated, and so I don't just ask for forgiveness but I try to go above and beyond to demonstrate my repentance. I'll let the buyer keep what I incorrectly shipped him, and then I'll Federal Express what he actually did buy to him. Being a Christian not only means being successful by serving, but also being humble when you mess up. Believe me, I have the opportunity to be humble a whole lot more than I'd like to be, but that happens in business. I think that it's the only thing that you should be.

BEN SETTLE: When you were talking about just telling the truth in your eBay ads, this is a very, very tried and true advertising technique. I call it a technique, but really it's just a principle in good selling. There's a lot of power in admitting the flaws of something. There was this ad in the early 1900s ran by a guy named Ernest Shackleton. It was in Britain and he was trying to get a team to go on an expedition out into the Yukon or somewhere bitter cold. That's exactly how the ad started. In fact, you know what? I'm not going to do this justice. I'm going to read this ad, because it's so telling. Maybe this would actually help somebody with eBay. Not only does it go against exaggerating and all that, but it's a good principle. Here it is. This was an actual classified ad in the early 1900s:

> *Men wanted for hazardous journey. Small wages. Bitter cold. Long months of complete darkness. Constant danger. Safe return doubtful. Honor and recognition in case of success.*

So you have six negative things, but then that one promise of recognition and honor in case of success is so much more powerful when it's surrounded by all the damaging admissions. You know what happened with that ad? Apparently half of England came out and responded to it. The guy was overwhelmed with responses, so that's something to think about.

GREG PERRY: It really is. I think that once in a while a direct marketer will mess up on purpose, and the next day say, "I'm sorry. I messed up." I don't know why I think that sometimes, but I do.

BEN SETTLE: There's a guy named David Ogilvy. I'm sure you've heard of him.

GREG PERRY: I've read his book.

BEN SETTLE: He was probably one of the savviest advertisers of the 20th century.

GREG PERRY: "The only sound you'll hear as you drive down the street is the ticking of the clock."

BEN SETTLE: Yeah, that was one of his famous ads and sold out the inventory of Rolls Royces. He told the story once about when he was with his wife and they were looking for some furniture, so they were at this furniture store. He was looking at this chair, and the salesman came up and said, "Look at this, there's a scratch on it. I cannot sell this to you unless you know that there's this scratch in the back," and he was just floored. He was like, "I can't believe that salesman just did that," and he practically kissed the guy's hand, he was so happy. Apparently that was a big revelation for him, and he started realizing you've just got to tell the truth in your ads. Not only can you sleep at night, but you might even sell more.

GREG PERRY: What happens when you do that on eBay? If I'm selling a rare book worth $1,000 in net commission and I say, "The problem is, the back jacket has a 3" tear. Someone's written an inscription on the inside, and three pages have dog ears. They've been folded down. We unfolded them, but you can still see where that was done." What that tells the buyer is that probably nothing else is wrong with this book, because you would have said if there is. A buyer that reads about flaws in an item, like Ogilvy – Ogilvy thought, "I can buy anything in this store and I can completely trust that I'm getting what he tells me."

BEN SETTLE: Absolutely, and think of that on eBay. It's hard to trust anyone. What if someone only has one feedback rating? But if you're out there telling the truth, man, that probably says more than feedback ratings.

GREG PERRY: It does, I think.

BEN SETTLE: Now I've got to ask you about his next thing, because really you're the one that kind of kicked me and got me going on this, and that is this whole idea of using media publicity. How does that work exactly, and how can maybe the average person who doesn't have a publicist and they don't want to spend a lot of money, maybe they have a smaller business, maybe they have a kitchen table business like you and I have – how they can use media publicity?

GREG PERRY: I would say if they hire a publicist, in most cases – especially for small timers like you and I, who have 0-5 employees – I would say if you hired someone to do your advertising in the media, probably it won't be done nearly as well as if you just do it yourself, and probably you'll get far less bang for your buck than if you just do it yourself. It depends on the business. It depends on what you do. I've given many media interviews, but even before I tell you what I've done, just right off the bat I think that you'll agree that everyone listening should know the name Paul Hartunian. Paul Hartunian produces probably the most famous press release "how to get publicity" package that's ever been produced. He doesn't cover all bases and he doesn't tell everyone how to get publicity in every manner and form, but he tells the entrepreneur, the business owner, the person who owns a small business especially – he teaches you a formula that is extremely simple on how to get interviewed. Whenever you get interviewed on the radio or TV, you are the expert. You automatically have this halo effect that says you know what you're talking about, or else they would have never asked you to be interviewed. If you think about anyone like Fox News, CNN, or you look on the average morning, they'll have 40 guests over a 2-1/2 hour time period. It's really not that big of a deal to be on one of these shows really in the whole scheme of things if you think about it, because every morning the producers on Fox News are thinking, "How in the world can we fill up today's 2-1/2 hours with a segment? We've got to get people, we've got to find interviews," so they're always looking for people. They do a lot of them, so it's not that big of a deal, but for a small business owner it can be extremely profitable to be interviewed by radio or TV nationally or even locally. If you're just a local guy, local interviews might even be more powerful, because you'll get people in your own town, who may even know your name, out to your business more.

You asked how I've had success with publicity. I've done mostly media interviews. I had guest-hosted a national television show, and I think that helped sell some of my books when I did that. That was in the mid- to late 90's. I've been on C-SPAN, I've been on one of Penn & Teller's Showtime specials, and I think I understand media. I've done about 80 or so national radio interviews about a book I wrote for Thomas Nelson a few years ago, and all 80 of those interviews were the result of me sending press releases around the country, with the sole goal of getting radio interviews. That's what I wanted and that's what I got.
It goes along a lot with what we've already discussed, and that is tell the truth, but we know the truth can be fantastical. It can be. So if I'm doing publicity for my *eBay Selling Tactics* – let me just tell you that – well, I'll just say it. I have an eBay course. I'm not doing this interview to sell my course, but I have an eBay course that teaches people who have never used eBay before how to become one of the most powerful sellers ever, and I call this

package "The most advanced eBay selling technique on the planet." That's what I call it. I don't say "one of the most," I say "The most advanced eBay selling technique on the planet." That's what I call my flagship product. That name sounds like an exaggeration, but I've looked at all the others. Well, that's using exaggeration. I haven't probably looked at every single package sold in every country in the world, but I've ordered every major package and I try to find them when they come out. I truly believe that one of my tactics is above and beyond, far better than anyone else. I cover selling topics that nobody else covers, and I do so in-depth and I give step-by-step on how to do it. I toss in all sorts of tips that are not published anywhere else. I've bought and reviewed virtually every other package out there, as I said, and mine is skyscrapers above the rest. Since mine is so good – and I know this doesn't sound humble – but mine is the best out there, so I decided to price it lower than anyone else's.

Most direct marketers who have brains like you would say that's not very wise, and it's probably not the best use of my resources, but I figure that people who need my package the most, the ones who really need that boost, are the ones who actually will take to heart my teaching. These are the very people who might need it most. The pros out there who've been selling for years, they think they know it all already. They actually have no clue, but in reality they're not going to think they need my product. They're not going to read it if they got it. They're not going to watch the DVDs and listen to my CDs, but newcomers, people who are struggling, who honestly want to make it, they have a need for my product, so I want to serve them. I sell this big, several-pounds of 3" thick stuff for $67. And again, I really didn't mean to get into that commercial, but let me get back to this. I really do believe it's the most advanced, and my customers tell me that too. You need to think about the words I just used. Whenever I do a radio interview, I use fantastical words like that. I say, "No, this really is the best," if I believe that it is. Or if I'm talking about a book I'll say, "No, there's no one out there that I have found who says the things that I say, and this is how it will help you, versus what you'll experience if you don't get it." You kind of have to use this fantastical language to get an interview, because a radio station might get 100 faxes and emails a day with press releases, and yours has to stand out. If you really have something to say, and if you truly have something to teach others, you have to make sure that you stand out or else you're not being a good steward of your resources. You have to tell the truth, and sometimes you have to tell the truth in a way that gets your press release to the top of the stack. Paul Hartunian talks all about this. I don't have any hesitation about using stories and wording and pictures in the buyer's mind and in the media's mind in order to get an interview, if I want an interview about a product that I have or a book that I've written, as long as I don't stray from the truth.

I have found media publicity is superb. Again, you're not selling something. You don't have to pay for it. You just have to pay for the fax or you might have sent letters or packages that had press releases in them. You might have sent them to the stations, so you might be out for stamps or something, but you're not out any money, whereas if you advertise you're out a bunch of money. Secondly, you're an expert. If you advertise, people think, "Well, they just bought time. I don't know if they really know what they're talking about." But if someone is interviewing you – as you're doing to me right now – they think I'm an expert, even though I have no idea what I'm doing, Ben. [laughing] Seriously, people view me as an expert because they trust you. They're already your customers. You took the time to want to ask me some questions, so there's an implied trust there. Kind of through you, they trust me more than they would if I were a stranger, and that is the power of getting attention in the media. So I strongly suggest that people learn more about getting media attention.

BEN SETTLE: As someone who writes ads, even besides the fact that you're getting on the radio, newspaper or the TV, which is all great and you can make sales, but there may be a lot of cases where you don't make sales if it's just a small station or whatever. But the inherent credibility by just being in the media, later on in your advertising you can say, "I was recently interviewed by XYZ station." You can be a brand new business, just hung your shingle out yesterday – like let's say someone's a lawyer (which I know is your favorite topic) – let's say for example someone's a bankruptcy lawyer. They advertise a lot. I just see them advertising all the time. So how do you stick out in the other ads out there of bankruptcy lawyers? Maybe all the other lawyers went to better schools and you kind of got C's at the local law school, but the fact that you were in the local paper or something, you're automatically perceived as being more knowledgeable than all the other high–falutin' guys out there.

GREG PERRY: Yeah, because you didn't have to pay for your advertising.

BEN SETTLE: Not only that, but they weren't in the newspaper, you were. They went to Harvard, but you were in the newspaper.

GREG PERRY: It's incredible leverage, just incredible.

BEN SETTLE: It's one of those things, and I'm serious. You're the one who got on me about that. I'm really glad you did.

GREG PERRY: I'm glad too. Being the author of a book or a magazine article also works the same way. It gives you that halo effect.

BEN SETTLE: Speaking of books, what advice do you have for Christian business owners who want to publish books or maybe just informational products like CDs or DVDs or something like that?

GREG PERRY: I think it's vital that every business owner has a book or CD or a product – or even better, several of them. A book gives you the halo effect we just talked about. People perceive you already as an expert, and Ben, every one of our listeners is an expert in something. I often give seminars on writing, and I'll ask, "Who in the room is an expert in something?" and hardly anybody will raise their hand. I say, "Wrong! You all are an expert in something. You don't understand. You don't have to be the best in the world to be an expert on a topic. That's crazy. You just have to know more than 90% of all people on that topic." It's not that hard to know 90% more than everyone else about a topic. That is not that difficult. I told you a lot of my early computer books were on programming. How many computer programming experts are there in the world – there are tens of thousands. There are probably 100,000 or more computer programming experts in the world, and most of them know more than 90% of the rest of the world about computer programming. There's like 100,000 or more of these people. What you do is take your field, which you know well – whatever it is – and you write a book or you produce an audio CD or a DVD. Even better, you write about a specific niche, or create a product about a niche in your field. Just write a little 25-page pamphlet or a short ebook, or just produce a 1-hour streaming CD that teaches someone how to do this. Teach them how to do this one specific niche.

Once you do that, you don't just have a CD to sell or a book to sell – you also now have several web articles, because you've gotten your material and you can now use that and leverage it in many different venues. If you have a magazine article and there's a magazine in your field – there are many industry magazines out there, a trade magazine about what you do – you already have an article that you can send in now. You have a chapter or two or three in a book that you're getting ready to write already written just by doing this one little niche subject. Once you have ten items, you are thought of as an expert, just as you are if you get media publicity. Now you can go to libraries, you can go to other business forums, you can go to live groups and give talks on your subject, and you're an expert because you wrote a book or you produced this how-to package.

Then you get business when you speak, and you get more business. Customers come to you and they tell you about their friends, and their friends call and say, "My friend, Joann, was at the lodge listening to your talk on your topic the other night, and that's exactly what I need. I need your business." People who read your magazine articles look at the byline at the bottom and they go to your website, so you get website customers that you would have never gotten before to buy products, because they have trust in you. It turns out non-fiction items are real easy to write, especially if you've never written before, because if nothing else, just talk into a recorder and record everything you know about a specific topic. Then you hire someone to massage all that into a book. You can go to Elance.com or call up your local college and find an English instructor and see if he or she knows someone who wants to massage material into a book. You pay them $200–300 and then they have something on their resume now that will help them. It all just balloons and just leverages, leverages, leverages on itself.

Or you can just self-publish, which I like to do myself. If you self-publish and you distribute a lot of books – whether it's an ebook or whether it's a real book that you actually have bound and everything – and you sell 5,000 copies of that somehow, you distribute 5,000 copies, the major publishers will have an interest in your book now, whereas they may not have before, because it has a proven track record. You can show your records that 5,000 of these have sold – or 3,000 or 1,000 – that publishers publish. They don't. Publishers are happy to just once in a while get one winner out of lots of losers. That's how they work. It's a numbers game. If you can prove and show that you've already distributed 1,000 of these things, major publishers will be far more interested in it than they would have before, and you didn't even have to be an author to write a book. For any business owner, I strongly suggest that you do this.

BEN SETTLE: It can really be super easy by doing what we're doing right now. I'm not writing this book. I'm interviewing you and some other people, just talking into a recorder. It will be transcribed. I don't even have to have it smoothed out by anyone. I just basically make sure the transcription is right and there's the book. I'm leveraging off all of your guys' expertise and credibility, which helps in advertising the book.

GREG PERRY: It sure does. You're absolutely right. Very good. Just interview an expert. If you're not an expert – or you might not think you are – interview someone who is, and you will be perceived as the creator of that product.

BEN SETTLE: Or just have your spouse or someone interview you. It doesn't even have to be a big deal.

GREG PERRY: That's true. Technology today allows all that. Thirty years ago it wasn't as easy. These days it's too easy.

Anyone can do it.

BEN SETTLE: It was a big production just to have a conference call like this. In fact, it was probably pretty expensive. You and I are talking on a free conference line. Anybody can go to the internet and just type in *free teleconference line* and there's plenty of them out there.

GREG PERRY: It's just not even fathomable to me that someone would offer that service. That's wonderful.

BEN SETTLE: This next question is a little bit longer. It's something that you said a long time ago that just really stuck out. That is, you told me that you wrote your first book because you wanted to be an author, and every book since that one you wanted to write to make money, and that you found the more money you make, the more people you were pleasing. What do you mean by that?

GREG PERRY: That is a long question, but the answer is actually pretty short. Everybody wants to see their book sold in a bookstore. When you see your book in a bookstore for the first time – or today's equivalent, when you see your book on Amazon for sale – it's really exciting. It really is. You might think, "That's not very humble." Right! It's not. It's really exciting, I'm just telling you, for about five minutes. You show all your friends and you call your relatives and you call your mom and dad if they're still living, and you call your grandparents. After you do that, in about five minutes you'll think, "Now, how can I sell more of these things?" and at that point writing becomes a business, just like any other business. That's what it is. You're producing a product that you need to sell. And if you write something that does not sell, you have just wasted resources and talents that are gifts from God. You just wasted some, because no one else is enjoying or learning from those resources. You've either overpriced it or you're selling it by lying about it. You'll have winners and losers, no matter how well you do, but if you don't do your best to get your product into other people's hands, you've wasted your time and your resources and your family's resources, and you're not being a good steward. It all goes to serving again.

I really liked seeing my book in Barnes & Noble. It was actually B. Dalton way back then in a mall, my very first book. I couldn't believe it! The second time I saw my book in a bookstore it wasn't really that big of a deal, and it all goes along with serving again. You will sell a lot of books if your writing serves a purpose, helps someone explain something, and even if your book isn't very good but you self-publish, you gain credibility in your field and get your foot in the door to help someone in a different way. So use your book or use your product in a way kind of like a business card to get more business by promoting your credentials. That's what I aim to do. I don't sell many computer books anymore. That's not really a major part of our income anymore. You can't really sell a book on Windows as well as you used to, the new Windows 7. Those Windows books don't sell as well as the Windows 95 books did. First of all, more people are growing up in the computer industry. More people have used computers from birth, it seems like, and computers are easier to use than ever before. Also there's the internet. If you want to know how to do something, just look it up on Google and you learn. You don't have to go to a bookstore and buy a book. But the fact that I've written so many books makes me a computer expert just in that, and I have to admit, I probably am a computer expert. But all of that is very important to me to promote me, so that what I endeavor to do next, I already have a built-in trust from the customer who's going to buy from me next. I think that for people who write books, you will see a sense of excitement, but you'll immediately start thinking it's a business, and it's a business tool. That's the way I view it and that's why I said what I said.

BEN SETTLE: It's so easy to get a book on Amazon. I don't think a lot of people understand that. I use a service that just does it for me. It's called LightningSource.com and it does it for me automatically. I don't have to do anything. It's great!

GREG PERRY: That's a great company. It's very good.

BEN SETTLE: They do all the printing, they collect the money, and they pay me a royalty. It's so easy. It's amazing that everybody's so in awe about that. Maybe that won't be the case in a few years, but might as well enjoy your notoriety while you can, I guess.

GREG PERRY: I don't want to minimize it. Producing a book or a product that can really be useful to someone isn't always for everybody the easiest thing in the world. Some people just aren't good at talking. I'm certainly not, but some people would be afraid to do what we're doing and to be on the other side of your microphone. Some people just have a blockade about writing something, so I don't want to minimize that. For some people, producing a product like a book or CD or DVD, a how-to in order to promote their product or service, for some people it's a challenge. It can be. There are hard parts about all of that, but in general it really pays for itself and it's worth overcoming those problems.

BEN SETTLE: Since you're a writer, you've obviously had to deal with that dreaded word "deadline," but everyone in business has deadlines. Whether they're a writer or not a writer, even like you were talking about earlier, just getting your tax stuff in on time is a deadline. What are some tips you have for anybody to meet a deadline? It doesn't have to be a writing deadline, but just general tips about deadlines.

GREG PERRY: That's one of the problems with writing, is the deadlines. The reason that I'm still in the middle of *Selling on eBay the Christian Way* is because I never set any deadlines for myself. It would have been done six months ago if I'd done that. I get that question a lot, "How do you meet your deadlines?" and I get that about as much as I get the question, "Where do I get my ideas for new products and books?" For me the answer is I don't have any idea really. Remember I said earlier I'm a little lazy. I feel as though I'm really lazy. I've written several million words and made money from several million words. I know that with one publisher alone I've sold more than three million books through that one publisher, so not only have a lot of my books sold, but I've written a lot of words through all the newspaper and magazine articles. I'll tell you, as someone who is primarily a writer, I don't have any incentive when I write. I get up to my keyboard and I'll think of 1,000 things I want to do instead of actually writing, and I never want to jump out of bed and go write. You'll see how this applies even if you're not a writer. If I'm out somewhere I'll have all these great ideas of things I want to write about, but when I get home and I'm actually at my keyboard it's like, "Eh, I just don't want to do that right now." I want to use this as an encouragement, because I've written 85 books that publishers have published for me, and with every one of those I had a hard time starting. Every one of those I had a hard time starting chapter 2, then chapter 3, then chapter 4 – and yet, they're done. I got them done.

What I do when it comes to writing is I drag myself to my keyboard, I force myself to type the first word, I force myself to write the second word, and really by the 3rd or 4th or 5th or 20th

word I just forget all about that and I'm just writing without any problem. I'm sure I'm paraphrasing this wrong, but there's an old saying that 99% of success is just showing up. I think that's brilliant. That was really shown in a book called *Outliers* by Malcolm Gladwell recently. *Outliers* is just a fantastic book. I strongly recommend it, no matter what you do for a living. I strongly recommend it. *Outliers* explains the concept that a lot of us really think of America as being a country of self-starters and we've pulled ourselves up by the bootstraps. He kind of crosses a line through all of that and says, "That's not really the way most things happen. Most things happen just because people show up and do them." That's really how most major things in life actually get done – just someone's there and doing the same thing over and over – and eventually something occurs that's wonderful. Some product is thought of and produced for doing something else.

First of all, you have to have deadlines. You must. As a business owner and an entrepreneur, you must make deadlines in order to meet them. If you don't have deadlines, you'll never meet them. This really helped me when I used to write a newspaper article every week. I didn't like it because it was a deadline every single week. It was an article on eBay and I did it for about two years for local newspapers around here. I enjoyed it, but I had a hard time doing it every week. Every Thursday at 5 she had to have my article, because I had an entire newspaper waiting on my article every Thursday at 5 if I didn't get it in. I had an obligation to her to be a steward of her time, because I made a deal with her that I would do it, and I had to do it. It was just something that I would not be comfortable missing. Every time I would write an article and have it in by 5:00 Thursday, I would lie to myself and say, "Now tomorrow I'm going to do next week's article. This isn't going to happen again." I think you should be truthful. I'm often not truthful to myself about things like that, but that deadline really helped me.

One of the keys to meeting deadlines is having deadlines and setting them for yourself. That's how you do it. If you have a deadline that you're not meeting regularly, you really need to step back and decide, "Do I want to change the deadline, or am I doing someone wrong by not meeting this deadline? Am I doing myself wrong, my family wrong, am I being the best steward of my resources by not meeting it?" Then if you decide, "Yeah, I really have to meet this deadline," then what you do is you just put one foot in front of the other and do what I do with my writing. Just write the first word, then the second word, then the third word, and that's the way you'll get things done. We talked about Dan Kennedy earlier. He writes something every day. He says, "I will always spend 15-30 minutes writing something. I don't like it, but I just do it," and it turns out every two months he has a new product that he's just written, that he didn't even think too much about doing it. So make deadlines and then just show up and you'll be successful eventually.

BEN SETTLE: About a year ago I started writing an email every day. It's interesting. I can get away with this because I really don't have a deadline, other than a self-imposed one. When I send an email out I'll often make a sale for something, so that's kind of a motivation. I find that just taking all the pressure off and actually giving myself permission not to do anything – my only goal is to open a text file. I don't have to do anything. It's funny, because you take all this pressure off. It's like being an athlete. An athlete who's all tensed up and everything often has trouble performing out on the track or whatever. But if they're loose and they're limber and they're just kind of athletically ready and they're just having fun, it might help. This is not for everybody, what I just said, by the way. There are a lot of people who that wouldn't work for, but maybe for people who, like you just said, it scares them so much. Now they're really scared they have to have a deadline, like me. I'm probably in that camp. Just take pressure off yourself and give yourself permission to fail, and you'll be surprised what happens.

That's really good advice you gave. Now we're going to get into some questions that I've really been looking forward to specifically. What Bible stories have had the most impact on the way you run your business?

GREG PERRY: Oh, that's real easy. What's just instantly coming to mind is a story in Matthew. It's the most important verse. It won't be all the things you expect. It won't be about truth or about resources. It's completely not what you're expecting. By far the most important set of scriptures for me in business, and the most vital for our listeners, is in Matthew 20, and it's all about the contract. Really, the contract does include all those other things, but this is such a great story. I just can't wait to step on some toes. The concept, Ben, of equal pay for equal work – you've heard of that concept; the Equal Rights Amendment and all of that – that's an evil, evil concept. Everybody's going, "Hey, what are you talking about?" That's really evil, and we can prove it in the Bible so easily. The simple concept is do what you agree to do, and the other party should also do what they agree to do, and it doesn't matter if it's equal pay for equal work. That actually has nothing to do with anything and it's a bad standard, because no one does equal work. Nobody works equally. The only time people are equal is in prison, and if you watch any prison movies you'll see they're not equal there either. Equality is just an evil, evil concept. Russia wants everyone to be equal, or they used to. They wanted everyone to be equal, and they really still do. In Matthew 20, Jesus is talking about this guy, and I'll just paraphrase this. This is such a great story. This landowner hires a guy to work for him, and he says, "Here's what I'll pay you," and the employee says, "Okay, that sounds fine," and the employee goes to work. Then all of a sudden someone else comes up and says, "Hey, I need a job," and the landowner says, "Okay, here's what I'm going to pay you," and the guy says "Okay, I agree to that," and he goes to work. The first guy finds out the second guy's getting paid more than he is, and he gets all upset. The landowner says, "Why are you upset? I'm paying you what you agreed to. I'm paying you what we talked about. I'm not going to shortchange you. I'm going to give you every penny we agreed to. Why are you getting angry?"

"Because you're paying him more!"

"That has nothing to do with the deal I made with you. It has nothing to do with that."

Jesus ends up saying – and I know Jesus said it, because it's in red – He said, "Shouldn't a man be able to do with his own money what he wants to do with his own money?" Shouldn't we be able to do with our own money what we want to do with our own money? Of course that's just ultra-brilliant. Of course the landowner is the one who's taking all the risk in having this business. The landowner is the one who has the money that he's getting ready to distribute to people who don't have as much as he does. This concept of contracts and work and payment for services rendered is a wonderful concept, and if you work harder then maybe he wants to pay you more. Maybe this landowner knew that the second guy was going to produce more than the first guy, because there is no such thing as equal work. And I'm going to step on some more toes here – maybe the second guy has a family and the first guy doesn't. The landowner just thought, "You know, I want to support a family man a little bit more than I want to support some kid who is a ne'er-do-well otherwise." I don't know what's in that landowner's mind, but it's his money. He's the one who agreed with these two employees, so that just is such an important concept in life, in business, in politics and our government. This equal work stuff is just putting a burden on people in a very bad way. If you make a deal with someone, if you have a contract, if you're in a covenant relationship with God, you need to uphold your end of the bargain.

I have a friend who also sells on eBay, and he sold four digital cameras about a year ago, and it turned out he only had three in stock, and here's what my friend did. I'm not proud of this fact. He told the buyer that bought the fourth camera, "Sorry, we only had three," and my friend got very angry when this buyer left negative feedback for my friend. The buyer said, "He said he had the camera, and he didn't. He sold something he didn't own," so the buyer left negative feedback. My friend is a believer too. That's a sad witness, but anyway, if I sell something I don't have, I immediately locate that item. As soon as I get payment I ship it to the buyer, or I have it shipped to the buyer, because it was my mistake. It's not your buyer's mistake. This is just an example. It's just anecdotal, but it illustrates the point I'm making that I said I would do something. My buyer said they would pay for it. We reached an agreement, and this has happened to me before. Probably in ten years of eBay it's happened seven or eight times. It's my mistake. I might be out an extra $10 or $15 because the only one I could find was retail and it sold for more than my buyer paid. So what? That's my problem. First of all, I don't even tell my buyer about it. It's not his problem. We have an agreement and it's up to me to fulfill it.

Paul talks a lot about stewardship also. He talks about stewardship a lot. Stewardship is kind of like a ranch foreman.

Did you ever used to watch those *Big Valley* reruns? I really liked *Big Valley*. I watched them all the time growing up. Heath Barkley was played by Lee Majors. He was always my hero. I know he was your hero.

BEN SETTLE: In *The Fall Guy*.

GREG PERRY: I'm older than you. Anyway, it's a lot like a ranch foreman who manages and hires the ranch, even though he's not the owner of those resources. The foreman is the steward of all those important tasks and cattle and people, and we are to be stewards of what God gives us. We've got to manage our family's resources. We're also balancing the stewardship of our customers. eBay's my deal here we're talking about. We use quality shipping materials. We make sure that we wrap things well. We reuse some shipping materials if the item can go in a reused box and it's the type of thing no one will care about. I can't think of anything right now, but I would never ship a rare book in an old beat up box that we got in the mail from something else, but I might ship a wrench or something – something that just doesn't matter. I can't think of an example now. We never want to compromise the condition of what we're shipping, so we try to balance our family's resources with our customer's resources, and be a good steward of both sides. At the same time, don't be a doormat. One of my favorite verses is in 1 Corinthians. Now half of our listeners will probably feel like this doesn't apply to them. "Act like men and be strong." That's what Paul tells us. "Act like men and be strong." I could just say so much about that, but the warrior in me just loves that verse. It's one of my favorite verses. There's another one that says stand firm against the schemes of the devil by putting on the full armor of God and all that.

I keep talking a lot so far about bending over backwards to serve your buyers – be truthful, be repentant when you mess up, be patient. I often sell new electronic disk drives, and I can buy some of these at way below retail and resell them. If I ship a buyer a brand new factory-sealed external disk drive, and he sends it back and says it's broken, and it's obvious to me that it's not what I shipped him – it's not in the same box, it's all broken, it's all dirty, I didn't ship him that item – there's no way I'm going to give him a refund. There's no way I'm going to do anything for that buyer if it's real obvious to me that there's some kind of fraud involved. Now I won't just jump the gun and assume there's fraud. I'll be polite, especially at the beginning. I'll be overly polite and say, "I really want to work this out. I've got some questions. I don't understand this," because maybe he shipped me the wrong thing and he found out later, I don't know, but there's no way I will give in to someone who's trying to do me wrong and if it turns out to be obvious. I will gladly accept negative feedback and I'll report him to eBay and PayPal, and I'll do my best to expose him, as a good steward to other sellers out there that might be caught up with him. I want eBay to know what he's doing. You have to show patience and forbearance if the buyer say is new to your business or is a new customer and just doesn't know how it all works, but if a buyer makes a demand that's unreasonable, first of all you do need to explain to the customer how and why it's unreasonable. You need to be patient and teach them and not be afraid to explain it, and don't over-react and escalate things unnecessarily, but you have to use discernment and wisdom so you don't give away the family farm.

BEN SETTLE: It's amazing when you talk about this, what you're talking about with eBay, how that just applies to any kind of business in any industry, online or offline. It could be a brick and mortar store. These are just really interesting concepts, because people don't consider them the most exciting things in the world, and yet this is what's going to help you sell more products and do it in a way where everyone's happy, you're doing everything right, and you can sleep good at night and not worry about anybody hating you the next day.

GREG PERRY: Exactly, and if you start doing it, you'll see the results and it will be feedback that will make you want to do it more and more. If it's hard to do now, it does get easier.

BEN SETTLE: Should Christian business owners be concerned with politics?

GREG PERRY: Should Christian business owners be concerned with politics? I get so frustrated with believers. People always ask me, "Why are you so hard on other Christians?" Well, because I expect more from Christians. I expect far more from Christians than from unbelievers. I know that unbelievers are going to lie to me, and I know that they're going to do me wrong or that there's a propensity for that, and I know that they don't think eternally, they just think short-term. The reason I'm so hard on Christians is I want more from them than other people. I expect more. I hold them up on a pedestal. I get so frustrated with Christians when it comes to politics and stuff because a lot of believers are out there – okay, let's say they want a plumber. They look in the phone book and they'll find one that has the Christian fish symbol on it, because when it comes to a plumber we want a Christian plumber, or some lady wants to buy a dress. She goes to that Christian-owned dress shop because they're so friendly and nice and have friends, and they seek believers whenever they find friends. They want to develop friendship with believers and they want to spend time with other Christians, but those same believers don't hold the leaders of the land to the same standard that they want their plumbers to hold.

They'll say, "Nobody but a Christian plumber's going to touch my toilet, but President of the free world? Well, you know, we'll just let Satan worry about him."

Of course, they don't see it that way. If you ever bring up the fact, by the way, that they prefer a Christian plumber to fix their toilet but not their President being Christian, it will really make them think by the way. That's a good line to remember. I know they never say, "Just leave politics up to Satan," but that is the end result. They have these false interpretations of Scripture that makes them think that – there's one that people think God always puts every leader in office. They think God puts every leader in office. So Hitler murders six million people, Stalin murders 20 million innocent people, the President of the United States comes along and has this strange, salivating lust to pass laws that encourage the murder of thousands of babies every day at Planned Parenthood. Planned Parenthood is the largest abortion mill in the United States and they say God moves the hands of the voters that put that person in office to ultimately murder millions of innocent people for some higher good purpose. I say we have a God of life, not a God of death. I say millions are slaughtered because of Satan, not because of the loving Creator God, who made us and who defines life and does not define death. The fact that we should not be concerned with politics, that is a lie from the father of lies, from the devil himself.

I say we should be concerned with politics. I say as business owners and as believers we should be concerned with politics. God told man in the very opening pages of the Bible that we are to be stewards of the earth. Man immediately gave that stewardship to Satan. Just handed it to him in the garden and said, "God gave us this amazing gift. Here, you can have it." Satan's had it ever since. I want to thwart Satan. I don't want to acquiesce to him. I want godly leaders in office who will protect the innocent, who will enforce contracts, who will do right.

God controls the hand of every leader in office? Then why did God say when they were sacrificing babies to Baal back in I think Samuel, they were killing babies as an offering to Baal. God said, and I'm quoting – I may not have the exact words, but I'm basically quoting – "It didn't even enter my mind that you would do such a horrible thing. It did not even enter my mind that you would slaughter babies as a gift to Baal." If it didn't enter God's mind that they would do that, then God did not move those leaders' hands, and I say no way, no how. I say we are commanded to be stewards of the earth. That starts with our nation, our local people, and our families, and we must speak loudly and clearly about our leaders when they're evil. When they do good deeds, we're to shout it from the mountaintops to give them the praise that is deserving of them. If a leader of a nation taxes 10%, Samuel called that tyranny. If only we had 10% taxation! One reason that 10% taxation is tyranny, we see it today. We see all these politicians that we've elected say, "The churches need to do more." I agree, but we have taxation now. When you add up every tax, regulation and every fee that you pay the government from your income, you're out 60 something percent right now just off the top. The government takes 60 something percent of our money before we have any. We're still supposed to tithe what, most believe 10%? I don't know that that's a firm law, by the way, but in general it's good to want to tithe maybe something like 10%. How can we do that when the government's taking 65%?

I don't know, but we still have to do it. We still should find a way to support the body of Christ, whether we are in tyranny or not. That's still our job is to build up the body, not to just let it decay. No matter what is against us, we still have our duty to do the right thing, but if we did not have the tyranny of 65% of taxation, we would see prosperity in this nation as never before experienced. We would see churches have far more resources to be able to do the things that they used to do, like build hospitals and Christian schools. You don't see churches building hospitals anymore because the money's not there. You see the government running health care because that's where the money is. Something's wrong with this picture.

Do we pray for our leaders as Christians? Are we supposed to pray for our leaders? Almost every Christian I know gets it wrong. They'll say, "Sure, you should pray for your leader."

I'll say, "Why should we pray for them?"

"We should pray that they're safe, first of all."

"Oh really? The Bible doesn't ever say that."

"Sure it does."

"No, it doesn't. The Bible never says that." It's just that they don't know what the Bible says about how to pray for leaders, and 1 Timothy 2 tells us exactly how to pray for our leaders. 1 Timothy 2 says that we are to give prayer and intercession and giving of thanks for all men. We're to pray for everybody, because your young cousin shouldn't have less prayer than the leader of Congress. Why should your young cousin get prayed for any less than the leader of Congress? God says through Paul in 1 Timothy 2, "Pray for everybody. Give intercession and giving of thanks for all people, supplication, pray." That all implies praying for their salvation. Pray for everyone. The salvation of the President's eternal life is not more important than your sister's eternal life. In God's eyes, that's not a more important life, so God says pray for everyone. Then he says, and this is the biggie, "For kings and all who are in authority, that we may lead a quiet and peaceful life." Paul says for anybody who's in authority, you are to pray that they leave you alone. That's what Paul says. No one can say I'm misinterpreting 1 Timothy 2. Paul first says pray for everybody, pray for salvation and all of that, but for leaders, pray that they leave you alone. That's what he says. "Pray that we may lead a quiet and peaceable life."

BEN SETTLE: If only they would leave us alone. That's a good prayer.

GREG PERRY: Yeah. I don't want their stuff and I don't want them to mess with my family. If I murder someone, I want the death penalty, by the way. I want to be punished, but if I'm not doing anything wrongly, I want them to leave me alone. That's my prayer. That's what God says, to pray for our leaders. I don't know of any Christian who does that, who prays that the leaders will leave us alone. They'll say it all the time, but then they'll get in Sunday school and it's like, "We should pray for the President and for the leaders of Congress and the leaders of all this and pray that they get saved." They don't really mean that. Most of them really don't care if those people are saved. They just want them out of office. They certainly don't get home and pray for that. They pray for other things. That's okay. What about Christians who run for office? I think that's great. I think that's wonderful. I think more should do it. There will be a lot of people that disagree, and I'm now left to call after I've said this, but I think Christians should be leading this country. I think God gave us stewardship over this world, and I think we have given it away and that we need to get it back.

BEN SETTLE: These are things that you don't hear a lot of people talking about.

GREG PERRY: Yeah, I know.

BEN SETTLE: I do want to get your opinion on something, and you've talked about this. This isn't necessarily a business thing, but I think it applies to what we're talking about and I'm just curious about your opinion. In the gospels when Satan was trying to tempt Jesus out in the desert and he was offering Him the world, he was like, "I'll give you all the kingdoms of the world if you'll bow to me," or whatever. Since God calls him the Prince of the Air, it always seemed to me like He gave this world over to Satan in a sense and that Christians are supposed to be the light to help everybody else out. It just seems to me that people get so wound up in trying to change the hearts of leaders and stuff, when really the leaders are the last people I'm relying on right now.

GREG PERRY: That's a good point. Of course, almost every leader in Scripture is evil.

BEN SETTLE: I inherently distrust leaders. I love the fact that we're supposed to pray to tell them to leave us alone, because they just corrupt everything. It's a corrupting world. People get power and they start going crazy with it. Look what we've got going on now. It's terrible.

GREG PERRY: Nothing would please us more then if we had a godly leader.

BEN SETTLE: I'd love it.

GREG PERRY: Wonderful, but the odds are that we're not going to. I think one reason God says don't pray that your leaders are saved – He never says that, He says pray for everybody – is that if some of these guys get saved, you've seen what Christians do to mess things up – big, national preachers and things that just blow it completely and just ruin the witness of every other Christian in existence at that moment in time. Just because they're saved doesn't mean they're really going to do much better. As a matter of fact, they might even do worse. They might. The best thing a leader can do is leave you alone.

BEN SETTLE: You were mentioning tithing earlier, and I don't have the answer to that either. To me, it's something that you do because you really want to help people, a church or whatever. In fact, one of the guys in this book Guy Malone runs a very, very unique ministry where he goes after people in the New Age occult world. He goes to their conventions and sets up a booth. That takes some serious something. They're very small. I've been helping out as much as I can. You do what you can. He emailed me and he goes, "I just want you to know that those checks you've sent" – these were not huge checks by the way, they were what I could do at the time – he's like, "It helped us pay to go to our last convention," some kind of New Age occult UFO type convention. He goes, "We were there and three people got baptized, including one new Christian." That to me goes so much farther than putting a new wing on a big church or something. Nobody was putting a gun to my head or anything. It's out of love.

GREG PERRY: That's exactly why you should do it.

BEN SETTLE: I'm creating another product right now and I said, "When I get this done, I'm going to donate all my products to your ministry." He likes to do stuff on the internet and that's how they do their thing. Any business can do the same thing, donate your time, your money. It doesn't just have to be money. If you have something that can help somebody that you sell, donate it.

GREG PERRY: That guy you were talking about, his initials aren't BL are they?

BEN SETTLE: No, his name is Guy Malone.

GREG PERRY: Oh, okay, Guy Malone. I don't think I've heard of him.

BEN SETTLE: You and I have talked about Genesis 6, the fallen angels, and people think they're UFOs. That's really what they do.

GREG PERRY: Okay. I think I've seen one of his videos.

BEN SETTLE: He was an experiencer as a child and he turned to Jesus, and they have 700 or 800 documented cases of abduction experiences that were stopped in the name of Jesus, just stopped. One of his partners used to be a researcher for MUFON. It's like a UFO network. He became a Christian because he noticed that they were getting just really dark testimonies from people whose lives were being turned upside down by this stuff. His girlfriend, who was a Christian at the time, said, "Put the crystals and new age nonsense away. You need something that can REALLY protect you." She gave him the Bible and he became a Christian. That's what they do now. It's amazing. These smaller ministries, people ignore them. They are really out there doing good work.

GREG PERRY: They're actually doing the work. You're right.

BEN SETTLE: I don't know what that has to do with anything. I just like to share that. People think that they have to donate thousands of dollars and they don't have, but just do what you can. You don't know how God's using you.

GREG PERRY: Yep, you're right.

BEN SETTLE: The next question I want to ask you is, what are some ways Christian business owners can prepare for hard economic times like we're entering now? I don't know how you feel about this, but I don't think we've even seen the start of what's really going to be going on here.

GREG PERRY: Well, I'm not a prophet. I think we have seen the last of good times for a long time. I think things will get worse before they'll get better, but I don't know. Like I say, I'm not a prophet, but I would say immediately every believer, everyone listening in the audience should read a secular book called *The Black Swan*. It's by this guy whose last name is Taleb, I believe. It's about the concept of the black swan. There are far fewer black swans than white swans. You hardly ever see a black swan. They did not think black swans existed until they saw one. I don't think Christians should believe in luck, but I have it on good authority of Jesus Himself that Christians should believe in chance. In Luke 10:31, Jesus talks about chance happening and it's mentioned at least one other time in scripture. The black swan really changed my perspective on hard times. I'm not talking about hard times like the Depression. I mean far worse hard times, like really, really bad times that are possible at any point in time. For 200 years, our nation saw growth and prosperity from its founding, and that's great. God does not like a government to strangle nations. God likes a government to allow freedom and freedom of commerce and God is a free market God. When a nation sees economic prosperity, often it's because the leaders did not shackle that economy. As soon as the US decided to reverse its course and put limits on freedom –

which really began in 1913, but it just grows faster by the week – that was the start of the big government. I think 1913 was when the IRS was created. That's right. We didn't pay income taxes till 1913, and somehow our nation survived 113-something years. That's when the Federal Reserve was created, and our freedoms have declined since that happened.

Ask yourself, why is this time any different from 6,000 years of hard times that most people on earth experienced? The earth has been around for 6,000 years. Some people would think it's much longer than that, but I think it's been around about 6,000 years. For those 6,000 years, most people have not experienced freedom and prosperity, and there has been a lot of misery in the world because, as you said earlier, the god of this world is Satan. I say that man gladly lets him have it and I think God says take it back from him as best you can. Either way, for 6,000 years, he has been the god of this world and there have only been short pockets of freedom here and there, and prosperity. It's an anomaly that America has prospered for 200 years. That's an amazing thing, that a country for 200 years prospered. Since the chance of continued economic freedom is not historical, then we are foolish to think that it's not possible that everything can crumble. We're fools to think that, if we do. Again, *The Black Swan* will help show you that the one thing that you don't expect probably won't ever happen, but it can. It's our requirement, especially the men, to protect our families from the thief in the night, the US government and the United Nations and the Federal Reserve. Those are the three thieves in the night right now in our pocketbook.

Is it all related to money? Yes. It really is, because when a nation is economically prosperous, then the people see a quality of life and that's important. People don't die of disease, starvation, sickness and all of that stuff, and dirty sewers running on the streets. People in nations that prosper don't suffer in those ways, and the quality of life, because it's economically prosperous, flourishes. Life flourishes. What do we do? First of all, we pray for wisdom, because God says if we pray for wisdom, He will give it to us. We pray for discernment, and then we start preparing for what we absolutely think might be the worst that can happen and we pray that the best happens. We pray 1 Timothy 2, that the leaders of our nation leave us alone, but until that happens, we have to do something to weather the hard times that might happen. You have to decide, what is the worst thing that you think might happen, and then you have to do step-by-step to help protect your family from that worst-case scenario. How far you take that, that's up to your wisdom and discernment. If you think it's all going to crumble and we're just going to have mayhem on the streets and the streets won't even be paved anymore and it will look like we're all cavemen or something – if you think it will get that bad, if you really think that, you should start making steps to protect your family. If you don't think it will get that bad, you still should take steps to protect your family. It's your job to do this. As believers, it's your job to protect your family, your friends and those around you, and to help build the body of Christ, because the world might get pretty bad pretty fast.

BEN SETTLE: Remember that interview with C.S. Lewis's stepson that I sent you?

GREG PERRY: Yeah.

BEN SETTLE: He was pretty convinced that this event – and I agree with him, unless Jesus comes back sooner than that – he thinks it's going to go back to an agricultural society. People are going to have to start learning how to farm and hunt again, because it's just going to collapse.

GREG PERRY: That's possible. I don't know that it will happen, but I think it's possible. I think it's bad.

BEN SETTLE: You're definitely prepared for that from talking to you. I'm grossly unprepared, but we're taking steps toward it. It's interesting because you've given me much advice on this and I always appreciate it. It's very good to know that.

GREG PERRY: I think it's important for you to pray for wisdom. Again, what do you honestly think the worst-case scenario should be? Even if you're an optimist, you should consider what the worst case should be in your immediate future and your 10-year and 20-year future, and then take steps to protect your family from the worst case, and hopefully it will never happen.

BEN SETTLE: That's actually very good business advice in and of itself too. You've heard of John Carlton, the copywriter?

GREG PERRY: Yes.

BEN SETTLE: He's got this very, very good piece of advice. He's an optimistic pessimist. He does everything he can to make sure everything goes right in a deal, but he prepares for if everything goes wrong so he doesn't get blindsided.

GREG PERRY: That's wonderful.

BEN SETTLE: It's the exact same advice that you were just giving, and it can apply to everything.

GREG PERRY: It always does. Truth always works in any scenario.

BEN SETTLE: What I like about what you just said was pray for wisdom. That's one thing a lot of people don't do. They pray for money, they pray for success, but they rarely pray for wisdom. What do you think about that?

GREG PERRY: I think you're absolutely right. They rarely do, and discernment comes with wisdom. As a businessperson, we can go off chasing some good deal or something, and we don't have any wisdom and it all goes haywire. We didn't do what John Carlton said. We didn't plan for the worst and we lose a big chunk. We have what some people call a blow up. Whenever people are investing in the stock market and they have a blow up and they just lose 90% in one trade, which is very common actually, they don't prepare for the worst. Pray for wisdom first and then you'll have the wisdom to know what to pray for to prosper and for your family to be safe and prosper.

BEN SETTLE: Terry Dean is in this book too, and if you've ever heard his story, he was very much in debt before he got into business. He was a pizza delivery man making $8.00 an hour, probably less than that. He said he was trying to run a ministry out of his home at the same time, so he was trying to finance that and they kept getting in more debt. Like a lot of people do, they were praying for money and all this and eventually he said he started praying for wisdom. Literally a week later, that's when he decided to get his computer and do the internet thing. It's just amazing how fast that can happen if you just pray for wisdom.

GREG PERRY: That's amazing. It's so easy. That's great. I've never heard that about him. That's wonderful.

BEN SETTLE: What advice do you have for Christian business owners as the world gets more and more secularized and anti-Christian?

GREG PERRY: When you act more as a Christian should act, when you are perceived as doing the right thing, the remnant will notice, the remnant of Christians who are left on Earth. That number, I believe, does get smaller every day, not larger. I think we live in a post-Christian nation here in America, not in a Christian nation. As you continue to do the right thing, no matter what happens because of it, the remnant should continue to do the same thing. The true believers should continue to do the same thing, and in a world that's becoming more and more secularized and anti-Christian, the Christians will stand out more. There will come a point where Christians are standing out and they'll get shot. History and most of Scripture proves that if the church is persecuted, the church grows much stronger. When we're fat and happy then we easily forget we need a Savior, but when times are bad and there's nobody to turn to, God is there for the believer, and God is ready to be there for the unbeliever upon their repentance. As the world becomes more anti-Christian, believers will begin to stand out more and more as they do business and as they interact with others. Believers in the tribulation are going to have trouble doing anything, I realize, but we're not in tribulation right now. Some people think it's in the future. Some people think it occurred in 70 A.D.. Whatever your belief is about end times, what matters is what's happening right now. That matters most as to how you should respond.

Let me throw out an example. We are in a post-Christian, anti-Christian world. It's going to get worse. It's not horribly bad in America right now, but it's going to get worse. There's a great example, which you may know about already called Chick-fil-

A. Have you ever eaten at Chick-fil-A? You may not even have them in Oregon. I don't know, but Chick-fil-A's this fast food chicken sandwich place and it's a Christian-owned business. I'm a big Chick-fil-A fan. They're a Christian-owned business and they're not doing it to be legalistic, but they always close on Sunday because they want their families to have the opportunity to be together. Even in a mall when every store is open on Sunday, if Chick-fil-A is there, they are closed. By the way, In-N-Out Burgers – I don't know if you've ever heard of those – those are fantastic. They're also a Christian-owned business. When you walk into a Chick-fil-A, you are entering an experience that you don't find at other fast food places. You look down at the floor and it's clean. You look at the employees and they look you in the eye and they smile at you. It's like they're home-schooled. It's like they're all intelligent. They smile at you. They're a lot smarter than I am and they're a lot happier and they're a lot more self-confident and they're not cocky. They are just what they should be; wonderful people that are there to help you. The food is fresh and it tastes good and it's fast food, but it tastes good. I think Chick-fil-A is like what we're saying here. As the world becomes more anti-Christian, these Christians will stand out even more.

I have a story about a Chick-fil-A real close to us. We know one of our neighbors just got a job at Chick-fil-A. She's a home schooler by the way. She started working there and she told us this story. This lady drove up and she had three kids in her car. It was raining and she ordered four chicken sandwiches and drinks. She paid and they gave her the drinks and then she said, "You know what? I've got these three kids. I really need to come in and eat. It's just too messy in the car. Do you mind holding my sandwiches indoors? Let me park the car and get my kids in and we're going to eat inside." The lady at the drive through, of course, said, "Yes, we would be pleased to have you do this." It's not like at most places where they'd go, "Huh?" She parked her car and when she got out of her car, there were two employees there with umbrellas to stand over those kids and that mom as they walked into the building. When she got in, all the sandwiches were there at a table and they put their drinks out and all their napkins and they helped get her three little kids there to that table and walked them in with umbrellas. Can you even imagine anyone else ever doing that at any fast food place?

BEN SETTLE: Uh, no.

GREG PERRY: No, that's just not going to happen. That's a great example of what it is like to be a Christian in an un-Christian society. You will really, really stand out. It's like the rewards in heaven. As a believer on Judgment Day, we aren't judged for whether we're going to heaven or hell. We're judged as to what rewards we get when we're in heaven. You don't do right to get the reward, but it's perfectly okay to get the reward for doing right. Does that make sense?

BEN SETTLE: It makes perfect sense.

GREG PERRY: That's a great thing. You will see Christian businesses stand out and be rewarded dramatically for these types of things, for just doing common sense, Golden Rule type of things. Christian businesses will really stand out as the world gets worse and worse, and that should be an incentive for you to continue to do the right thing in all that you do.

BEN SETTLE: That is really good. It keeps coming back to what you've been saying about serving other people.

GREG PERRY: That's all it is.

BEN SETTLE: How does spiritual warfare affect Christian business owners?

GREG PERRY: That's really timely because I just finished this book actually called *God at War* and man, it just changed everything for me. It just changed my entire view of spiritual warfare. If you can find *God at War*, it's really an amazing book, but in most churches today, and I know this because I go to a lot of churches – Why do I go to a lot of churches? Because I can't really find any that I think are good churches and I'm still looking. We live out in the middle of nowhere, just to say we really are kind of in a physically bad location. We don't have mega-numbers of churches all around us, so it's difficult. Anyway, in most churches you walk in and there's not one indicator that we're in the middle of a spiritual battle. Not one. The battle between good and evil is real and it plays out in the heavenly all around us. We learned this in the early part of Daniel, that spiritual battles often get played out there, and those spiritual battles physically often get played out on earth as well and they're related to the spiritual battles being done up above.

The physical battles on earth that we experience as people often have those spiritual battle roots. When there's a battle on earth of any size, whether it's between a husband and wife or two nations, it often has its roots in a spiritual warfare as well. I don't think the feel-good theology has really any biblical grounds right now. I think churches that no longer preach about sin and repentance are making it very difficult for unbelievers to get saved. I think if a Christian business owner does not see his or her business as being part of a spiritual battle, then guess what side of the battle that Christian business is already on? They're on the losing, evil side. If you don't see as a Christian that you are playing a part in a spiritual battle, then you're on the wrong side and you don't even know it. Every decision you make has to be in the light. You have to understand darkness wants to take hold of you and your business and your family, and darkness wants to run your decision at every turn, but as a Christian you have the power, the ability, to overcome those decisions very easily. There's a reason Paul says to pray continuously. A lot of people just dismiss that and say, "I can't just go around with my head bowed praying all the time." That's not what he means. He means you're always in this battle and every thought and deed should be filtered through scripture. Every single decision you make, you should filter it through the Bible. That means you have to know what the Bible says about a lot of things, but the Bible's actually easy to understand about most things. That means you've got to know your Bible. Don't read books about the Bible all the time, just read the Bible. When a passage seems confusing, the first thing you should do is just assume it literally means what it says. That often helps you understand difficult passages. It may not. There are some verses and some passages that are allegorical and that are not literal, but most of them really are pretty literal. Don't spiritualize everything. A lot of times it really means just what it says. You're going to learn a whole lot if you just take that simple approach to the Bible. You're fighting for evil if you ignore the spiritual battle. You're on the losing side and you have to get on the winning side.

BEN SETTLE: Very good stuff. That's interesting when you bring it back to the book of Daniel. I find it very fascinating that when you go back to the Hebrew and all that and some of the older Old Testament passages, that there's a lot more at work than what it looks like on the surface. This gets deep. This isn't something I would actually debate anybody on, but I've just been studying this Hebrew scholar lately named Michael Heiser, and he does a lot of stuff for Bible software and translations and stuff. He's really into this stuff. He was translating some of the words from the earlier books of Genesis when the nations were being divided and there's actually, I don't know if you want to call them bad or fallen angels or whatever you want to call them, they call them gods (little g) in some cases.

GREG PERRY: Yeah, the Bible does use that term.

BEN SETTLE: Each of those countries kind of had some entity over it and that was what God gave them and God kept Israel for Himself. I can't go into all of it right now obviously, but it's very fascinating. If you look at it that way, you start thinking there is a lot more going on with spiritual warfare than what people are maybe thinking about. What I keep hearing from a lot of the people I've been interviewing here is that the marketplace is actually a hotbed of spiritual warfare. Do you agree?

GREG PERRY: I fully agree with that. I fully agree. Every decision we make is part of the battle, and that really means Christian business owners have a higher responsibility than unbelieving business owners. More is expected of you because more is given to you. You have to fight. You're part of the battle even more than if you weren't in your position.

BEN SETTLE: A lot of times it's easy to think, "Well, that's the pastor's job or whatever, to deal with this stuff," but churches aren't filled with unsaved people. The unsaved people are out in the world and they're not in church.

GREG PERRY: Right, exactly.

BEN SETTLE: Where can people get more information and learn more about you? You were talking about your eBay course. Do you want to give your URLs or website information? Where can people find you?

GREG PERRY: I can give you about three links. I don't really care if people learn more about me, but they can see what I do. This has been an eBay-centric interview, and so if you wanted to look at our auctions at any time, you can go to www.BidMentor.com. I really don't like that term, but that's my eBay ID – BidMentor – because I mentor people on how to get more bids, and so I call myself BidMentor. Believe me, I wish I had a better name, but that's what I have. If you go to www.BidMentor.com at any point in time, it will give you a list of all of our auctions. I think we might have 30 up right now. We had a hard time getting to auctions in the last few months, but we will have up to 200 at a time, depending on what's going on. You can see how we sell. I don't care if you steal my language; steal what I do, great. Anyone in the reading audience, if you can learn from me, great, just learn from me. See what I do and see I'm successful. Look at my closed auctions, and if there's anything I do that you think is neat, be sure and do it.

If you really want to learn how to sell more, I do have the package I told you about. I am not embarrassed to tell you about it at all, because it is the best package out there, but I'm also not on this call to sell it, but you can go to www.MostPowerfulEBay.com. It will take you to the eBay auction where I'm selling that package. I feel the best place to sell this is on eBay. That seems to be where it gets the most interest. So if you go to www.MostPowerfulEBay.com, you can read about all the most advanced selling techniques on the planet, which is the name of my course. It's a huge course for $67.00 at the time of this recording, and you can look at what I say. I think even by reading the ad you'll learn something, I hope.

I've started a blog, thanks to a friend of mine. I forget his name. I think it was Ben Settle. I don't know if you've heard of him or not, but he kept encouraging me to start a blog. I've been slow at starting it and it took me forever to actually get it started. It's taken me just as long to get content up there, but it's called www.RightNerve.com, like I hit the right nerve, except a lot of people will think I've hit the wrong nerve because they're not going to like what I have to say.

I don't ever take any prisoners when I discuss God or the government or guns or lots of stuff. I talk about God, the government, guns and lots of things. I'm very pro-gun. If you believe the Bible and somehow think Christians should not judge, then you should not be looking at my blog. I think only Christians should judge and that Christians should do a lot more of that, and I based that on what Paul and Jesus and a lot of other people in the Bible say. I am gathering up a bunch of articles on eBay for my blog and I'm hoping to get those up there by the end of the week. I should have a lot more content up there pretty soon.

BEN SETTLE: Finally, there are still a lot of people who are going to be hopefully reading this book that maybe they're not Christian yet, but they're very curious. Maybe they've been reading this book, maybe something you've said they're thinking, "I want to do this. I want to be a Christian." What should they do if they're at that point?

GREG PERRY: That's the easiest question you've asked. All they have to do is just send you and me a bunch of money. Seriously, that is the easiest question that you want me to answer. How does someone become a Christian, because everybody listening may not realize this, but every person has a soul. That soul is eternal and it's completely up to you right now to decide what you want to do in eternity. It's up to you. Every one of us can decide what we want to do in eternity, and eternity is a real long time.

If you think about, by God's standards, we're all really a mess. All of us have lied and stolen, even something small, but we've all stolen something. We've all lusted after people we shouldn't lust after and so on. On Judgment Day, every one of us, even those of us who think we're good, will all be standing in front of God. And if He asks us if we've done anything other than be holy and pure, everybody here is going to say, "Yeah, I've done a lot more things besides being holy and pure."

Even though God is all love, He's also all justice. That's one of His loving attributes is justice. Justice is not something other than love. Justice is love. It's part of God's love. If God loved us hypocritically, He wouldn't care about us and He would just ignore the bad things that we do, but He can't do that because His standards are really high. That's a great thing. Let's say the environmentalists worship the creation, not the Creator. Their god has pretty low standards. They worship dirt. We worship the Creator. We want to be accountable to an authority who is fully just, fully loving, and fully holy. We want to be accountable to someone who is fully good. We fall short of any standard that our Holy God could ever set for us. You and I fall short of his standards. His standard is high because He is holy. There's nothing we can do about it. God is really smart. God is so very smart, he knows that there's nothing we can do about meeting His expectations. We choose to not meet God's expectations but He sent somebody to take our punishment. Let's say He just sent somebody a little bit better than us to be punished in our place, then who would be punished in their place? If someone's just a little less bad than we are, then who's going to pay the price for that person then? They wouldn't be any good. God knew that. God knew that the price had to be paid fully for our sin and since He's holy, the only way He could spend eternity with us who fall far short of what He wants us for us, the only way He could make this happen, was to take the most innocent and most sinless person who ever walked the earth and have that person pay the price and accept our punishment.

That's the only way we could go free, because God can't look the other way like a lot of judges today do and say, "I'll let you go on a misdemeanor when you're guilty." God can't do that. He's a just and loving God. Someone always has to pay the punishment or else He's not just. He can't ignore our sin. If He did that, they wouldn't be just. He says our sins have to be paid for. We're not good enough to pay for them, so God sent His son, Jesus. It's really neat because Jesus is fully equal with God and Jesus is part of the Godhead. Jesus is God, but He came to earth as a mere man and he lived a sinless life so that at the age of 33, he could be slain to pay the price for all of our sins. In other words, He never shows us mercy. Instead, He sent somebody to pay the price for us. Justice is always served with God, but since Jesus died, justice was served for us and we are free to be with God forever. God made sure that our penalty was paid for, but He still can't let us into heaven quite yet because we haven't said we wanted to be there.

We have a healthy God. We don't have an unhealthy God. He would never force people on earth to do what they don't want to do. If someone on earth doesn't want to spend eternity with God, He says, "Okay, I'm not going to make you." God asks the easiest thing ever asked. All He asks is that we turn to Him and just say how sorry we are for the wrong we've done and to thank Him for sending someone else to take our punishment. If we look to God and say, "We want you to be our God now. We're tired of money being our God. We're tired of the world being our God. We're tired of sports being our God. We're tired of our business being our God." If we turn to Him and say, "Not even our families are our God. We want our families to be number two to you, God," as long as we tell Him that we are going to trust in Him from this point forward, God says our punishment has been paid for and that He will gladly let us into heaven when we die.

He does not lie. He cannot lie. He tells us, "Not only do I not lie, I can't lie." Once He says we are forgiven, once we say we want to be with you, God, forever and we want you to be our God and we want to love you, and we're sorry for what we've done, God doesn't go back and list our sins. He doesn't even remember them. He says that. No matter how bad we've been, you can never be as bad as Jesus was good, so your punishment that you deserve has been paid by His Son, and God wants nothing more than for you to want to be with Him.

That's all you really want. If that's what you really want, then in less time than a blink of an eye, you will be filled with Him and live forever with Him instead of eventually spending forever in hell, because that's the other alternative, the fires of hell. That's it. Just say you're sorry to God for hurting Him and for hurting everyone around you. That's what we do. Promise that you will turn to Him and that you want to trust in only Him for your eternity, and He will make you His forever.

BEN SETTLE: Very good. Greg, I appreciate you doing this.

GREG PERRY: It's been fun. I appreciate your asking me.

Christian Business Bonus Tip #2

Following is a Bible-themed article written to my website newsletter subscribers. To join my free mailing list and access 700+ pages of advanced web marketing tips, go to:

www.BenSettle.com

"Bloody" Effective Levitical Salesmanship

Today's marketing tip is a bit graphic.

Viewer discretion IS advised… and if you're easily grossed out then, well, you've been warned.

Still here?

OK, then here's the scoop:

Yesterday I did a podcast (that'll be posted next week-ish) about sales and marketing lessons in the Bible.

Now, this topic can't be done justice in an hour.

Or even 100 hours.

There are WAY too many lessons to choose from. One of my favorites (we didn't have time to cover) is in the Book of Judges. It's about a wandering Levite (the "priest" tribe of ancient Israel) and how his concubine was viciously raped to death by some psychopaths who lived amongst the Benjamites.

The Levite (understandably) wanted justice.

But due to the times (mass anarchy and moral apathy), he knew he had to do something radical to get anyone to care.

So what did he do?

Beg for help?

Start a posse?

Give up?

Uhm… no.

What this dude did was cut his concubine's corpse into 12 pieces, and sent a piece to each of the 12 tribes!

Now THAT'S impact.

There was no hemming and hawing.

No "brushing it off."

And no ignoring the message.

And you know what?

Great marketing also has this kind of hardcore impact, too — and asks the exact same question the Levite no doubt did: "What's it gonna take to get peoples' UNDIVIDED attention?"

Obviously, don't do anything gross.

I mean, let's keep this in context, okay?

But the mere act of asking the above question will generate all kinds of profitable ideas that make you instantly stick out.

Make it impossible to ignore you.

And… yes… put more profit in ye olde pocket.

Ben Settle

For over 700 pages of advanced web marketing tips and secrets, go to www.BenSettle.com

How To Have "Supernatural" Success In Business

Interview with Gina Parris
www.GinaParris.com

BEN SETTLE: Gina, how did you first get started in business and what were some of the challenges that you faced along the way?

GINA PARRIS: I sort of got started in business because my first job was in sales, so my dad taught me at a young age that if you could be great in sales, you can do anything. In our country especially, that sales is the great equalizer. Even as a young teenager, he had me cutting my teeth on sales books – either that or stock market stuff, which was really funny. When I went to college, it was actually to be a full-time minister. When I started doing that, I realized how much I missed being outside of the church walls and really basically in the marketplace. Several years ago I started coaching because I thought that was a great blend of everything I loved about business and ministry together – really helping people master their mindset and strategize everything they needed to really market and master all the five steps necessary to build any business. That's how I started.

The challenges along the way were that I don't really like to do what's not fun. It was a challenge to really discipline myself to do the work when I didn't want to. That meant that I had to bring people on to coach me and not just the feel-good kind of coaches. I had to bring in people that were willing to ask, "How direct can I be with you?" My coaches will say, "Gina, on a scale of 1 to 10, how direct do you want me to be with you today?" That's their nice way of saying, "How hard can I kick your butt today?" That's been a really helpful key to overcoming my challenge, which is inherent to my personality. It's great that I can make things fun, but it's sort of detrimental when I need things to be fun. That's been a challenge and a victory.

BEN SETTLE: Didn't you have some challenges early on, like when you were just getting married and everything and you guys were struggling a little bit? Were you doing business by that time too, or was that before the college stuff and all that?

GINA PARRIS: I was not in business then. We moved to Europe right away after about a year. I left the ministry, moved to Europe, and did a little bit of sales repping, but then when the babies started being born, I was a stay-at-home mom for a while. That was probably the hardest season.

BEN SETTLE: Being a mom, that's a sales job in and of itself. What are some lessons you learned just from raising, what was it, four children?

GINA PARRIS: Yeah, four. One, we just had his baccalaureate today. He's graduating high school next week.

BEN SETTLE: One of them is really cool because he's into comic books.

GINA PARRIS: Yeah. That's one of the twins. That is a lesson in sales. The biggest thing is to master your ability to understand the different personality types. Everything is sales. My worldview, I think, is the most beneficial for them. I need to sell them on how to create habits that are going to work for them because, God bless them, they're almost all wired just like me. The most helpful thing is really understanding and mastering different personality types and how to train them all. You know how the Bible says, such an interesting phrase; "Train a child in the way he should go," – it literally means according to his own bent, "and when he's old, he'll not rebel against it." That's been so powerful. In fact, in the conferences that I teach, I get that all the time that learning about personality mastery in order to sell better has actually transformed their marriages and home lives. That's the most thrilling thing I can hear.

BEN SETTLE: This is a little off topic, but it's not at the same time. There's this really bizarre show that Tanna and I started watching called *Dexter*. This is kind of weird, but it actually goes with that scripture you're talking about. It's about a psychopath. He has the urge to kill people. They're sociopaths. They have no feelings for anyone or anything like that but he vents his urge to kill onto other bad guys. He goes after people who got away with murder, because his dad, when he was a kid, brought him up that way. His dad knew what he was. He's like, "I'm going to have to teach you right and wrong, because you won't understand it. You're not wired to understand it." A lot of the show was about him at least trying to follow what's right by the way his dad brought him up. It's funny how that lifeline can actually save somebody from really doing something evil and bad. Hollywood embellishes these things, but it still is a good illustration for it.

GINA PARRIS: I love the way you're able to just tie everything. You're the master.

BEN SETTLE: That's going to be in an email this week. Honestly, I've been thinking about that since we started watching it. Some people are just born with bad wiring.

GINA PARRIS: Exactly.

BEN SETTLE: But if they have that biblical upbringing and are trained by good parents, it can guide them and prevent them from doing bad things to people.

GINA PARRIS: Oh, my gosh. We all have bad wiring. We all have great strengths that are our greatest weaknesses, and so the ability to know how to recognize that in ourselves and others is life changing.

BEN SETTLE: What are some tips and biblical examples of how to "kill the giant," things that harass you in your life and in your business?

GINA PARRIS: David is probably my very favorite character in the Bible apart from Jesus, and I love watching his whole story. Sometimes it's just awesome to read almost his whole life in one sitting, but the first thing I say about being able to kill the giant is everybody wants the big victories, but literally the victories that you win in private are what earn you the right to win in public. Who you are when nobody's looking is huge. All those years that I was in Germany in a little village where no one really knew me, they're priceless to me because I knew exactly who I was and who God was to me. Win the battles in private. Then when you look at the whole giant story, you look at how David was victorious and King Saul went absolutely insane with jealousy. That is such a lesson to me to stay away from this competitiveness. This idea that somebody has to lose in order for me to win in the kingdom is absolutely not true. There's no life that ever manifests as a result of jealousy. I say to stay away from jealousy.

Also, I think a huge thing is to be attached to a cause that's bigger than yourself. I know it's almost embarrassing for me to admit how easily I've struggled in the past with just becoming selfish, fearful, and greedy because I started to focus on trying to make money instead of trying to build a cause. David was able to look at his brothers who were making fun of him when he came to this battle scene, and he looked at his brother and said, "Is there not a cause?" He says, "Who's this uncircumcised Philistine to defy the armies of the living God?" When we totally identify with something much bigger than ourselves, then we're unstoppable.

BEN SETTLE: That's pretty good. You brought up something really interesting there and I would love to get your opinion on it. I've only just recently started getting introduced to this sort of mindset. It's this whole idea of competition. You know who C.S. Lewis was, right?

GINA PARRIS: Yes.

BEN SETTLE: His stepson or his adopted son, I can't remember, once was being interviewed about the Narnia movie, *The Voyage of the Dawn Treader,* and he was talking about this. He's a very strong Christian. That's his whole life. Even in Hollywood, he doesn't budge on that which is really nice, but he was talking about how great it would be for society to get rid of this whole idea of competition. What do you think about that?

GINA PARRIS: It's a conflict of course, because one of my niches is working with athletes, so I am very competitive when it comes to sports. We'll put that aside as sheer entertainment and personal development. Like I tell my baseball players, "The point is who baseball makes us." In the business realm, I am convinced there is a battle right now over the ability to create business that gives life and creates what some people call enlightened wealth versus these people who have won for so long. They've dominated the marketplace with businesses that steal, kill and destroy – the drug trade and human trafficking, and arms, weapons, and war. There's just a wickedness and there's an absolute line in the sand, I believe, of whose side are you going to be on? As Christians, it's ludicrous to play business by those rules of darkness. There are people that aren't even Christians that have way better revelation of this no-competition, kind of victorious business model. The truth is that when we all do what we're called to do, there's more than enough. There's no shortage of money. Money's not even tangible. It's this energy that is made by what we all agree it is. If we all say that there's all this value, then it exists. If everybody gets in fear, then we can contract the amount of money that's flowing in the marketplace. If we will stay out of fear and we'll all create value and serve and not be afraid of what we're worth, there's no lack. Nothing's impossible in the marketplace. I think there's no more exciting place to serve the living God than in the marketplace.

BEN SETTLE: Why do you think that is the case? A lot of people would say if you're serving God, you have to be out there in the jungles of Uganda somewhere, leading a church or something. This is one of the things that I notice a lot of Christian entrepreneurs will say is, "A lot of the battle is fought in the marketplace." Do you agree with that?

GINA PARRIS: Absolutely. Oh my gosh, yes. I'm the first one to say let's go to Uganda and let's teach them how to build a business. Even in the USA, we're working right now to have entrepreneurs really link arms with charities and empower people and teach them how to think differently in ways that build success and ways that buck the machine that's trying to make them dependent on a hand-out. Absolutely. I think church is made to be a place where we can gather together, worship God, and be equipped. The Bible says that ministry gifts, like pastors, teachers and evangelists, are given to equip the saints so the saints can do the work of the ministry, which means it's not what's happening at church. That's not the ministry. The ministry's what happens out in the marketplace.

BEN SETTLE: Yeah, you don't see a lot of unbelievers in church.

GINA PARRIS: Exactly. They love coming on the phone calls we have for Christian professionals. You get a bunch of millionaires talking about how to really make business a biblical way and that you're totally non-judgmental to people who are not Christians. You want them to come on your call, that's attractive. My organization has seen 35 clients become Christians because we've earned the right to be heard.

BEN SETTLE: Yeah, you take that pressure off – you're not saying, "Come here, we're going to descend upon you and we're going to pressure you into this new cult over here."

GINA PARRIS: "Lucky you, you could end up like us."

BEN SETTLE: It's terrible. It really is a bad, growing thing right now I think. We went to a local church here a couple years ago and you could feel the manipulation and trying to separate us. I was like, "I can see what you're doing. This isn't what it's about. I'm not here to play games." I can imagine how an unbeliever would feel coming into that. I'm a believer and I'm turned off by it. Imagine someone who's not a believer.

GINA PARRIS: I'm convinced there is a whole new way. God loves His people everywhere. He's got his people everywhere that can hear his voice saying, "There's a better way of doing business, of raising a family, of being redeemed and living the life of the redeemed." There's no greater story than the redemption story. Count me in.

BEN SETTLE: You're a coach. In your business I can only imagine that you probably see this a lot, this whole idea of fear of failure. Why is that such a stumbling block for Christian business owners and how do they overcome that?

GINA PARRIS: That is the million-dollar question, isn't it? I think my own issues were fear of success. "What's going to happen when they realize I'm just normal?" The fear of failure, it's everything. It's the same story whether you're a baseball player afraid of striking out, a fighter afraid of getting knocked out, a sales person afraid of being disliked for making a sales call, or a business owner afraid of loss. Napoleon Hill talks about a fear of poverty, and so I think all of those things, for one reason or another, trigger a pain feeling in our body and we just want to avoid pain. We'll do more to avoid pain than we will to gain pleasure. All of it has to do with our story, the story that we buy into from how we were raised and mostly, although not always, a lot of it was unspoken. A lot of it was spoken too. Some people were told, "You'll never amount to much, don't get your hopes up, we'd hate to be disappointed." All kinds of programming that we get. It runs counter to this science of success.

BEN SETTLE: Gary Halbert had that problem apparently. A lot of people know him as being this marketer who just made all this money, which he did, but he also would lose it. I know one of his good friends, Doberman Dan Gallapoo, was actually his roommate for a while. He said he was amazed how this guy could make money and he would just lose it. He asked Gary this. He said, "I don't understand, you made all this money with that coat of arms business. You got all these clients just throwing money at you," and yet the guy died broke. He asked Gary about that once and Gary said, "My dad told me I'm a Halbert and Halberts will never amount to anything. We'll never be anything. You need to know your place," and that sort of thing. It's really terrible.

GINA PARRIS: I have had people tell me that after seminars. They tell me my dad always told me, "Don't you be looking at those people thinking that's us." That's remarkable. As Zig Ziglar says, "It is impossible to consistently act in a way that's inconsistent with how you see yourself." Absolutely. Whether you're sabotaging your back nine on the golf course to lower your score again back to where you normally golf, or your income, it's exactly the same as your self-image. Oh gosh, that breaks my heart.

BEN SETTLE: How does somebody get past that? Is it something you just pray about? Is there any work associated to that too? What does God say about that?

GINA PARRIS: Once I think I'm past it, I see my own issues. I don't know if we ever fully get past it. I do know that the fullness of who we are is revealed in Christ. When you look at the Word and you're able to see who God is, then it so much enlarges your worship and you can be focused on who God is inside of you instead of how tiny you are in the marketplace. I have these three steps that I always go through. They are:

- Acknowledge the distressing belief, emotion or thought, whatever it is.

Write them all down. "I've never succeeded. I've always quit before I've been victorious. I've never made more than ___ per year." One lady was right at $20,000 a month. She thought, "What? I'm totally capable of doing way more." It doesn't mean that it always manifests at a certain poverty level. It can be in any level.

- Offer acceptance and forgiveness.

Just accept yourself in that belief, because it's part of your story. I had one client who said, "Money's the root of all evil." I said, "You know, that comes from the Bible." I think she was maybe Jewish. I said, "Is that an empowering thought or not, to think that money rather than the love of money is the root of all evil?"

She says, "It's just the truth."

I thought, "In a way, the love of money is the root of evil." It's the truth. It so depends on how you apply it to your life. When you acknowledge that and accept that belief, then you can create an empowering choice.

"Even though my dad said that I'll never amount to anything, even though my dad's business failed and he really doesn't think I can succeed either," you say, "I totally accept myself and my story and I choose to do whatever it takes to learn the science of building a great business." We always have the power of choice.

BEN SETTLE: You talk about building that story, you get to write your own story in a sense.

GINA PARRIS: Heck, yeah. I love that.

BEN SETTLE: You can give it a happy ending if you want.

GINA PARRIS: Exactly. On our very worst day, we are redeemed from the curse of the law. Most people might know Galatians 3:13 says, "For Christ redeemed us from the curse of the law," but I bet no one in the church I go to knows what the curse of the law is, but it's written in Deuteronomy 28. It says, "If you do all this, you'll be blessed coming in and blessed going out, and your business will be blessed, your flocks will be blessed, your children will be blessed, all these things will be blessed." And it says, "If you don't obey the Word of God, then you'll be cursed." It names poverty, sickness, confusion, and rebuke. All those things are the curse. If you know that you're blessed, then you don't have to fear the curse, which brings me to another point. When we talk about who we are, how we're going to succeed in the marketplace, writing our own story, and living our own programming, that's from our parents and not from the Word. So many things go back to the law of faith where Jesus always told people, "According to your faith, be it unto you." People would be healed. It wasn't just because He was God. In almost every single time that someone was healed, the way it was recorded in the Bible, He looked at them and said, "According to your faith, be it unto you." They believed. They heard Him speak about who He was and faith grew in their hearts. For one reason or another, the faith was there in their heart to lay hold of a miracle. I tease my spiritual friends. I call them my friends who vibrate with the universe. They call it the law of attraction and it just cracks me up because *The Secret* came out and it was this big deal. I said, "That's the exact same stuff I've been teaching for 20 years and it's called the law of faith."

BEN SETTLE: It's old hat.

GINA PARRIS: Exactly. I know it. What we really believe to be true, positive or negative, tends to be what we receive, what manifests. I know there's just been a lot of danger. Something I caution against in the church is where we talk about spiritual warfare and when we take these scriptures from Ephesians 5 and different places that say to put on a full armor of God, for our battle is not against flesh and blood but against principalities and powers and spiritual forces of evil in heavenly places. Christians make the doctrine out of that, that if we step out for God then you're going to make the devil mad and he's going to do all this bad stuff to you. You hear Christians say little catch phrases like, "Well, higher levels, higher devils," like you're going to get promoted and have the Big Kahuna demons after you. They totally build the faith for tragedy and stuff. When ordinary crappy stuff happens to them, like the same crappy stuff that happens to people who are not stepping out for God, they say, "Oh see, it's the devil." I think there's a real danger in making your devil be so big, because there's no way that a created being like Satan and all his minions come close to the power of the living God and the Redeemer who fills us with His power. I think when it comes to spiritual warfare it is so important to know that we are already seated with Christ in heavenly places and truly this has become my mantra. I don't hear anyone say it, but I say that the battle is not ours to win, the victory is ours to enforce.

It's just crazy to think that we're this vulnerable little orphan out in the marketplace trying to battle these big old demons. It's just not like that. Especially when we're talking about principalities and powers, some people say those are hierarchy of demons and others will say those are philosophies, that we take every thought captive to the obedience to Christ. The battle's for our mind and it's for how we think and how we believe, and so I think the worst thing we can do is open ourselves up to fear. To think that in order to be a soldier for God, the devil's going to be able to give us cancer, or all these things that we're redeemed of, to say that because we're stepping out for God that the devil's going to be able to put all these elements of the curse on us, that is an absolutely dangerous place to go, because ultimately according to your faith, be it unto you.

BEN SETTLE: What's that one story? I'm going to get the verse wrong. I'm not even going to try to quote it. There's that story when Jesus was talking, and I think this goes in line with what you're saying. He was talking about wicked spirits inhabiting a person. He gets kicked out and he brings seven more back that are worse, unless he has the Holy Spirit in him and then they don't want anything to do with you if you've got the Holy Spirit in you. They're fleeing from you, not actually attracted to you.

GINA PARRIS: I think that's exactly right, because the house is swept and empty.

BEN SETTLE: Yeah, that was it.

GINA PARRIS: How do we not be swept and empty but be filled with truth? Meditate. This is the only word that you see successful in. It was in Joshua when he told him, "This book of the law should never leave your mouth," meaning don't stop talking about it. You should always have the Word of God on your lips and meditate on it all the time, think about it all the time, be muttering it, saying it, and especially so you'll do it. He says, "Then you'll make your way prosperous and successful." That's exactly how you fill your heart. Where the Word says that the devil goes around like a roaring lion seeking whom he may devour, that's who he may devour, the ones who are totally clueless about who they really are in Christ and what their authority is as a believer. To think, "God's testing me sometimes with evil stuff. God is testing me or the devil's testing me," it's like you don't even know what's going on. It's just stuff. I had a pastor who said, "We used to put on these conferences and bad stuff would happen and we'd say, 'Oh no, it's the devil.'" He said, "Finally we figured out, 'It's just the toilet, call the plumber.'" It's just stuff that happens.

BEN SETTLE: When you're in a flesh body, it's going to get sick if you don't take care of it.

GINA PARRIS: Exactly.

BEN SETTLE: What do you mean when you say to focus on the promise instead of the problem during times of struggle or fear?

GINA PARRIS: We'll always have opportunity to get in fear. We're in a challenging market right now. There has to be a promise that you cling to. In fact, I would say if you're a Christian entrepreneur, the best thing you can do is be able to point to when God told you to start doing what you're doing. Did God tell you to do it or did you just get this hair-brained idea? That's really important. If you can write down or remember when you decided to do something and you had total clarity in your heart, you knew it was the right thing, then you can focus on who God is. He's the one who's faithful. Find a promise that he'll make your way prosperous and successful, that he'll meet all your needs according to Christ, that the Christ is being formed in you, whatever. Focus on the promise, because otherwise, if you get your eyes off of that and just look at the problem, your problem will get bigger and bigger and the power of God will, in your mind, become smaller.

BEN SETTLE: How does one tap into abundance from a biblical perspective?

GINA PARRIS: There's two extremes here, isn't there? There's this extreme that maybe poverty is virtuous. So let's all be like Mother Theresa – who had access to as much money as she wanted any time. She had private jets. She could do anything, go anywhere. She had access to it, so she chose to live how she did and in a lot of ways, she's so rich. Man, it's beautiful. And I'm totally just as comfortable in a third-world village as I am in a five star resort. I love them for different reasons. So how do we tap into abundance without then becoming so greedy and selfish? I don't know where we get this idea that abundance equals greed and selfishness, because I know for one thing, when I didn't have any, I was a lot more thinking about it all the time.

I think the best way to tap into abundance biblically is to quit looking at all the stuff. Like Paul says, fix your eyes on Jesus, the author and the finisher of our faith. When we can look at who God is, who Jesus is and all through the Word how God reveals himself as in the Old Testament, he says, "I am El Shaddai," which means literally means a multi-breasted one, which is really into their kind of symbolism, that He's got more than enough to nurse all His children. More than enough is who He is. More than enough. More than enough. When we focus on how huge God is and how purely loving He is and the unlimited power that is always available to us, and that we are empowered to do everything that He's called us to do in the marketplace, it just takes your fear off of looking at something little tiny like a profit and loss statement. You tap into absolute scientific laws that always work. There are scientific laws about how to build a business, how to identify your targets, how to prepare a message to deliver a marketing message, how to know what people's wants and needs are, and how to understand their personalities so you're ministering to what they really need. How to handle pre-sales, how to really make a sale, how to service a client in a way that just really blesses them and how to do follow-up, how to create a client for life and then how to systematize all that - all those things, there's a science to it. It's not like, "Every single thing in the universe runs by laws, oh, except business. Business is mysterious. It's sometimes you can do it, sometimes you can't." God doesn't even work that way. To tap into abundance spiritually is to focus on who God is, and then naturally learn the stuff. It's not rocket science, but even rocket science works by science.

BEN SETTLE: It's not brain surgery, but brain surgery is a science.

GINA PARRIS: Exactly. So yeah, the abundance is there. The Bible says that if He didn't even spare His own son, how would He not also with Him freely give us all things? Jesus said, "Don't be afraid, little flock, my Father's been pleased to give you the kingdom." It says in Ephesians that we've already been blessed with every spiritual blessing. I mean the abundance is a done deal. The redemption? It's a done deal. All of the rest is just us learning how to apply it.

BEN SETTLE: I think this dovetails really nicely into another question. I remember when you put this YouTube video out and I thought, "This is really cool." That is, does God want Christians to be rich?

GINA PARRIS: Oh, exactly. Does God want you rich? I'm convinced the answer is God wants your heart, so it's totally irrelevant. That's like saying does God want you to wear the plaid pants or the shorts? It's so irrelevant to serving God. And yet I've had people really close to me that get their eyes off of the Lord and become so caught up in greed that when things were tough – somebody came to me, she was nearly hysterical through the challenge, and she bitterly said, "I thought Christians were supposed to be blessed." She was angry and resentful at God for some challenges in their business, so that's one ditch, that you get angry when stuff's stuff. We said, "What makes you think this is the end of the battle? You keep going."

Now, a few years later, their net worth has gone up to millions and during this real estate thing they're kind of breaking even. They're still making a six-figure income, which is a lot more than when they were struggling, but they kept going.

Does God want you rich? I say God wants your heart. And in that video I compared it to baseball. Of course it's spring time, so baseball's always on my mind in the spring, but last night I was at the Little League field looking at all the little kids that try out for Little League and you can ask, "Does God want them all?" People say, "Well, obviously God doesn't want everyone rich, because everyone's not rich." Well, God did his part. I look at all these little baseball players that think, "Well, obviously God doesn't want them all to play major league ball because, number one, there's not enough room for all these players." But the fact is most of them will lose interest. They can't even have fun during one whole inning in the outfield, let alone work as hard as some of my clients work week in and week out putting in the 10,000 hours that it takes to master something. So, does God want you rich? I think He doesn't care. I think if you want to play the money game, play the money game and win it. If you want to play the baseball game, play the baseball game and win it. If you want to live in a third world nation and touch tons of lives, play that game and win it, but don't put rich or poor on God. Don't blame Him for your poverty, because He's no respecter of persons. He treats everyone the same. Everyone has the same ability to increase their own talent.

BEN SETTLE: You were talking about how somebody might have challenges and they'll say, "Well, I'm supposed to be blessed," and I'm sure this was the case with you and probably everybody that has succeeded in any way, shape, or form at anything, business or not. Of course, you don't grow unless you have some pain.

GINA PARRIS: Right.

BEN SETTLE: If anything, I'd want God to make me excel at something. I have to expect some kind of growing pains. He's not like a genie, just rub the lamp and bling, all the sudden you're just really good at something.

GINA PARRIS: Exactly. If you're going to double your business, you probably cannot do it by tweaking what you have. Hopefully, as a business coach, our goal is to always set up systems that are totally scalable, scalable, scalable, so that, in my case, we hope that your business can make a profit without you in about two years. But it is not comfortable, even where I'm at with my coaches. Oh my goodness. There's days that they'll say, "Gina, how badly do you want this?" Part of me thinks I was sort of comfortable before. Can I lower my expectations? Absolutely. With growing you always will have to break through new ceilings and new dimensions, and it's never comfortable doing that.

BEN SETTLE: What's the difference between being driven and being called?

GINA PARRIS: I'm not fond of being driven. The Bible talks about us being driven and tossed, like being driven like by the waves of the sea and tossed by every wind, even if we're purpose-driven, which was marketing genius right there. We have a purpose driven life. That could be probably a pretty good way to say it. But ultimately that goes back to in my mind to Saul and David, how Saul was so driven. He was so driven for the need to prove something, the need to be the best, to prove something, which is so sad because when he started he was so humble. Like Tiger Woods said, "Somewhere along the road I reached a place where I thought the rules didn't apply to me." That drive just causes you to implode and self destruct. The difference is being called means that you're led from the inside and you're operating out a congruence to your values and your calling and your purpose, and it's a beautiful place. It's a place of faith, and faith has rest. It's completely different than striving and striving. I've worked with so many men, and ultimately the reason they're striving has to do with wanting to prove something to their dad. Winston Churchill when asked on his death bed if there's anything that you wish, any regrets over your life at all, would you have any? He said, "You know, I wish my dad just could have lived long enough to see that I really did amount to something." Kind of interesting.

BEN SETTLE: That's also interesting from someone who wants to sell to a market. That's one of the questions in this little questionnaire I have whenever I start a new copywriting project. The people in this market, is there somebody they want to impress – a girl, a guy, whatever. It could be a parent, boss, to get back at somebody, or an enemy. It's such a powerful emotion and it can take over somebody's life if they let it.

GINA PARRIS: That's true, and as a copywriter you'll stir it up, you'll go with it.

BEN SETTLE: Well, yeah. In a way you do, you have to at least acknowledge it, because otherwise it's almost like they expect you to understand where they're coming from.

GINA PARRIS: Absolutely, like Dan Kennedy. Dan Kennedy talks about if he's selling something for balding men, he wants every bald guy who felt okay about himself to feel horrible by the end of the ad. Like, "Oh my God, I'm so ugly."

BEN SETTLE: Yeah. That's unfortunate. Usually I don't even sell that kind of stuff where you have to really mess with someone's head like that. No pun intended. [Laughter] What is the law of faith?

GINA PARRIS: What you believe is what you receive, basically, and how Jesus said, "According to your faith, be it unto you." Our friends that vibrate with the universe, they call it the law of attraction, that we manifest what we continually think about. So if you're worried all the time, the power of your worry cancels out the power of your faith. So there is a lot of quantum physics to it. It's powerful. The law of faith is what you believe really is what you receive. We don't get what we deserve, we get what we expect. It's powerful.

BEN SETTLE: There's this girl on my list and she's into coaching and stuff, but I don't think she's a Christian. She seems to be like one of your tuning-in friends. Nice girl though. I wrote this email once about how I was walking the dog for a couple years at the same spot on the beach, and I always noticed these seagulls and I was thinking they're going to poop on me one day. Like three years later it finally happened. She goes, "I can't believe it took that long, the way you were thinking about it the whole time." I mean, it was bound to happen whether I was thinking about it or not with all those pooping birds flying over me each day.

GINA PARRIS: The extreme of that belief is that we cause every single thing that we experience, so ultimately, even if tragedy strikes, we caused it on some level. There's no way that I'm going to believe that. If you're in a car accident, they're going to say, "Well yes, you were on some level vibrating that.

BEN SETTLE: You were tuned into that one.

GINA PARRIS: You were, you were tuned in. And then where the Christians would say, "No, it was the devil," I'm just going to say there's a good chance, number one, that God might have said something to you that you were too busy to hear, like slow down.

BEN SETTLE: Things happen.

GINA PARRIS: Things happen. We live in a fallen world. One thing you don't have to believe God for is challenges.

BEN SETTLE: Have you ever read *Influence* by Cialdini? I've never read this whole book because I get bored by it, and I know every marketing person's supposed to have it under their pillow, I guess. I just get bored to death by it.

GINA PARRIS: I just told my coach to read it.

BEN SETTLE: A lot of people like it. I just can't get into it for whatever reason, and this is no reflection on anybody else but myself. But I do remember the story in there that kind of was interesting, and I don't know if it relates to this exactly or not, but I would like your thoughts on it since you've read it. There's that part where he was saying he wouldn't even fly on certain days anymore if a tragedy had struck on that calendar day, or something like that. Do you remember that part?

GINA PARRIS: No, that's hilarious. That's why I got through it.

BEN SETTLE: It was really strange. He actually sounded scared, like if there was a lot of suicides on one day – and I don't remember what his example was, because this was back in 2006 when I read it – he'd done all the research and found out that probably because people who are already feeling suicidal might have tapped in and said, "Huh, this is a good day to do it," – I don't know what their reason was, but it was interesting how everybody kind of thinking together, not like there was some mystical thing going on, but just like it was convenient for them to kill themselves on that day.

GINA PARRIS: Yeah, my mom says the opposite, that anytime she gets on a plane she hijacks it in her spirit so it'll get there. She's stranger than I am. I just figure I'll hijack it in the spirit that we're getting where I'm going, and everybody's safe. In her mind, everybody is safe because she's on the plane now with her spirit of faith.

BEN SETTLE: Do you think a lot of people are scared of dying? This is an interesting question, not just from a business point of view, but just in general. Personally, I have no fear of death whatsoever. I'm actually kind of like, "Bring it on." I don't really care.

GINA PARRIS: Oh, that is so funny. My husband talks about this time when we were in a taxi in Mexico. He says, "I was never so scared in my life." He said, "I mean, if I was sure I was going to die, I wouldn't have been scared, but the way he was driving."

BEN SETTLE: I agree, more scared of pain then dying.

GINA PARRIS: Yep, he said, "I'm going to be maimed and be in pain."

BEN SETTLE: The first time I ever went on a jet plane I was like 19. We got up in the air and there was one of those, "Ding, we have a problem" type things. Apparently, the wheels wouldn't go back in. It's better than the wheels not coming out, it was the wheels didn't go back in. I've never seen such panic and it didn't even make sense why they were all panicking. My friend's panicking and I've got my headphones on. I'm like sleeping through it. I just remember thinking, "What is this obsession with dying everybody has?" I mean I don't know. Have you seen that, with people just so scared of death that's all they kind of worry about, as a coach?

GINA PARRIS: Just a few. One that was a fairly famous athlete and it was interesting. But the Word talks about setting people free who all their life were held captive to the fear of death. Isn't that interesting?

BEN SETTLE: Yeah, it is.

GINA PARRIS: As believers, that's part of our calling is to help people become set free who feared all their life, so obviously it's been a problem for quite some time. Ultimately, I wonder if people are more afraid of the fear of death or the fear of pain, because everything goes back to our fear of pain or our quest for pleasure.

BEN SETTLE: That's an interesting thing, because how many of us would not really care if we just died peacefully in our sleep anyway? But who wants to rot away from a disease or something?

GINA PARRIS: Yeah, exactly. So I think it's maybe a fear of pain.

BEN SETTLE: That's an interesting thing just to think about from a marketing point of view, too. People avoid pain and gravitate towards pleasure. That's something for the readers to think about.

GINA PARRIS: That's one of my key questions right off the bat. I make really quick calls all the time just to check in with people, I always ask, "Which of these four pains would you be most likely to avoid?" Or I might call them frustrations. "Which of these would cause you the most frustration or pain?" I always say, "Things being done improperly or out of order, things being out of control, things being no fun or boring, or conflict with others." The order in which they answer that question from four, three, two, to one gives me huge insight into their personality and how and why their business is where it is, and how I can minister to them fastest and most effectively. It's huge, understanding how people perceive pain.

BEN SETTLE: Is there an answer that comes up number one most of the time when you ask those questions?

GINA PARRIS: No, it depends on the group of people. It's very interesting, because the real driven people who tend to be entrepreneurial, they're almost always pretty much a driver personality and they don't like things being out of control. They're kind of controllers. They make things happen. The real analytical guys that tend to be much more engineers, they like security. They're not always entrepreneurial. Their greatest fear might be things not being done correctly. But we see the gamut. I was surprised that the things being boring, among entrepreneurs, is often their least concern, and it was where I test out the highest. I can't stand stuff to be boring.

BEN SETTLE: Well, if you're going to have a problem that's probably not a bad one to have, if that's your biggest frustration. You can always make business not boring.

GINA PARRIS: Yeah, I married Mr. Parris, he kicks my butt when I get bored. You have to do stuff that's not fun.

BEN SETTLE: He'll put you to work doing something. "You're bored over there? I got work for you to do over there."

GINA PARRIS: Exactly. That's our answer.

BEN SETTLE: There's this e-book that Gary Halbert wrote back in 2005. You can't even buy it anymore. I got it as a bonus for something I bought. It was about the core desires and motivations of different groups of people. It was different professions, different age groups, and different races, which was very interesting. Not the most politically correct book you'll ever read, but it was interesting. He said executives who are always in leadership positions, they want someone to sell them something that doesn't take any responsibility for them to use. Like they're craving leadership, basically.

GINA PARRIS: Oh, absolutely. That's why anytime we can do 'done for you' business – and I don't offer anything that's 'done for you' – that's brilliant, and the wealthiest people will pay the most for it. "Do my marketing for me, write all my stuff for me, shop for me, do everything for me. I just want time."

BEN SETTLE: Yeah, time is that big motivating factor. Everybody thinks money is, but are you seeing that time, at least amongst maybe higher income people, is way more important?

GINA PARRIS: Absolutely, and just the peace of mind.

BEN SETTLE: Now here's something you mentioned a couple times throughout this talk I've noticed, so this is probably a good time to ask it. What is the Biblical model for marketing a business?

GINA PARRIS: I think it starts with the mindset that people need us, literally. Because a lot of Christians are so sweet, in their sweetness they don't want to bug anybody. They don't want to seem pushy, they don't want to be sales-y, they don't want to make anybody uncomfortable, therefore, "I will not make sales calls." The mindset is that we are a conduit of hope. Everybody out there, like we've said, has got pains, they've got fears, and if we have any way at all to answer their fears and give them hope, then that is our job in our marketing. The Biblical model is to identify the target. "Who are the people that need me?" Jesus came to His own, and His own received Him not, but then He always knew He was going to come for the whole world. So you identify the target of who really needs what you have, and literally understand their pains and their concerns and develop a message that's about them, not about ourselves.

Then it's about utilizing as many tools as efficiently as you can so that you can automate as much as you can through using technology to reproduce yourself, and to bring them into a system where they screen themselves, and where you can really find the people the fastest who are going to benefit from what you have. I think it just is so powerful to know that your marketing blesses people. Whether somebody buys my service or not, part of my marketing is to get in front of them and speak, right? And my goal is that everybody is completely blessed when they leave one of my seminars, even one of my free ones or inexpensive ones. It's marketing for me, but I'm satisfied because I know that they'll go home that day blessed whether they buy from me or not. So a lot of it is just being out there to serve as powerfully and efficiently as possible. That's the difference between trying to go hurt people, use people, lie, cheat, steal, whatever it takes to make a dollar.

BEN SETTLE: And that's the huge irony of it. People are afraid of being pushy. If you want to sell, those are the last things you should be doing anyway – pressure and all that. That's the last thing I would do.

GINA PARRIS: Oh, my gosh, there's a pretty well-known coach online and I took one of his free strategy calls. He was sort of interesting. I might have said this to you, because you gave the point that sometimes all you need to do is ask the prospect, "What do you want me to do?" He made me uncomfortable and I thought, "No." At first I thought, "Yeah, this is a good idea." Then I called him and said, "Sorry, it's not a good idea," and he was so mad at me. He was totally yelling at me. He's telling me how we're out of integrity with each other. He made me feel like I was four years old. He insulted me several times in the call. I just thought, "What about that exchange made me in any way admire who he is? All he had to do was say, 'What would you like me to do?" and I could have said, 'Tell me for sure why this is for me.'" But it was crazy.

BEN SETTLE: That was straight out of Jim Camp. He's the world's greatest negotiator and he's the one that teaches that. I thought, "Gosh, that is so good because you're giving them the power to choose. You're giving them the right to veto, and they need that."

GINA PARRIS: Exactly. I learned it from you.

BEN SETTLE: I learned it from Jim Camp, he's awesome. What is the best time management tip you have for Christian business owners?

GINA PARRIS: To know that time is such a gift, really. I've made a video where I drew out like a 30-year timeline on a piece of note-book paper, it might have been longer, but every line on the note-book paper was a year and I turned it sideways and drew it all out. I saw how your life goes by in a flash, how tiny the little inch was where my kids were home if I was raising kids. It made me just want to be just a good steward of time. One of the natural laws is that if we're a good steward of our own time and other people's time, that we'll get more, and so really start with the end in mind and block things together. Block out the most important money-making tasks right off the bat and do them. Record them and make yourself accountable to get them done.

BEN SETTLE: Start with the end in mind. That's from *The 7 Habits of Highly Successful People*?

GINA PARRIS: Yes. Stephen Covey used to say it. Absolutely.

BEN SETTLE: Was that a book that you learned a lot from?

GINA PARRIS: I think I liked it more the second time around several years later, but that's kind of the only one that meant a lot to me.

BEN SETTLE: Yeah, that's the only one I got out of it.

GINA PARRIS: Sharpen the saw and all that stuff, but that was for sure my favorite one.

BEN SETTLE: The beauty of all these e-books today is that people are just taking what these 300 page books say and saying it in 30 pages.

GINA PARRIS: I know. I went on that Harvard Book Review thing where you get the Cliff Notes version.

BEN SETTLE: I don't know how people read these long books. I have a book here from this lady named Janine Driver, and she's a body language expert. I've seen her on like *The Big Idea* with Donny Deutsch and stuff. I thought, "That's kind of cool." She's got this book, but I can't read it. It's just too much fluff. Can't you just put it down into the 10 pages of stuff that I need?

GINA PARRIS: I know. Absolutely. That's probably what people are thinking reading this. They're like, "Man, they went on a lot of rabbit trails."

BEN SETTLE: Maybe, but I think you're actually giving away of lot of really good information. I've had many discussions with Matt Gillogly. He runs ChristianBusinessDaily.com and we've talked about this a lot. A lot of Christian business owners are just really bound up in guilt because their churches are not telling them this stuff. They're telling them to get on a committee and learn how to do it that way. Most of us hate committees. We don't want anything to do with committees.

GINA PARRIS: Especially if you're entrepreneurial and know how to be successful in business. If you go to a small church where the pastor is not very gifted in leadership, it's so hard. Or if you go to a big church where he's a control freak, you're going to butt heads.

BEN SETTLE: They're just not getting this very many places. What's the most important business success secret that you've learned from the Bible?

GINA PARRIS: It's the parable of the talents, that it's really not God's job to make the money come into my bank account. It's my job to develop the talent, and really, it's not about me. It's easy for me just to get comfortable and sit back. I can think there's a million people saying what I say, what difference does it make? But the truth is, God has given all of us talents and He expects us to develop them to His glory and trade. I love that He said trade until I come. It's pure marketplace scripture right there. So it's my responsibility to get in the Word and learn what He says about being around people who know how to do it right. Here's another thing. In Psalm 1 where He says not to hang around mockers and scoffers, but the person's blessed whose delight is in the law of the Lord, that was something I had to learn. I started becoming indignant that a lot of my friends that we mentioned earlier, that vibrate with the universe, seemed to be having so much more success, and so I started taking all their counsel and hanging around with a lot of people that don't honor God. It really didn't go well with me. I'm doing much better now with coaches, executive coaches, being surrounded by my teammates and colleagues who have built multi-million dollar businesses and charities and have done it all because of their relationship with God. I'd say, man, get biblical counsel. Surround yourself with biblical counselors and develop your talents, because it's ultimately not about ourselves.

BEN SETTLE: You mentioned somewhere at the beginning of the call, the book *Think and Grow Rich*, and I just think it's kind of interesting because I don't know what his faith was, Napoleon Hill, but it didn't seem necessarily Christian to me. It's interesting that he died broke.

GINA PARRIS: Nobody acknowledges that.

BEN SETTLE: There's something missing there, and I have this feeling it's the "C" word, Christ.

GINA PARRIS: I know. Or the C word Cause.

BEN SETTLE: Or Cause, yeah.

GINA PARRIS: Was it to get rich? Everything was about riches, riches, riches. Well, what the heck does it profit you if you gain the whole world and lose your soul? Absolutely. It makes a big difference doing it God's way.

BEN SETTLE: Where can people learn more about you and your services?

GINA PARRIS: My blog is just always in limbo. I look at it and think, "Gina, that's so fluffy." But my blog is over at www.GinaParris.com, and I invite everybody reading this to get a free online mini-business x-ray. This is so powerful for anybody to log on here and just answer these questions. It takes about 10 minutes and it will really, really help take a look at your business, and I invite anyone to take that for free. I got a bit.ly for that and that is http://bit.ly/minixray.

I'd love to just help people really take a look and see if they're scientifically building their business correctly, because if we can succeed in the marketplace, then we have influence and we have the right to be heard and to share the love of God.

BEN SETTLE: The last question is this. If someone reading this is not yet a Christian, maybe they're kind of on the fence and maybe this book is introducing them to this whole new world they've never experienced, what would you tell them if they were standing in front of you?

GINA PARRIS: Well, I'd say get into the Word. If you don't have a Bible, then go online to www.BibleGateway.com and start reading the book of John and find out who Jesus really is.

If you maybe grew up in church and there's a part of you that says, "I really know. I believe in my heart that Jesus is God and that He's able to make my life new," then it's really just as simple as believing that in your heart and saying it with your mouth. "I believe Jesus is God and I want him to be my Lord." Just pray. Just as simply as it takes, just say, "Lord, I know I'm not perfect and I invite you to take away my sins and make my life new and I'll live for you." It's not complicated.

In fact, that word sin, if that word scares anybody, I just want you to know that literally it's an archery term. When we hit a bull's-eye, we say "Bull's-eye," and in Hebrew, they'd say "Paga." If we miss, we go, "I missed." And they go, "Oh, sin." It's the word for missed. It means that you've fallen short. The target is the glory of God. Oh my goodness, it's the best place in the world to be. So I invite you to hang out with any of us who love God and learn everything you can. Welcome to the family. It's really a great place to be.

BEN SETTLE: You've seen lives change when they do that. How did your life change when you became Christian? Do you remember when that was?

GINA PARRIS: You know what? I cannot remember ever not loving God, but I never knew about making a decision, saying it so out loud that I was choosing to live for God. I just remember that day that I made a decision and I prayed with some friends. I was 12, and I've never ever looked back.

BEN SETTLE: Great. Thank you for doing this.

GINA PARRIS: I love it. My pleasure. Thank you so much.

BEN SETTLE: You did all the work. I just held the clipboard.

GINA PARRIS: It's a great conversation and I'm just thrilled to help out anywhere that I can.

Christian Business Bonus Tip #3

Following is a Bible-themed article written to my website newsletter subscribers. To join my free mailing list and access 700+ pages of advanced web marketing tips, go to:

www.BenSettle.com

The Bible's Secret Email Marketing Lesson

One of history's grooviest marketers is Bruce Barton.

Back in his day (early to mid 1900's) he was a household name, a giant in the advertising business and even an advisor to presidents. One of his best teachings (in my humble, but accurate, opinion) was in a 1924 radio broadcast about when the Biblical patriarch Joseph was the second in command in Egypt.

Joseph was "it."

Egypt's top dawg.

Everyone was commanded by Pharaoh to follow his orders and his name was as familiar to every Egyptian man, woman and child as their own, until...

> "And Joseph died...and there arose up a new king over Egypt which knew not Joseph."
> (Exodus 1:6-8)

Boom!

Almost overnight all Joseph's power, prestige and name recognition vanished like a fart in the wind. He went from being "the man" to being a footnote in some hieroglyphic somewhere -- completely forgotten.

There's a HUGE lesson here for us today.

And that's this whole idea of how easy it is to be forgotten.

Happens ALL the time.

One day you're "Joseph" and everyone in your market knows who you are... the next they've forgotten you or have found a new king to hang with (and buy from).

Anyway, this is why I'm so big on email.

And why I think email kicks so much gluteus bootyus.

Do it right and it's almost impossible for your list to forget about you (in fact, you'll always have "top of mind" status).

It's the #1 skill to have.

Nothing else even comes close.

Ben Settle

For over 700 pages of advanced web marketing tips and secrets, go to www.BenSettle.com

Ancient Business Secrets Of The Bible

Interview with Matt Gillogly
www.ChristianBusinessDaily.com

BEN SETTLE: Can you tell us about your background and that shake-up that you recently had in your life that sort of got you on this new path to help Christian entrepreneurs?

MATT GILLOGLY: You got it. My background is that I worked in the golf business for a number of years. I used to run private country clubs. I was a turn-around expert in the golf business. At one point in my life, I was a PGA golf professional, but I never played on tour. If you've ever been to a resort or private country club, those are the kind of places that I ran and built. I always had a heart and a desire to be an entrepreneur and like most people, I read *Rich Dad, Poor Dad*, and it completely changed my life. I didn't realize how miserable I was working for someone else until I read that. So I started learning about real estate, and right about the year 2000, I started working on buying my own investment property. We were living in Baton Rouge, Louisiana at the time. My first real estate deal that I did, I think I lost $60,000 cold hard cash. My second deal I lost $30,000 cold hard cash. So you can see I was really moving in the right direction. Then I decided to finally break down and invest in a kit online. The internet was in its infancy then. I went and attended a Robert Allen protégé program, which really was nothing more than $6,000 to get pitched every 90 minutes. I spent $15,000-$20,000 on stuff and was off and running. Within 90 days, I did $90,000 worth of real estate deals, cold hard cash into my pocket. Another guy, not Robert Allen, who was mentoring me took me under his wing and before I knew it I was coaching investors. I'm no longer actively involved in real estate. I've sold my entire portfolio, but I've been involved in over 150 real estate transactions. I've coached 28,000 real estate investors nationwide.

But to back up a second, I started investing, and I gave my life to Christ. My whole world started to change. I started wanting to know really truly what does it mean to run a Christ-centered business. I grew up Catholic but never really understood what it meant to have a personal relationship with Christ. So when I gave my life to the Lord, I just naturally assumed there was a biblical way for running a business. I could find zero resources then. There wasn't a book at the library. I went to my pastor and said, "Hey, I'm now a believer. I've given my life to the Lord. How do I go about running a Christ-centered business? I'm an entrepreneur, so how do I go about doing that?" No joke, Ben, my pastor said, "How about we start with you running the bake sale?" I went, "What? What does that have to do with…" He said, "Well, you know, we can get you on some committees. That will be really good for you as an entrepreneur to be on some committees." I don't know about you, but my whole goal in life is to like get rid of committees. I couldn't see how a committee was going to solve this. So I started going on this quest about what it means to run a Christ-centered business. About two years ago I had a business partner in my coaching business, and we're still very good friends today. I literally heard the Lord speak to me and say, "Alright, you've been talking about helping Christian entrepreneurs, it's time for you to go." I said, "God, I can't. I'm making too much money at this other coaching thing. Let me go make a lot of money, and I'll get back to you in two years." Well, God didn't really like that answer, so he started taking me through a 24-month period where He dwindled my business down to almost nothing until He got my attention and I said, "Okay God. I guess I have no choice but to work with Christian entrepreneurs." And it is amazing, because there are very few if any resources out there.

There's a lot of stuff about working in the marketplace, but as entrepreneurs, we don't want to know how to get along with everybody in the company. I want to know what God says about using debt to grow the business. How do I go about examining opportunities that come my way? Because not all opportunities are good. So God takes me through this, and I'll tell you right now, Ben, He has cleaned me out. He has sucked dry basically every account that I have, all in an effort for me to completely understand what it really means to be a Christian entrepreneur. I won't tell you that I'm 100% there, because I never will be. He's just really taken me through the wringer. For the most part it's been exceptionally humbling, because I've always prided myself on making money at will. That is one thing that God has taken away from me. He has done a lot to me in this time, and He's completely changed my heart – the way I think about business, the way I approach business, and the way I look at opportunities. He's completely turned my world upside down. It's been frustrating. It's been painful. There's been a lot of tears shed, but I wouldn't change it for the world.

BEN SETTLE: Just to clarify, when you say "The Lord cleaned you out," what kind of numbers were you doing before the shake-up happened?

MATT GILLOGLY: $150,000 a month. Now remember, I had a business partner. I was walking out with about $30,000 a month. That was my net.

BEN SETTLE: Most people can barely make that in a year.

MATT GILLOGLY: Yeah, that's like real money the last time I checked. I haven't pulled a dime out of the company in five or six months. There's nothing to pull out. I'll put it into an even greater perspective. We were netting $30,000 a month; I'm now losing $10,000–15,000 a month.

BEN SETTLE: It's a good thing you had savings. That's devastating to think about.

MATT GILLOGLY: I'll tell you right now, I've had some nights where I've been pretty hacked off. There's been a lot of tears shed. I'm laughing today, but I could be crying tomorrow. It's exceptionally humbling to me. I was a guy that first got exposed to Dan Kennedy in 2004. By 2006, I was one of Dan's golden boys. He was sticking me on stage every chance he got, doing million dollar events and just killing it. I got pretty full of myself and thought I was pretty damn good at what I did. That was kind of one of the lessons that God showed me through this whole thing. The reason why I'm so open, Ben, is that the enemy wants us to feel shame when we have failures. I've been through that emotion. All that shame gets you is more frustrated and more heartache. I have joy about the situation that I'm in because I know God's doing some great things through me and in me. We need to just be flat-out more open about the skeletons in our closet. I've always said that if Bill Clinton were to have said, "You're right. I screwed up. I've been sleeping with everything that's got a pulse for the last 25 years, and I enjoy it." If he were to have said that, probably 85% of the people would have gone, "Well, okay."

Some people are like, "Oh gosh, I can't believe that just happened to you." I'll tell you right now, I went from a big chunk of cash in the bank, the kids' college accounts taken care of, and driving a nice car, to $750,000 upside down. It's time to sell the car and dump the house. I'm sure this is really motivating to people, but there are people who are listening to this right now that are in that exact same situation. What I found about being open about this is that everyone is like "Wow, these guys are real." We're real people. I don't know about you, Ben, but I'm just as screwed up as everybody else who's reading this. I share this because I find every time I share it, people are encouraged by it. The business is coming back, and we're picking up speed and all that good stuff. God will restore it. Notice I'm saying God's going to restore it, because I sure as heck tried to restore it for the last 24 months and all I did was screw it up more.

BEN SETTLE: What exactly does it mean to run a Christ-centered business? I assume that's what you're talking about here. You're letting Him take care of it. What does that mean exactly?

MATT GILLOGLY: To run a Christ-centered business is to go against pretty much everything that's been drilled into our mind in America and in the media. If you watch TV you get bombarded with, "Manifest Your Destiny. Look deep inside yourself, and you'll find the answer and what you're supposed to do. Do what you want, where you want, when you want, with whom you want, and whenever you want." Do you ever watch Boston Legal? William Shatner plays Denny Crane. He's kind of like this spaced out attorney. They come into the office, and he's got his hand up to his forehead and his eyes squinted. You can tell he's really concentrating hard, and they go, "What are you trying to do?" He goes, "I read *The Secret* last night, so I'm trying to manifest Raquel Welch." So the next scene they come in and all of a sudden they go, "Denny, you've got someone to see you." He goes, "Who's that?" and they go, "It's Phyllis Diller." Here is he trying to manifest Raquel Welch and he gets Phyllis Diller. My friends always go, "Well, it's a start." My reply is, "Have you seen Phyllis lately? That's a long, far cry from Raquel Welch."

I used to be in a mastermind group with a guy who was really big into The Secret. He got indicted, lost everything, and went to jail. The big question in the group was, "Did he manifest that?" This is really hard for Americans, and especially entrepreneurs, to get. We become entrepreneurs because we want to control our destiny, right? Then as a Christian, they say, "I'm just going to ask God to bless everything that I do." Because God is a genie? He's the ultimate genie, and if I'm a business person and I'm a Christian, that means everything is going to be blessed? I can tell you, it doesn't work out that way. What it means to run a Christ-centered business is that it's all about His purposes. It's not about our purposes – it's about His purposes. This is so hard and so contrarian to the whole message of being an entrepreneur. "I'm going to work from home. I'm going to work a four-hour work week." Well, if you were to ask Timothy Ferriss, he doesn't work four hours a week. I know people who know him, and they say the guy works incessantly. His whole concept of taking eight months off work a year, play golf, and go live in the French Riviera – that sounds great from the stage, but I know a lot of the top speakers and none of them do that. We were made to work. Genesis tells us men were made to work (and women, don't send me an email saying I'm a chauvinist). We are made to work. We are made to till the soil and reap the harvest by the sweat of our brow. Frankly, it's unbiblical to not work. Who wants to go to Florida and play golf for the last 20 years of their life? It's boring. I'm a recovering golf pro. I go on a week-long vacation, and I can't wait to get back in the office. That's not because I don't love my wife and kids, but God created me to work, and I love to work.

I spent the first 40 years of my life trying to do what Matt Gillogly wanted, and it got me broke. Now I'm going to spend the next 120 years of my life doing what the Lord asks me to do, and it's going to be about His purposes and His desires. I always like to refer to Matthew 6:33, "But seek first His kingdom and His righteousness, and all these things will be given to you as well." Most people want to focus on just the last part of that verse – all this will be given to you. You've got to seek God first, and you have to seek His righteousness. Righteousness is not a bad word. Everybody goes, "Oh, gosh, righteousness – what are you, a Southern Baptist? What are you, Pentecostal? Catholic?" Pick one to offend. Righteousness is just His right ways of living. So what are His right ways of living? His right ways of living begin and end with the Top 10 – the Ten Commandments. So what's the First Commandment, and I'm going to paraphrase this – *You should have no other gods before Me*. We think it's our ability to create money, to do things like we're going to make money to go buy a brand new car and a big brand new house. Again, there's nothing wrong with having a nice house and a nice car, but as we go through this, you'll understand that after you go through this true understanding of what it means to be a Christian entrepreneur, none of that stuff really matters. It's about the matter of the heart. When we really start to understand all the different gods we place in front of God, all the different things we put more value in, we realize we don't do a very good job at following the first commandment.

God convicted me one day. He said, "Matt, you know all those books you have on your shelves?" and I spent like a couple hundred grand a year on this stuff. "You know all those groups that you belong to and all those events you go to? Never once have you asked Me what I think about any of those business things you're doing." It's kind of like when you're an eight year old kid and you just got busted looking up Mary Jacob's skirt or something like that, and you couldn't deny it. It's like breaking Elmer Fudd's window with a baseball bat or whatever it was. It was exactly like that. I had my hands behind my back and I was pawing the ground with my foot, looking down, trying to come up with a cute, clever answer, and I couldn't. To run a Christ-centered business means I'm going to co-labor with God. It's going to be about His purposes and His desires, and it's not about my purposes and my desires. It's not about going to God and saying, "Okay God. I really love you. I've got this deal closing on Friday. We're going to make $30,000 and you get 10%. Since you're going to get 10%, have it close without a hitch." What if we instead went to God and said, "Lord, I just love you so much. You are my daddy. I just love you so much, God, and I know you love me unconditionally. What do you want me to do? Do you want me to go do this deal where I'm going to JV somebody's product? We can go do it for the money, or, God, what's part of Your plan in this?" I totally ignored that for a significant portion of my life as a believer. So to run a Christ-centered business, first and foremost, it's about His purposes and His desires.

The second thing is about putting God in front of everything. All these books I have on my shelves, all the newsletters I get, now when I read them, I ask the Lord to show me the things he wants me to pull away from these newsletters. If we read it unchecked with just our own personal fleshly desires, all the ideas sound good. But we approach it with, "God, I know there's a lot of great ideas in here. I know there are a lot of different ways to go. Lord, show me the one thing or the few things if any in here that you want me to start installing into Your business." This is really hard for entrepreneurs to get. They all bristle when I tell them this. This is not my business, it's God's. I'm just simply like the general manager, and I've got a really good profit sharing program. I am a steward and I've got to check in with my chairman and CEO on a daily basis. What if we were to just go to God and say, "Look, do you want me to work with this client or not?" What would it be like if God was co-laboring with you when you were writing copy? What if you were moving in His power and not ours? His power is way better. For me, a Christ-centered business is that it's not just Sunday, it's every day. How I'm a Christian reflects as much about how I treat my kids at WalMart when they're screaming out for a chocolate bar as it does when I'm sitting at church looking all righteous. It's in everything we do.

BEN SETTLE: You were saying God might want you to do something different than what you want to do. Have you found in your life and in others where you've observed this that what God wants you to do is actually more fulfilling than the thing you thought you wanted to do originally?

MATT GILLOGLY: Oh yeah, it's way better.

BEN SETTLE: So it's not something people should be running away from, thinking they don't want to ask God because they don't want Him to tell them something they don't want to hear.

MATT GILLOGLY: Yeah, that's going to happen because they're all afraid God's going to tell them to sell everything and move to Ethiopia. I've got a feeling about entrepreneurs. Not only are we control freaks, but we actually love the adventure of it. I know your background of you living in your office and having to shower in the sink. In its own strange way – and I don't want to necessarily say you remember it lovingly or fondly – but we all have kind of this sick point of our life where things were absolutely going nowhere and we all go, "Boy, those were the good old days." Think about the joy and adventure of waking up on Tuesday and having to get rent in by noon, and you're overdrawn by $1,500 in your account, and you've got no prospects on the horizon. Isn't that what entrepreneurs live for?

BEN SETTLE: When you're doing it, you're not real happy about it, but when you solve the problem, you're like "Hey!"

MATT GILLOGLY: Yeah, you high-five the mirror and beat our chest. We tell everybody that will listen just how great we are. The reason people love becoming entrepreneurs is they're bored out of their flipping mind with what they're doing. They want excitement back in their life. Be a faith-filled entrepreneur where you're going to trust in God. What better way to go and just really live life on the edge. For some people, living life on the edge means not having any money in their bank account. For other people it will mean other things. It doesn't mean God's going to suck you dry and take away all your money. Just because it happened to me doesn't mean it's going to happen to you. There is some great wonder and amazement to see how God can work. I just think we miss out on so much in enjoying the ride and enjoying what the ride can be as entrepreneurs, because we're unwilling to let God take control. We'd rather fly the little Cessna all on our own than be the co-pilot in the F16 fighter jet. Granted, the ride in the F16 fighter jet is scary, but boy it's a lot of fun.

BEN SETTLE: I'm just wondering, when you were told to get out of the real estate thing and do the Christian entrepreneur thing, was it a gut feeling or how was He talking to you?

MATT GILLOGLY: No, He talks. I hear His voice. Now people are going to go, "Oh gee, this guy's off his rocker." But I hear it. I hear the audible voice of the Lord. If I don't pay attention to that, one of two things will happen. The Lord will come and visit me in dreams. It's not God standing at the base of my bed going "Go work with Christian entrepreneurs." It's kind of like a hidden thing. The thing that He does that really just whacks me out is He'll start having people that don't even know me, like the old lady at the grocery store when you're picking out tomatoes, who comes up next to you and goes, "You know, I just sense that you like to work with Christian entrepreneurs." You'll be totally wigged out. [laughing]

BEN SETTLE: So you'll get little clues.

MATT GILLOGLY: Yeah, like the Bible will be open to something specifically that the Lord put on my heart. I'll give you an example of this that totally freaked me out. This was at the end of January 2008. I went out to a place called the International House of Prayer in Kansas City. They have a 24/7 prayer room. They go 24/7, 365 days a year. They've been going since 1999. They do events with a group called The Joseph Company. The Joseph Company is for marketplace leaders and entrepreneurs to come to. It's like a six-day leadership retreat to understand how to pray and all that fun stuff. It's really an amazing trip. So I go out there and, like most entrepreneurs, I've got my guard up. This prayer thing is fine for people who are intercessors. I mean, God visiting in a dream, that's good for you guys who have prophetic skills, but I'm a business guy. Give me a balance sheet, right? So the first day everybody's walking around the room talking about how tough they are. By day three, they're all weeping like little kids, because the Lord has touched their heart so much. In day two, we go to the prayer room in the morning. It's a big old converted grocery store, so there's like 400 people in there. They've got music going with a band up there. They do this thing called rapid fire prayer. They go, "Okay, anybody who's here for The Joseph Company event, stand up. Come out in the aisles and people are going to pray for you." So people are putting their hands on me and praying. There are like five or six people around, and I don't know any of these people from Adam. At the end of one of the prayers, this guy goes "Deuteronomy 8:18." I go, "Okay, thanks," and I don't even bother to look it up. I was just like, "Thanks, weird intercessor guy." Later that day, I'm back in the prayer room and they do another rapid fire prayer thing. I stand up, and afterwards one of the other people praying looks at me and goes, "The whole time I was standing next to you, I kept seeing Deuteronomy 8:18 over your head." I'm going, "Okay, this is getting really weird." Day three. Deuteronomy 8:18 pops up. Intercessor prayer of, "I really get the sense that you're in this difficult season and the Lord wants you to know Deuteronomy 8:18." After about the fifth time, I go and look it up. It is, "But remember the Lord your God, for it is He who gives you the ability to produce wealth."

Now God had been placing that on my heart like saying, "Remember, I'm in charge," but I wasn't letting go. He kept putting Deuteronomy 8:18 in front of me constantly until I finally decided to open this up and read about it. Then I started reading the corollaries to it, because I have this study Bible and all the verses that relate to it. It was all about the Israelites who have a history of prospering. They're dead broke without a country. They seek God with, "Oh God, we love you. We love you." God blesses them, and they have a bunch of successes. Within three generations the kids have false idols in the house, they're watching MTV, and driving a Mercedes-Benz. Wham, God takes it all away from them and throws them into captivity. They are like, "Oh Lord, we're sorry, we're sorry." He waits for that generation to die off and lifts up another generation. He blesses them. This happens constantly in the Old Testament about Israel's straying from God, God getting ticked and taking away their country, their wealth, and all their riches. So Deuteronomy 8:18 is what God told the Israelites after they had been wandering through the wilderness for 40 years. They kept going around the mountain for 40 years until that unbelieving generation died off. As they were getting ready to cross over the Jordan River into Israel to take the land that God promised them, God says for them to wait a second and not to forget – "But remember the LORD your God, for it is He who gives you the ability to produce wealth, and so confirms His covenant, which He swore to your forefathers, as it is today." What does the world tell us? The world tells us we have the power to get wealth, and we don't. We do not have the power to get wealth. Only God has the power to get wealth. It's when we seek Him and go after Him that this prophetic word written in Deuteronomy 8:18 comes true. I'm not talking about what you're going to order at lunch when you go to Denny's. Don't sit there and go, "Oh Lord, illuminate what I'm supposed to have for lunch." It's not that.

I have friends of mine, Ben, who are real estate investors who pray over their deals. One of these guys, an acquaintance, was sharing this story with me. He's down in Wilmington, North Carolina, along the coast, and this is at the beginning of summer. The real estate market was not doing well, and he said, "God, I've got all these deals." He said, "Basically what I do is put vacant land under contract, and I flip it to a developer and make $500,000 or whatever. That's all I do. I've been doing this for 25 years." He said he knew what were deals and what were not deals. He said, "The market down there is really bad. Developers aren't buying vacant land. I'm praying over these deals, and God keeps leading me to this very below-average deal." He said it was like God was illuminating it. He said, "God, you're nuts. There's no way that's a good deal. This is a bad market. You must be crazy." So he tried to go do a couple other deals and those don't work. He kept coming back, and every time he got back into the office, God was shining his light on this deal. He said, "I have a long enough history with God to realize I should be following this." He said, "I decided I would move forward in this deal. I put this deal on a contract (and I don't have the numbers exact, but you'll get the idea) for $1.2 million. My goal is to flip it to a developer for about $1.6, 1.7 million. It's about 120 acres right along the Intercoastal

Waterway. It was a nice development property." He continues, "We go into our phase two analysis of the property, and we realize there's $3.5 million dollars worth of sugar sand underneath the ground." Now, sugar sand is a big commodity. They harvest this sand at other places and put it on beaches that are eroding. He said, "There's $3.5 million dollars of sugar sand, and it's going to take 3–5 years to harvest it." So I asked, "What happens to the land you have now once you harvest the sugar sand?" He goes, "I have lakes on my property, and the value of my property goes up exponentially." He said, "I got that deal because I had a history in developing my prayer life with God. I remembered that it's God, not me, who gives me the power to get wealth. I wouldn't have done that deal at all."

And, Ben, if I can tell you that story one time, I can tell you that story 100 times about other people with similar situations in business. Guys who the Lord puts on their heart to get out of a particular stock and sure enough, a couple weeks later that stock is tanking. Guys who are told to buy things, and the stock market increases. This is what it means to co-labor with Christ. This isn't some shaman thing where I'm rolling my third eye up, sitting in the lotus position, and I'm inhaling some funny smelling grass. This is the God of the universe and this is real stuff. God is real. There's no doubt in my mind that God exists. Unquestionably, the Bible is the most historically accurate text known to mankind. Atheist archeologists all use it to find ancient cities in Israel. It's a historically accurate text. So if that's historically accurate, why wouldn't God want us to prosper? This isn't the prosperity gospel where we're saying give $500, here's the mailing address, and God will give you $5,000 back. This is about co-laboring with Christ. I can tell you that's way more fun than trying to do it on your own.

BEN SETTLE: Is that why some Christian entrepreneurs profit while others don't, because one group is listening to what God is saying and the other isn't?

MATT GILLOGLY: It comes down to one thing and that's about the heart. Listening to God is 95% of it, but an even greater portion of it has to do with what's the condition of your heart. In Daniel 1:8 it says "And Daniel purposed in his heart that he would not pollute himself with the king's delicate food..." This was after Daniel had been dragged away from Jerusalem into Babylon. He's 15 years old, and Nebuchadnezzar, who is basically a head lopper, is going to say, "You're going to eat my food. You're going to learn the wisdom and writings of the Chaldean. I'm going to reprogram you and you're going to stay in this palace. You're going to have all this luxury, but you've got to do things the way we do it here." Daniel basically says, "I'm not going to defile myself with the delicacies of the king." And sure enough, Daniel doesn't, and God blesses him. The reason why is that Daniel stayed true to God. That's why some Christian entrepreneurs profit and others don't. The Christian entrepreneurs that are willing to stay true to God and do what God wants, to surrender their hearts and minds completely, surrender their business completely, and to really just have a passion about serving God – those are the one that traditionally prosper. David was that way. Daniel, Abraham, Joseph, and Job were all that way. David didn't care about being king of Israel. He cared about his relationship with God. When David's son, Absalom, rose up against David to take over the kingdom and the city is being ransacked, David is getting ready to flee, and his chief priest, Zadok, says to him, "David, what are you going to do? You're going to lose your kingdom. You could wind up being dead." David said, "I don't care about the kingdom. I don't care about being king, the palaces, the horses, none of that stuff, as long as I've got God."

For some people, God's cool as long as He takes care of me, but what if God doesn't bless you? Are you still going to love Him unconditionally? Are you still going to have a heart for Him? Let's say He calls you to go do a business and for 20 years it doesn't work. You go through bankruptcy after bankruptcy. You lose your house and wind up living in a smelly cave with a bunch of other broke, bankrupt people. Would you still love God? That's what David had to do. David was living in the palace, and before you know it he's living in the cave of Adullam. Here's what God sends him, 400 other people who were broke and bankrupt. Not in all cases, but in most, what I find is deep down inside they're still waiting for God to be the genie without doing any work. There's that four letter word – w.o.r.k.

BEN SETTLE: You teach that a Christian entrepreneur's duty is to fund the Kingdom. What do you mean by that exactly?

MATT GILLOGLY: Here's the deal. I'm going to use you, Ben, as an example. What is the thing that's near and dear to your heart? Something you want to cure or fix or fund. Is it battered women, homeless children, save the whales, whatever? What's one thing you have a great passion about from a philanthropic standpoint?

BEN SETTLE: I have a big passion for dogs and dog shelters.

MATT GILLOGLY: So the natural progression is that people go, "I have a passion for dogs and dog shelters. That would be a good thing for me to give money to from my business. Hey God, what do you say you prosper my business and I'll give to dogs and dog shelters." Right? That makes sense. It's a pretty normal thing. So here's my question. What if God doesn't prosper you and you aren't able to fund dogs and dog shelters? Would you feel like a failure?

BEN SETTLE: You know what, that kind of happened to me. Last year I thought dogs was the market I wanted to go after. This is what I thought was so interesting about what you were saying before. I thought it was dogs. I love dogs. I have a dog. I've always loved dogs. I wrote a book pretty easily about dogs. All of that only to find out I'm really not all that into dogs. [laughing] I was on the radio doing radio interviews and stuff. I have two boxes of books here that I still haven't sold. I just kind of lost interest in it. I remember praying about it, saying "God, I get the feeling dogs isn't really the thing I'm supposed to be doing." I just had no motivation to do it. I recently found something else that fills that void a lot better; but it's funny that you bring that up, because that was kind of my thing. "I'll donate a bunch of sales to the dog causes and stuff," and it just didn't work that way.

MATT GILLOGLY: I'll over generalize, and I'm not going to say this is exactly how you were thinking, but deep down inside, the normal thing is for people to say, "I'll attach to dogs." They hear all the new aged stuff of giving 10%, and the more you give the more you get back. What if you gave and got nothing back? My question for everybody is, "Doesn't God want me to take care of dogs?" I don't know if God wants you to take care of dogs or not. I can promise you one thing. God doesn't care about dogs and he doesn't care about feeding the homeless people in Philadelphia. He doesn't care about the widows in Buffalo. At this juncture, all He cares about is your heart. Now in the big picture, certainly God does care about all those things. But right now, all He cares about is your heart. Most people, if you were to pump them with two bottles of wine and some truth serum, they'd say, "Well, alright. I'm really just doing the dog thing because I want a Mercedes-Benz 500 series car. I want to be hog-nasty rich, live in a big house and have a mountain place. I'm just using the dog thing to make it sound better and hoping God blesses me." God sees right through this. I teach that it's Christian entrepreneurs' duty to fund the kingdom. What I really mean is it's their duty to take back the mountain from the enemy. That's their duty. Ben, do you watch TV at all or go to movies?

BEN SETTLE: Sometimes, just depends.

MATT GILLOGLY: Okay. If Christians are ticked off about what they see on TV, they have nobody to blame but themselves. We advocated our role in media a long time ago. We freely and easily handed it over to the enemy without even thinking about it. So as Christians, we say, "I'm going to get in my own little private bunker. I'm just going to go to church. I'm going to homeschool my kids. We're just going to live in our own little private Idaho and not pay any attention to the world. That's what God really wants me to do." No, if you're gifted at business, then go get in the business arena and slay the enemy. People get all put out because McDonald's has made it their number one initiative that they're going to support the gay & lesbian Chamber of Commerce, and they've made a major contribution to that. McDonald's gets a couple seats on their Board and all that other fun stuff. So my buddy sends me this email and goes, "It's time to boycott McDonald's french fries." I sent him an email back saying, "That's really noble, but I've got a 2-1/2 year old so I ain't got a shot. Besides, I really like McDonald's french fries." If boycotts worked, we never would have had to take care of Saddam Hussein. If boycotts worked, Castro would have been out of power decades ago. If boycotts worked, we wouldn't have to worry about that crazy guy in Iran making nuclear power, or Sun Yung Su or whatever the heck his name is, Kim or whatever, that beady little guy with the funny little glasses and the $2 haircut in North Korea, whoever he is. He would have been long gone.

Boycotts don't work. Instead, let's play, Take Down the Enemy. If we're really hacked off about the fact that McDonald's is funding the gay & lesbian Chamber of Commerce, let's do something radical. Let's buy McDonald's. Let's go greenmail McDonald's. Let's put together a Christian hedge fund, and let's go buy 10% of the stock of McDonald's. We send them a nice little note and say, "We want four seats on your Board or you're going to have an ugly proxy fight." McDonald's hems and haws, they think about it, and they go, "How about three seats." We say yes, and now we put three righteous, praying men and women on that Board who have a heart for God and don't care about the size of their house or their car, and they have hearts pure for the Lord like Daniel 1:8. They're not going to defile themselves with the delicacies of the king. When they come in, the armies of the angels of the Lord are going to be a hell of a lot more powerful than the one-third demands that are floating around that room.

BEN SETTLE: What you just described reminds me so much of a pastor that I have studied with. He calls that being wiser than a serpent.

MATT GILLOGLY: That's it, man. Everybody goes, "I want to fund the Kingdom, I want to help orphans." The heck with that. I want to put together a couple of Christian hedge funds, and I want to buy ABC, CBS, and Fox News. Not because I want to make them all Christian stations, because that would be boring. Let's beat the enemy at his game. Let's be stealth bombers for Christ. Let's take back Hollywood. Let's not pray for Ellen DeGeneres to get saved, let's pray that the camera guy gets saved. Let's pray that instead of Christians thinking the only way they can serve God is by being a pastor or by going to Uganda, let's raise up guys like you and I. People who are totally sold out to the Lord and love the Lord with all their heart, soul, and mind, but get the heebeegeebies about sleeping in a tent in Uganda.

Let's raise guys like you and I up, Ryan Healy, and a bunch of the other guys you've put me in contact with. Guys like my buddy, Bob Regnerus, Chauncey Hunter and Nate Hagerty and all these guys who run successful businesses. Let them be financial eunuchs. Let's not run a business so we can have a $28 million dollar retirement parachute, although that is nice. Let's run it so we can then go and buy other companies. This battle and this war that we're raging against the enemy is a multi-pronged attack. There's a reason why when we invaded Europe, we had a number of different fronts that we fought on. We came up underneath and went through North Africa and through Italy. We hit them from the eastern front from Russia. We hit them from the western front. We engaged the enemy at multiple different places along an extended line, and we strung out their resources so they couldn't compete with us. The great thing about WWII is we just had more planes, more trains, and more automobiles. We had more people and more guns and bullets. They just couldn't keep up. We have two-thirds the armies of the angels of the Lord. The enemy only has one-third. Don't you think our two-thirds is a little better than his one-third? The devil is good at his job. He is very gifted at what he does. But the bottom line is, if we engage the enemy on multiple fronts and don't sit there going, "The enemy is attacking me. My life is horrible," so what? You've got God. You've got the maker of heaven and earth on your side. Get your dad involved. My dad's a lot better at beating up the other guy's dad because my dad is God. Let's just get after it.

People complain about the public school system. It's like, "I've got an atheist teaching my kid science." Well, what have you done to talk to that atheist about the truth of God? What have you done to raise up your daughter or son to make them warriors for God? Or do you just take them to church on Sunday from 10:30 to 11:30? What are you doing with the other 4,000 hours that you've got your kid? Are you putting that responsibility on the church 40 hours a year, sending them to Bible study camp where they're going to learn about Shadrach, Meshach and Abednego and everything's going to be hunky-dory. No, they're going to go to college. They're going to get introduced to the sex, drugs, and rock-and-roll. They're going to have a weak phase and wham, they're playing for the other team before you know it.

We've got to raise up warriors for the Lord. It starts with being businessmen and businesswomen. Entrepreneurs change the world. All change happens in business, even in the Bible. Abraham, David, Isaac, Joseph, Job, just go through it. Paul made tents. Peter was a fisherman. Matthew as a tax collector. Heck, Jesus Christ was a carpenter. He wasn't even a technically trained Rabbi. I help so many people out because I'm like, "So you've been to seminary. That's great. I tended bar. What does that have to do with anything?" So what if you're more technically trained in Greek than I am. I've got a lot of good friends who go to seminary, and I really appreciate and respect their knowledge, because when I don't understand something and I want to get the Greek etymology and all that fun stuff, I call them. But this whole concept of the only way I can serve God is by going to seminary, I've been through all this. They don't want me at seminary. [laughing] They'd be like, "God, get him out of here." There's only one way to the Father, but there are many ways to Christ.

I've got a friend who led this Bible study group that I went to for years. He goes down to Myrtle Beach once a month. He's an insurance salesman and they have a retirement place down there. He said, "We go to church at a bar." Church on Sunday morning is held at like the Pink Pony or something like that. The owner's there and all hung over, but guess what, the owner gave his life to the Lord. The pastor weighs like 280 pounds and always wore Hawaiian shirts, flip-flops, and a pair of shorts. He was like 68 years old. This is a guy who is on fire for the Lord and is holding church in a bar that smells like beer and urine. They're packing it out. They're leading people to the Lord left and right. God doesn't care. There's going to be somebody reading this who has been on the fence about giving their life to Christ. They're going to hear us talk and go, "Oh my gosh, I can be a Christian and not have to sell everything? I'm not going to have to go be a eunuch for the Lord and go to seminary?" No. Look at Ben and I. We're pretty screwed up, right Ben?

BEN SETTLE: I'm definitely far from perfect. What are some more of the business lessons you've learned from reading the Bible and praying? What answers have come to you?

MATT GILLOGLY: My two favorite books about business in the Bible are Proverbs and Ecclesiastes. I just love those two. In fact, I have a membership site where I work with Christian entrepreneurs and do these video trainings. I send them 30 minute video trainings every two weeks. I was shooting this on Camtasia and I taught on Proverbs 2. I won't give you the full teaching, but basically if you read Proverbs 2:4 it says "…if you seek her as silver and search for her as for hidden treasures…" and *her* is meaning *wisdom*, "…then you will understand the fear of the Lord and find the knowledge of God." This one was given to me about 10 months ago. The most important business lesson I've learned from reading the Bible is, am I spending more time trying to find the buried treasure that God has me on a quest for, for the silver that he has me on a quest for – am I spending more time reading the books of the world to try and find those answers, or am I spending more time seeking God for those answers? That's probably the biggest, most important business lesson is that God's in control. It's not how much debt should I carry? Direct marketing plan? Should I write an eBook or sell audio tapes? Should I have a newsletter? Those are all secondary to the primary thing, and that is seeking God like we would a buried treasure and silver. There are so many great verses in Proverbs. Proverbs 3:9 "Give honor to the Lord with your wealth, and with the first-fruits of all your increase," Proverbs 3:13-14, "Happy is the man that finds wisdom and the man that gets understanding. For her profit is better than the profit of silver and her gain better than fine gold." Solomon asked for God to give him wisdom. God will generously give you wisdom if you seek Him out.

BEN SETTLE: We were sort of alluding to this earlier when you were talking about taking things back from the enemy. Let's talk a little bit about that. Let's talk about spiritual warfare here and how does that affect Christian business owners.

MATT GILLOGLY: I'm convinced it impacts it more than somebody who's called to be a pastor. And this isn't just my opinion. It's the opinion of a couple of other business guys I know and me talking to pastors and intercessors that I know. I have a couple of intercessors on staff, and we have a prayer room in our office. They come in a couple times a week and we pray and talk about this quite a bit. These are people that pray 50 hours a week. That's their job. Satan realizes that one of the missing ingredients in the church is money, and not to build bigger sanctuaries. So let's think about this. If the enemy realizes that if I were to have profitable businesses that are throwing up $100 million dollars in cash, don't you think I could do some damage in the world with that? Whether it's $100 million or $100,000, I can do some damage with that. That's not just buying beds at the local homeless shelter. Again, that's very noble and great. The Bible is very clear that we are to take care of the poor, the widows, and the orphans first. But let's use a coffee shop as an example. Let's say I'm running successful businesses. I go out and decide to buy a small chain of like two or three coffee shops. Coffee shops are a unique place, and the reason why Starbucks and all these coffee shops are so successful is that people are craving for community. Ben, you work out of your house, right?

BEN SETTLE: Right.

MATT GILLOGLY: I have an office and today my other guy isn't here. He's out of town for the rest of the week, and I'm bored. I'm lonely. People are lonely in their lives. We all hide behind a computer screen and chat, we text and use cell phones, and things like that, but you cannot replace sitting down face-to-face with somebody and having a meal or a cup of coffee and talking with them. You and I have known about each other for about three years throughout the blogs and stuff. We just talked for the first time a couple weeks ago. We have this little bit of friendship going, but if one of us were to get on a plane and go buy the other dinner, we'd have a completely different level of friendship. A meal is one of the great ways for us to be able to share with one another and get to know each other. The same thing with a cup of coffee. So let's say I was profitable enough in business and I go out and buy three coffee shops. In those coffee shops, what I do is create an environment where people not only can share, but let's say we let everybody know there are intercessors on staff. How about, during the hours of operation, there's a guy over there playing guitar, and he's singing about Christ. Now, not Jesus oh Jesus, oh Jesus. There are a number of different songs that can sound very mainstream that people would start singing and not necessarily know what the lyrics really mean. The staff walk around and while they're cleaning up, they ask, "Is there anything I can pray for you today?" Satan realizes that would have as much impact, if not more, on leading people to the Lord than it would at a church. There are people who will never go to church but will go to a coffee shop. It would be highly unlikely for me to get my next door neighbors, Tom and Melanie, to come to church. He went one time and he ain't coming back. He enjoyed it. The music was great. I go to a non-denominational church, so it's like a rock concert, right? But I would have more impact on him by having a cup of coffee with him in an environment like that than I can by taking him to church because his guard is up. So see, the enemy realizes we can be stealth bombers. Let's say it was a dry cleaning place or a grocery store. What if we had a prayer room in the grocery store, and we made it voluntary that anyone on staff can come in and pray. There's a bank in Elk River that is known as the praying bank. It's called the *Elk River Story*. I highly recommend you read about it. People know if you need prayer, you go to the Elk River Bank. It's a community bank. When you make your deposit, the tellers ask if there's anything they can be praying for you about. People have been loving the Lord in the teller line.

You see, the enemy realizes this is the final frontier, and he will do absolutely anything to make sure business people don't succeed. He'll hit our greed gland, he'll bollocks up our communications, he'll prevent emails from going through. Satan can't do anything without God giving first approval, but God really wants to make sure we're not just putting on a show about us running this Christ-centered business. He really wants us to contend for it. If you're really going to run a Christ-centered business, it's more than saying, "I'm a Christian. Let me stick a fish on the back of my car. Isn't it great at Christmas time we bought turkeys for the homeless?" It's about the Spirit. It's about praying.

The battle here on earth cannot be won until the battle is won in the heavenlies. Isaiah 45 tells us if you want the double doors of prosperity to open up over your life, if you want God to make the crooked paths straight and to break the iron bars and to smash the bronze gates – if you want God to do all of that as He did in Isaiah 45, you have to understand what happened prior to that.

Daniel prayed and fasted for 21 days. He had to win the battle in the heavenlies before winning the battle here on earth. I actually do a whole teaching on this, which we can talk about later. I did like four hours of teaching just on this. If we think there is not spiritual warfare, that there are not battles that are fought, come spend a day with me. Now, I get the fight more than I think most do because I'm really up front with my stuff. I like to go "Nanny Nanny Poo Poo" to the enemy. I like to stir the pot. This makes a lot of people uncomfortable. But if you were going to say, "I'm going to run a Christ-centered information marketing business, and I'm going to write copy that brings glory to the Lord even if I'm selling something like male enhancement prosthetics, there would be a serious tug-and-pull that would go on.

Again, this is just being real and understanding about everything that's really going on in this whole thing. When I put a prayer room in my office and told my wife that I was going to do this, when I told her I was going to start working with Christian entrepreneurs, I told her she better get ready. She didn't buy into it. She was like, "If God wants you to do this, God will bless it." I said, "No, God's going to sort and sift me (us) like wheat," and that's really what He has done. I'm not saying you all have to go through bankruptcy. We all have to go through different things. For some people it's losing all your money. For some people it's cancer. For some people it's losing a child. Whatever. There are different things. This whole concept that as Christians we're not going to have a hard life is a bunch of crap. It might have been easier to do business as a heathen, but I'm a heck of a lot happier doing business as a Christian. We think prosperity in America is a big house and a nice car and staying at the Ritz-Carlton. Prosperity in God's view is way more than that. Nowhere in the Bible does it say, "I'm going to prosper you and stick you in a gated community with a big pool, tennis courts, and horses. You'll live on the 17th green." Right? God prospers in a lot of different ways. He prospered with camels. Camels smell.

BEN SETTLE: They fart.

MATT GILLOGLY: They fart and spit. They're nasty creatures.

BEN SETTLE: How is running a Christ-centered business, especially the way you've been talking about, going to affect not only a Christian's business but their personal life too?

MATT GILLOGLY: I'll tell you. I've been married for 15, almost 16 years. I've been with my wife for 18, almost 19 years. I'm not going to lie to you and tell you everything is always hunky-dory. We've been through a lot. We've had to lift up the bandage and look at the pussing, oozing scab that neither one of us wanted to look at, pick at, and fix. We're no different than any other couple, and we have issues. I'm different than she is, and sometimes I hack her off and sometimes she hacks me off. But I'll also tell you that the number one unifying thing in all of this is that my wife and I have committed to praying together two times a day. Sometimes the prayers are great and we've got tears rolling down our eyes. Other days, it's like "Baby, I'm running late. Let's do prayer in the car or call me on the cell phone and we'll pray." But when we do that, our days are a lot better. My intimacy with my wife is off the charts, and I didn't get Blue Steel cream or anything like that. My marriage with my wife has never been stronger. My relationship with my children, because I'm praying with them and being very open and upfront with our lives and my business, has never been better. My 10-year-old and 12-year-old know my business has been struggling and we may have to move and sell the big house and all that stuff. Again, I'm not trying to demotivate people and I'm not saying everyone's going to have to go through this, but it has made my relationships much stronger, not only with my wife and children, but I've realized who my real friends are. I know now who are my marvelous comrades and who are in the battle with me. I have a list of like 8-10 guys that we text each other when we're traveling or something.

A friend of mine, Bill Collins, is in the energy business. He insulates chicken coops and dairy farms. He cuts people's propane costs in half. It's a pretty nice business to be in these days, and he's doing very well. His supplier that he gave the formula to for making this stuff has ripped him off. He's now in competition with him, and he's basically selling it at like 50% off. He's just killing his business. He has a major meeting with all these attorneys and all, and we were praying for him. He came out of that meeting, and these guys basically admitted they stole his stuff, they were sorry, and what could they do to work together. That's the power of having this in your business. I'd rather have 10 friends who will stay in the fox hole with me and will fight it out to the bitter end than have 200 friends who are going to run for the high ground as soon as things get a little sticky and a little rough. The Lord has brought to me all kinds of great people who are just going, "Man, this is great." They're encouragers. Of course, I have my share of people who are saying, "Don't you think you should go get a job? Have you thought about applying at McDonald's?"

BEN SETTLE: No, but you've been thinking about buying their stock.

MATT GILLOGLY: [laughing] Yeah. Right now as we're recording this, gas is something like $4 a gallon. I'm just like, "You guys have got this all wrong. If you want to feel better about the price of gas, go out and buy some Exxon stock. That way, every time you start pumping gas, you realize you're putting money back in your pocket." Who's happy about the high gas prices? The guy who owns a million shares of Exxon. He's telling all his friends to go buy a Hummer.

BEN SETTLE: Let's switch gears a bit and talk about actual biblical examples of sales, persuasion, and marketing that people in the Old and New Testaments have used, not necessarily for selling, but just basic general persuasion principles you can apply to your business today. What are your ten best examples?

MATT GILLOGLY: It's funny, because we've talked about this a couple of times and we've always just kind of thrown some things out, so Ben actually forced it and he said, "Do you have a list of 10?" So I guess what I'm going to go through is I have a bunch of things down here. They're not like in any catchy bullet points, and sometimes I'm going to fumble on the biblical reference, but I'll get the right book. I may not get the right verse, you have to go find it on your own, so you can tell I'm not theologically trained, folks. The only time I've been to seminary is when I was a bartender. I'm Irish, and you're either going to be a priest or a bartender, and there is an argument that they are one and the same. It's amazing what people will tell a bartender. It is amazing what things they'll confess or share that's in their heart. They're probably more real when they are in a bar than when they are in church.

We'll go Old Testament before the cross first. Some of these I guess are going to be some marketing, and I can't help that some of them will be kind of some basic business principles as well, but probably one of the biggest marketing lessons that I see in the Bible – and specifically this is the book of Ecclesiastes; I can't remember where it is – but it's about casting your bread on the water. In order for you to get something, you have to go out and do something. I'm looking for it, you can hear me flipping the pages, but basically the whole concept is that you've got to be marketing every single day. As I work with business owners – and some are Christian, most are not – most people don't do something every single day from the standpoint of marketing their business. That's something that I learned and I do something every single day. My goal is to prospect, write a blog post, do an email to the list, or do something every single day. I just spend two and a half to three hours a day feeding the system, doing something to convert the leads that are coming in. In today's digital age everything is kind of automated on our end with Google and with SEO and with the magazines and all that stuff, but people just don't do enough to market. They do like one little thing. What Solomon is sharing with us in this book is specifically you've got to do something every single day. You've got to constantly be casting your bread upon the water. So that's kind of my first big one. Do you have any comments?

BEN SETTLE: I guess God would be a big advocate of a daily email then, or daily blog post, or a daily something every day; either written, audio, maybe a video or something every day. A daily email is very powerful, or a daily podcast, or daily video, or something daily like an article. That all kind of goes hand in hand with what you were just saying.

MATT GILLOGLY: That's the thing, is you've got to be doing something every single day. Kind of a subset of that that I want to put in there is, and I think a lot of entrepreneurs get caught into this trap, is the same thing in the book of Ecclesiastes. It says, "Two are better than one, because if one falls down, there's another one to pull you up. If you're cold at night, the other one will keep you warm." While this is not necessarily a marketing principle, I think it's a business principle that people should abide by, which is you never want to do this alone. I'm a firm believer of partners and partnerships, because I find that when

I'm having a bad day or a down day, then there is somebody else there to pick me up. I think that's just real key to have, and that's kind of really I guess an offshoot of the two that I found in there. Do you have any thoughts on those? I've got one more in the Old Testament that I want to share, which ties into Jesus' perspective, and then we're going to talk about the apostle Paul, which is really kind of a big crescendo of the whole thing.

BEN SETTLE: Yeah, I was just thinking back to how it seems like a lot of the people God called, he didn't have them do everything alone. Moses had Aaron, and there are other examples of this, but none of those guys are really loners in that sense, where they did everything by themselves. It's almost like everybody's got their own unique gifts, and when you can combine that gift with somebody else's gift, that's when things really happen, not when we're just trying to do it all by ourselves. For example, I could start up a business and I could try to do the traffic and the lead generating and the copywriting and the content creation. But I'm really only good at the copywriting part, and I'd probably fail miserably at the other parts.

MATT GILLOGLY: From my standpoint in my business, I'm not an exceptional copywriter. I can write basic copy, but for me it's about converting them into a buyer. That's the unique skill set that I bring. So yeah, that's good. So let's go into – this one is going to be Old Testament, New Testament. My wife and I were in the car together this morning, and I was telling her about this call. She said, "Well, what are you going to talk about?" I said, "I really frankly don't know yet, but I have a couple of basic ideas." She goes, "Well tell me, what are some of the marketing lessons?" So I told her the first one. Then I told her this one. I said, "Do you remember watching *The Ten Commandments* as a kid growing up?" I always thought it was funny that you watched *The Ten Commandments* during Easter. I'm watching a Jewish show during a pagan holiday. She said, "Yeah, I remember watching *The Ten Commandments*." So I said, "Do you remember when Charlton Heston as Moses went to Pharaoh's place of business?" He went into Pharaoh's place and he was relatively unannounced, he was unwanted, and he tried to convert Pharaoh's heart with amazing feats of strengths, if you will. All it did was further cement Pharaoh deeper into his beliefs that there is no God. He makes the Nile bleed, frogs fall from the sky. I forget what else. A big marketing mistake that I see people make, and a lesson that you can take, is most business owners go in with the belief that everybody needs what they have. So what they try to do is they spend all of their time, money, and energy trying to convert the most skeptical of the skeptical, when they aren't spending their time picking the easy fruit. There's an Old Testament example of how Moses, even with God's incredible miracles, couldn't convince Pharaoh to let his people go with all these incredible miracles. Then if you look at it from Jesus' standpoint, Jesus didn't send his message to the Pharisees. When he did, Jesus got frustrated. Jesus' message was best received by the people that were looking to fill a hole in their heart. They knew they had a problem and they were looking for a solution. So the marketing lesson in this is when you market, first and foremost, target those who have a burning desire for a solution.

I just had lunch today with a guy, and his business idea wasn't bad, but there was no proof that anybody wanted it. He thought it was a unique idea because nobody was already doing it, to which my answer was, "Well, the reason nobody is doing it is because you can't make any money doing it. Nobody wants it." I think it's a big mistake that a lot of people make. They try to come up with the big thing that nobody realizes that they want it, when in reality, Jesus made a great example out of this of saying, "Look, I'm going to give the people exactly what they want, and I'm going to go out and give it to the people who are most hungry for it." Think about all the different people that Jesus talked to and that he touched figuratively and spiritually, but think about everybody. They were absolutely dying for a miracle. They were so hungry for what He had that they would work their way through the crowds like the woman did, and just touch His robe. Those are the type of people that you want to target with your marketing. You don't want to target the Pharisees, who think they already have all the answers. Those are the worst people in the world to sell. You want to target the golfer who has tried everything to get rid of his slice, or the guy or gal who's trying to lose weight, who has tried to do everything to lose weight. When you look at it biblically, and you can look at it throughout both the Old and New Testaments, and specifically in the life of Jesus, who did He hang out with? He hung out with the people who are hurt the most. Too many marketers try to hang out with the people that are hurt the least, and it backfires on them. Jesus was admonishing the Pharisees, and they said, "Well, why are you hanging out with the hookers and the tax collectors and the unsavory characters?" He's like, "Those are the people that need us most." Which leads me to another point, that many times the last people I want to hang out with are other Christians. I want to hang out with the people who are hurting the most, because they are the people who need us, and need that salt and light in their life. That's a whole other topic. My standard joke is if I'm going to have people over to my house, the last people I want to have over are the Christians. I don't know what I'd call that marketing lesson, or what the bullet point on that would be, but I think you get the general idea.

The next one I have written down is, Ben and I will talk about marketing from the standpoint of direct response. You've got to have a great headline, you've got to have great bullet points, you've got to have all this stuff in order for it to work. But there's another marketing lesson that is a bit intangible that I think a lot of people miss. In today's day and age, business is about what you can get. Jesus spoke about this in Mark, the fourth chapter, verse 21 is where it starts. I'm reading from *The Message*,

Jesus went on, "Did anyone bring a lamp home and put it under the washtub or beneath the bed? Do you put it up on the table or on the mantel? We're not keeping secrets, we're not telling them, and we're not hiding things. We are bringing them out into the open. Are you listening to this, really listening? Listen carefully to what I'm saying and be wary of the shrewd advice that tells you how to get ahead in the world on your own. Giving, not getting, is the way. Generosity begets generosity, stinginess impoverishes.

Now, we could go on this whole topic about tithing and offerings and giving and all that other stuff. This example I'm going to give is really prevalent in the world that Ben and I live in and work in, in the direct response world. If you want to get time with a big name, you've got to jump through a lot of hoops to get to them. While I agree with that conceptually, I don't agree with that biblically, because you didn't have to jump through hoops to get to Jesus. You didn't have to jump through hoops to get to the apostles. People could have direct access. That's the whole beauty of why Christ came is that we now have a local call to heaven to talk to the Lord. It's no longer a collect call or a toll call like the way it was in the Old Testament. Most business owners, from a marketing standpoint, their marketing is focused on getting. I like to position our business's marketing lesson as giving. My basic philosophy of this is that if somebody wants to talk to me, I'm more than willing to talk to them. I'm more than willing to get on the phone with them for 15 minutes, even if they're not a perfect prospect. Now I know that's really counterintuitive to what a lot of people have learned. But the Bible is very clear. We are here to serve our fellow man, and generosity begets generosity.

Now, I don't go at it with an ulterior motive. I'll have a number of phone calls throughout the week, and I know the person is not going to be a client of ours. I know that they can't afford to hire us. I know that they're not the target market that we have, but I'm willing to spend 15 minutes on the phone with them. I'm willing to take that time out of my day because you just never know how that conversation is going to positively impact somebody else. So when I sell I take that same approach. My role is to bless that other person, and I tell them that. When I'm doing a sales call, we have a process. When people do get to me and they're a targeted customer, I let them know, "Look, I want to be really clear about the purpose of this call. My purpose of this call is to serve you. If I can help you solve some business problems, I'm more than happy to do it. If it leads to you hiring us, fantastic. If it doesn't, fantastic, but let me help sow into your business, and if I can't solve your problem or if we're not a good fit, I'm going to point you in the direction of somebody who can." It's amazing how that changes the tone of a conversation right off the bat. At first they're really leary, but I say, "No, I'm dead serious. My role here is to help you, to serve you." Yeah, I'm taking 30 minutes out of my day, so what? I mean, it's not all about charging and getting as much money as you possibly can.

I'll never forget this. As I was going through some business stuff over the last number of years, over time the Lord just kept bringing me back to that verse of love your neighbor as you love yourself. Over time, I'd like to tell you that God spoke to me, but he didn't. Everybody goes, "What does His voice sound like?" So the Lord is taking me through this and He said, "Let's begin unwrapping love your neighbor as you love yourself," which is actually another marketing principle that I have. He said, "How much do you love yourself?" Now, the answer to that question is I think I'm pretty good. I think I'm pretty cool. I think I'm kind of a big deal. So He just starts taking me through this process of unwrapping that and He says, "Do you love your neighbor?"

I said, "Well yeah, I love my neighbor."

"Would you love your neighbor if you neighbor was a homosexual? Would you love your neighbor if he was homosexual and he had a live-in person, mate, significant other, partner, and they invited you to the wedding?"

"Would you love your neighbor on the other side if she was a single mom and had a boyfriend and got knocked up and got pregnant, and she had two other kids by her other husband? Would you love your neighbor across the street if he was an atheist? Would you love this person, and that person?"

He kept saying, "Would you love them…"

"Yes."

Then finally, "But would you love them as you love yourself?"

So as I started to unwrap that over the course of 12-18 months, it really started to take on this whole other genre and whole other meaning to me. It took me to this place of I used to have contempt for the person who didn't have money to hire me. Now I have love and compassion for the person who can't hire me. I'll tell you, from the standpoint of selling and liking what you do and what we do and what we charge for our services – I mean, to hire us for a year is like $100,000 or more, and our partnership program is significantly higher, and that's a lot, so there's always a series of phone calls that I have to go through. When I started approaching those calls with love in my heart for my person, and not looking at their credit card or the balance in their bank account, or I started looking at and I wasn't saying, "Oh geez, we land this customer and it's $10,000 a month, or $15,000 a month, or whatever it is." I started taking the approach of, "I'm just going to love them, and I'm going to love them well. I'm going to love them as I love myself. I'm going to treat this person as my neighbor." We didn't close any more business. It wasn't the magic secret sauce that all of a sudden took us from $100,000 to $100 million, but I will tell you this. I enjoyed the conversations even more. I enjoyed the process that I was in with those people, and some of those folks aren't even clients and they've become friends. I've always said, "Look, if you've got a question call me. I'm more than happy to answer it for you." I think this whole thing of loving unconditionally, loving people where they are in their process, changes the way you write copy. It changes the way I do my sales calls. It changes the way I deal with a difficult vendor. Not every time, I'm a human being. I have my moments where I'm not too nice. But from a marketing standpoint, it just completely changes.

I see this in your copy, Ben. You don't write hype copy, but it's almost like you are writing copy almost from like a love standpoint of saying, "Hey, let me share some real information with you. Let me share with you what the real deal is." People read that and they see through it. That authenticity really plays out well. I remember Gary Halbert when he was still on the earth, he took us through this. He'd take out two pieces of paper and say, "You're going to write two letters to your mom. The first version is for those of you that hate your mother. The second version is for those of you that love your mother." He said, "You've got to write that letter like you are writing it to your mom." From a marketing standpoint, I don't want to use any language, I don't want to use any tactics, any neurolinguistic programming stuff. There's nothing wrong with any of that, but it's the intent of it…

I'll paint an example I think that most people can understand. Everyone digs sex, right? Sex is really enjoyable. God created it, right? When you have love in your heart for the other person, sex turns into intimacy. It turns into this incredible thing. When you don't have love in your heart for the other person, it turns into pornography. The point is, when we sell just for the sake of selling and when we market just for the sake of marketing and we get contempt for the other people, it is pornography. When we have love and compassion and mercy for the other person of where they are right now, then it becomes intimacy. It completely transforms the conversation. It completely transforms the relationship. That's probably the best picture that I can paint.

That brings me to the next point, and this is a big shift that I've made in my marketing over the last two years. So that people understand, I've been a front of the room pitch guy and worked in a number of different niches and worked in the direct response world for seven years, so I've got a lot of different experiences in this. I used to be just about the sale, and again, this is going to kind of piggyback into what we were just talking about. If I'm going to market biblically, I'm going to care about building a true relationship with the people that I want to do business with. Again, it comes with no agenda. If I have true love in my heart, if I really do love my fellow man, a relationship takes times to build. Now let me give you an example in my marriage. My wife Sara and I have been married 18 years. We've been together 21 years. We met in college. We met in a bar, and yes, we'd been drinking. She lived across the street from me. I had a reputation at that time of being a bit of a playboy, if you can say that while talking about biblical marketing. I was very concerned about the number of notches on my bed. I wasn't really concerned about anything else. So I meet this gal and I can tell immediately that she's somebody I'd like to bring home to mother. This is somebody who I'd want to raise my kids – the other ones, you wouldn't even want to be around children – but she was dating somebody else at that time. Instead of me pushing to close the deal and get her into bed, I took time to build that relationship. We went out on like three dates before I kissed her. I wasn't aggressively trying to get her into the bedroom. I'm just being real, folks. These were my pre-Christian days, and frankly I've probably known quite a few Christians that did this.

BEN SETTLE: Yeah, in college.

MATT GILLOGLY: Yeah, I mean, I'm just being real. But I took time to build that relationship and to nurture that relationship. This was in March. By the time June rolled around, this other guy she was dating wasn't really serious. There were a lot of guys interested in her, and I just kept sticking around. When I would see her at the bar at the local small college that we went to, she might have been there with another guy that was interested in her that she was casually dating, and I would just go up and say hi to him and I'd say hi to her and I'd talk to them a little bit. Then I'd go on my merry way. If I stopped there and she was with a group of her sorority sisters on campus, I'd come over and I'd say hi. I didn't have an agenda, I just came over and I said hi, because again I had love in my heart for her. Over time, what this showed was that I was different than the other guys that were knocking on her door and that were interested in dating her. I'll never forget one time standing on the porch and Sara lived across the street from me and we were talking, and all of a sudden one of her ex-boyfriends who was still kind of floating around in the picture a little bit shows up. He's like,

"I've got to talk to you right now."

Sara looked at me and I said, "Hey, no worries, go talk to him. It's fine. Call me when you're done." She said at that moment she knew that we were going to be married.

The bible is about relationships. Many people, when it comes to their marketing, they are concerned about the Old Testament rules. "I've got to do this to get that. If I do x, y, and z.." That's the Old Testament – "If I do x, y, and z then I'm going to get this." But when you have a relationship with somebody, you do something and you have no expectations of what the result is going to be. Now this is really kind of below some people's theology, because this goes against the attraction strategy, this goes against the "name it and claim it" theology that is out there in the Christian world. This goes against the whole thing of pay it forward. In all those instances, the ulterior motive is that you do have something that you are looking to get. In the Bible, Jesus poured into people's lives. So did John, so did Paul, so did all of the apostles. They poured into people's lives with no expectation whatsoever of any return on their investment. Again, they did it because of love. The Old Testament is about rules, and rules without relationship equals rebellion. Rules without a relationship equal rebellion. Think about this – God still loves you, even if you don't accept his Son. Think about that. Wrap your arms around that, and then apply that to your business. God loves the drunk who's doing heroin as much as He loves the guy who's sitting in the pew every single Sunday. If you don't believe me, think about this. What if those two people were your kids? Would you love one child less than the other? No, all you have to do is look at the prodigal son to answer that. The one son sticks around, he's the good son. The other son, he blows his inheritance. Wine, women, fast cars, or fast chariots or horses, or whatever it was at that time. He winds up working in a pig stall. And yet when he comes back, the father runs to greet him because he is so happy that he has returned. His love in his heart never stopped.

So from a relationship standpoint in your marketing, you've got to be willing to market to that person from now until the end of time, and for them to reject you, because that's what God does to us. He's willing to market to us, to send His message over and over again to us. He's willing to do that even if we never say yes. In the case of the prodigal son, the one son wanted his inheritance now, so the father gives him his inheritance, and he goes and blows it. The older son is still there. He's doing everything his father has asked him to do. So now the younger son comes back, and his father welcomes him back with open arms, right? This means that the older son's inheritance that was 50% is now 25% because the younger son is going to get half of what's left, and here he is being the good kid. From a marketing standpoint, folks, you never, ever know – I could tell you right now, I have people that will say, "I've been on your list for three and a half years, and I'm ready to do business with you now." It just never ceases to amaze me, and that's because biblically I do not look at them as a transaction. I look at them as a living and breathing human being. I'm more concerned about the relationship than I am about the results.

So let's talk about this a little bit. Again, I'd like to put this in context. Paul is kind of like the Elvis Presley of his day. Everybody knows who he is. He just didn't have like the black leather suit or the jungle print. Paul is known before he even gets into a town. Everybody knows who Paul is. He's kind of a big deal. In that day and age, there is no email, there is no cell phone, no iPods, iPhones, iPads, computers, there's no internet. Al Gore hadn't been born yet, so the internet hadn't been invented. There is no mobile marketing. There is no fax machine.

There is no telemarketing, there's no direct mail. The printing press was invented in the 1400's, which is why Martin Luther was able to get his 95 theses out so quickly, because they had just invented the printing press.

BEN SETTLE: The internet of its time.

MATT GILLOGLY: Yeah, to get paper and ink to write something out, and then the ability to write something and convey it on a piece of paper was an exceptional skill. So when Paul was in a Roman prison and he wrote Romans, or when he wrote First Corinthians and he wrote it to the Church of Corinth – imagine this. In First Corinthians, it's the people of Corinth, and they had this reputation in the ancient world of being these unruly, hard-drinking, sexually promiscuous bunch of people. Sounds like today, huh? When Paul arrived with the message and many of them became believers in Jesus, they brought their reputations with them right into the church. Paul was the pastor, and then he left. This first letter that he wrote to them is about his pastoral response, affectionate, firm, clear and unswerving in the conviction that God is among them. In this he was talking about how Jesus is revealed and present in the Holy Spirit, and that continues to be the central issue in their lives, regardless of how much of a mess they have made of things. This is a letter to them where he is kind of admonishing them. They basically go back to their old ways after he left, so for Paul to write this you've got to think about what he had to go through. He had to acquire paper, he had to acquire ink, he would dictate this to a person and they would write it out, and he had to think out exactly what he was going to say, because if they made a mistake he couldn't just tear it up and start over again because paper was so hard to get a hold of. It would then be sent to them, so there was usually one, maybe two copies. It was sent to them, and when it would come everybody would stop what they were doing and they would gather and they would listen to somebody read the letter to them. They didn't have billboards, they didn't have CNN, they didn't have the 5,000 media messages like we have today. Paul was really the first direct mail person. He heard about an issue, and then what he did was he wrote specifically to that issue. Now if you look at the way that he wrote his letters, he always started out his letters in humility and he always started out his letters in love. He didn't start out admonishing them right away. So they'd go through this. Now this would be a big deal that he would send them this letter, and these things were long. Corinthians is 16 chapters.

I love today when I hear people say, "Matt, you're going to email somebody once a week? Isn't that a little rude? Don't you think that's a little bit over the top?" My response is always, "Well, Paul did it, and he had to do it twice to the church of Corinth because they didn't get it the first time." Right after First Corinthians comes Second Corinthians, and this is Paul going back to them. No sooner did Paul get one problem straightened out in the Corinth church than three more appeared. The reason for Paul's second letter to the Corinthians was that they were attacking his leadership. In his first letter he wrote most kindly and sympathetically. He didn't mince words. He wrote with the confidence and authority of a pastor who understands the way God's salvation work. But they bucked his authority, and they accused him of inconsistency, impugned his motives, and questioned his credentials. They didn't argue with what he had written, they simply denied his right to tell them what to do. Here's this guy who came in, and he is educated. He is the Jew's Jew, and then he comes to Christ. I mean, he is one of the most learned and educated men of his day. He writes this letter to them, and he admonishes them, and what do they do? They thumb their nose at him. Maybe like 2% got it, then the other 98% are like, "Ah, I'm not going to believe that." So what did he do? Paul was the original multi-step marketer. He wrote a second letter to them. He didn't care that they were upset. He didn't care that he offended them. He didn't care that he was speaking truth to them and they didn't believe it. He went at it again. To me, that is a big lesson for us from a marketing standpoint of saying, "Look, there's a reason why you have to mail multiple times." Now Paul is doing this in an age where there is no other form of communication, and a letter is a big deal. Yet in our businesses, we go, "Oh, I could never email every single day. What about those people that opt-out?" Well, who cares? What about those people who stay in? We'll send 18,000-40,000 emails out in a day and we might get 40 opt-outs. Big deal, who cares? I really don't care, but I want to keep hammering on that message. You'll notice that Paul did this. He did it in First Corinthians and he always goes back to the fundamentals. He just reads it in a different way, which is another marketing lesson. You never ever stop marketing those fundamentals. Now, you know these letters were shared, and this information was shared, but he had to send letters back to the Church at Ephesus, the church of the Philippians, he had to do it to the Thessalonians not once, but twice, he had to do this to Timothy once and twice, and Timothy was a guy that was studying under him. Just time and time again you see that Paul had no issue with continuing to communicate with the people that needed to hear his message, and communicate to them over and over and over again until they got it.

So then, if I want to summarize the marketing lessons of the apostle Paul, one is that he always started his letters with humility. Two, he always moved to love. Then third, he started working his way through the particular issues one by one. He would knock them down with proof, which to me is a great way to market. If you come in from a marketing copy standpoint and you say, "I'm just a regular Joe just like you are. The reason why

I'm doing this is because I want other people to know what I have found out." Then you start lining up each one of the individual issues, and you line up an issue and then you refute it. You show how Christ on the cross came to solve that problem. That's what he does in every single one of his letters, and it took him 16 chapters to lay this out in First Corinthians. Here are the number of topics that he hits in Corinthians. The cross, he goes into the mystery of sex, he goes into whether or not to be married or single, freedom with responsibility to honor God, spiritual gifts, the way of love, prayer language, the resurrection, and then, "Oh, by the way I'm going to come see you." He comes in with a close, and at the end of it he comes full circle in all of his letters just like we do in marketing. He comes into a close and he goes, "Hey, if Timothy shows up, take good care of him. Hopefully I'm going to be there soon. I appreciate your love offering that you've given. I can't wait to see you guys." There's even PS's, like in chapter 16.

So for us as marketers, if Paul can do this 2,000 years ago and he realized the importance of laying out a well-documented position and argument and working his way through it point by point, and laying out and always bringing them back to the basic solution, that is the cross, the love of Christ, why can't we keep doing that if we're selling weight-loss or vitamins or a solution to somebody getting more customers, or copywriting skills, or whatever it is. Whatever you're selling, you've got to hit those points dead on. You've got to be willing to prove that your solution provides that, and you've got to be willing to keep going through that. Be patient to go through that, and then at the end you've got to be willing to mail them again and again. You've got to re-email them again and again, and fax them again and again, and make an offer again and again, because it just never stops. Paul had to do it 2,000 years ago twice. Who's to say that we don't need to do it 200 times in order for people to finally see the light?

BEN SETTLE: Can you imagine if Paul had email?

MATT GILLOGLY: Yeah, no kidding. Can you imagine text messaging in the Roman prison?

BEN SETTLE: Twitter?

MATT GILLOGLY: Twitter. "I'm still in chains. They're around my ankles. They just gave me a hunk of bread with worms in it. Can't eat this." Then there would be a lesson in it. It's kind of like false doctrine, you know? You owe them 140 characters. Can you imagine Paul being limited to 140 characters? Man, that would probably drive him insane. I know that these aren't like specifics like, "Do this, do that, do this," but here's what I've learned in my life. So the lesson from me of where I've gotten to in this place in my life is there are a lot of great marketing principles out there. There's a lot of great marketing rules and do's and don'ts, and buy these kits and here's my 500 rules that I never violate every time that I market. I think that if you just come out with authenticity and love, the cross allows us to be true-faced and authentic with each other. When we do that in our marketing, when we become authentic and real, we become more like Christ. People are attracted to authenticity. They are attracted to when we share the realness of who we are through our marketing. Whether it is personality-based marketing, or corporate-based marketing, product-based marketing, or whatever it is. People enjoy that realness and that authenticity. At first they're not going to believe you, and secondly they are going to think you have an ulterior motive. But as they get to know you, they're going to realize that you're doing it because you love them unconditionally, whether they buy from you or not. To me, that's incredibly freeing. I don't get as concerned about the results of my marketing as I do about the impact of my marketing. I'm more concerned about the relationships that we build long-term than I am about that result on my bottom line each and every single day.

So here's my challenge to you. For the next six months, what would happen if you love your neighbor, business associate, or prospect as much as you love yourself? I think if you ask God to help you wrap your arms around that and unravel how that plays out in your life, I think there's an opportunity for a dramatic change in the way that you view the people who are coming into your list. Just unwrap that for six months. Keep asking God to show you what that looks like in your marketing. I'd love to hear some of those comments. Post that, what that looks like to you, because I'd love to hear that. There are two sites you can go to. The first is www.ChristianBusinessDaily.com, owned with my business partner Bob Regnerus and I. We do podcasts and we'll put this interview up there. We post things when we feel like posting it, and you can comment there.

The other is our site, which is www.CapstoneStrategicPartners.com. That's more of a corporate site, but if you really want to post a comment on Christian Business Daily about this topic, there's a place to post a comment. Bob and I see it all the time, and if you want to speak specifically to me about something or post a comment, I'll see it. If you don't want me to share it with the rest of the world, please put that in there and I won't, but I will reply to you. If you post on ChristianBusinessDaily.com, I will reply to you. If it requires a phone call and I think that makes sense, then hey, we'll do a phone call.

BEN SETTLE: I assume you're not afraid of anyone who would disagree with anything you said, and in fact would actually welcome the comment.

MATT GILLOGLY: Please, my whole goal is to tip over the tables in the temple of life. I'm on Facebook. Just type in Matt Gillogly. We have a fan page for Christian Business Daily on Facebook. You won't be the first person who sends me a long dissertation as to why I'm wrong. Understand that I'm a recovering bartender, I haven't been to seminary, I'm not a theologian – I don't even know how to spell it. The only Greek I've ever known is the guy who worked in Greektown when I was in my fraternity. I don't know any Hebrew. I don't care to ever know any Hebrew. I failed Latin miserably. I got a D– in it. I'm just a normal guy who's just trying to figure this out.

Christian Business Bonus Tip #4

Following is a Bible-themed article written to my website newsletter subscribers. To join my free mailing list and access 700+ pages of advanced web marketing tips, go to:

www.BenSettle.com

A Marketing Tip Of Biblical Proportions

Remember last week's tip about the Bible's marketing secrets?

Well, another big one just occurred to me.

And that is storytelling.

Just about everything Jesus taught was in "parable" form. And I reckon that's probably one of the main reasons why the Bible is one of the longest enduring texts in human history — and why even people who have never so much as flipped through it can recite some of its stories (i.e. Adam and Eve, the nativity, etc) due to hearing them told as kids.

Not too many dry, "lecture" texts that do that, are there?

And guess what?

Stories can give your marketing lots of "staying power", too.

I don't fully know exactly why they work so well.

But it probably has something to do with the way our minds are "hard wired" to process and remember stories (or so I've been told by some smart people who study neurology). And that makes it very easy for people to start reading (and KEEP reading) ads in story form — regardless of how good your actual "writing" is.

I've seen this phenomenon many, many times.

Frankly, the ads I've written with stories weaving in out of them have always put a beating on ads I've written without that "story factor."

Same with other marketers & copywriters I know, too.

So what's the big lesson here?

Facts tell... but stories sell.

Use 'em and watch your sales multiply.

Ben Settle

For over 700 pages of advanced
web marketing tips and secrets,
go to www.BenSettle.com

Survival Of The Wisest

Interview with Ryan Healy
www.RyanHealy.com

BEN SETTLE: Ryan, how did you first get started in business and what were some of the challenges that you faced along the way?

RYAN HEALY: Well, let's see. I thought I was going to talk about my freelance copywriting business, but that's actually not the first business I started. My career as an entrepreneur started somewhat early, probably like a lot of guys, where you mow lawns, babysit, shovel snow and stuff like that. I did all that stuff. I got a job, I'd say it was a job, at age 12 watering plants at the model homes in my neighborhood and they paid me $5 to come down and water all the plants in five homes. I thought that was a sweet deal. I was always trying to make money. Later on when I turned 18, my parents had been involved in Amway for a while when I was younger, and I always remembered that. So as soon as I turned 18 I said, "Well, I'm going to do this Amway thing." I did Amway for three years actually. I basically just spent money. I didn't make any money. If anybody's been in Amway or Quixtar who can relate to that, I followed their plan and called friends and family. I had some pretty strong reactions from people early on. They got really mad at me for even calling them. Anyway, I moved on from there and never gave up the entrepreneurial dream. It wasn't so much that I wanted to be an MLM guy, I just wanted to be in business for myself.

I ended up getting into a vending business. This company out of California, called The Antares Corporation, sold vending machines and helped people place those vending machines and start a vending business.

One of the testimonials was from this couple down in I think Kentucky. They were just making cash hand over fist and I thought, "Wow. If only I could do that." I was 22 at the time, I think. So here I go and get a second mortgage on my condo. The market had been going up quite a bit, so I had just enough equity in my condo from the market going up that I was able to afford these vending machines. They cut you a deal if you buy five machines, instead of three, up front. I'm like, "Well, I can lower my per unit cost if I buy five." So like an idiot, I went ahead and I signed up for five of these vending machines. The funny part is that I had actually gone to a bank to attempt to borrow the money before I took out the second mortgage. The guy who was there was, believe it or not, an honest banker. That sounds like an oxymoron, but in this case it wasn't. He was an honest banker and he sat me and my wife down at a table, took us back, and he said, "Look, I would love to make you this loan. I really would. But I have to tell you, vending businesses have one of the highest failure rates of any kind of business. I strongly advise you to not take a loan for whatever reason to start this business." Here I am, 22, young, stubborn, I'd just gotten out of Amway, and in Amway they talk about dream stealers, "Oh, he's trying to steal your dream." I'm kind of like getting this stubborn thing going on and I'm like, "This guy's trying to steal my dream."

BEN SETTLE: The only banker that wasn't trying to steal anything from you.

RYAN HEALY: Yeah, he was the good guy! I go get the second mortgage and I plunk down all this cash. A few weeks later a big ol' semi backs into my condominium and unloads these pallets. It was like an up and down ramp. I got my vending machines. One of the things that sold me on it was they were going to give me these mailing pieces. They're like these postcards, pull-out postcards with a tear-off response postcard attached, and a mailing list. Basically, you would take the mailing list, take all those labels, slap them on these postcards, and drop them in the mail. You had to pay for the postage, too. That wasn't even included in the purchase. By the way, I spent $30,000 on these vending machines. Just so you know. Then I spent more to send out these mail pieces, and I got a very underwhelming response. I started to have some doubts when I began to look at the list and I saw Borders bookstore. I was thinking to myself, "Now, I'm pretty sure if Borders has vending machines in their place, it's probably going to be done at a corporate level, and sending a postcard to my local Borders is not going to get me in." I started to look and see some of these corporate addresses. I'm thinking, "Well, that's not going to work. You have to go to the top." Anyway, I mailed it out. I placed a couple of machines. I found it very, very hard to keep up with filling the machines at different locations in town while I had a full-time job, because I could only service the machines during the day, which obviously was when I was working. There were other obstacles. How do you keep chocolate from melting while it's in your car, and your car is parked out in the middle of the parking lot all day during summer? I didn't have time to go drive home and then drive back out again anyway.

Long story short, I was able to pawn off the vending machines to a really smart vending business guy who paid me like $1,500 for all of them, after I'd paid $30,000. Thank God that I was able to sell the condo, get my money out, and basically broke even. When I sold my condo, I had to bring about $1,500 to the closing table. I had to pay $1,500 to leave my condo when we sold it.

That was much better than actually having to come up with $30,000 of my own money, so God was gracious in that circumstance.

It was after those experiences that I eventually became a freelance copywriter. That was after actually trying to become a financial planner. I got a series 6 license and quit my job to become a financial planner. I even partnered with this other financial planner who was supposedly making $500,000 a year. I thought, "Who better to learn from than somebody who's making that kind of money?" Well, our deal was that I would be paid. He was generating leads through the newspaper, and I was supposed to call these leads and get them to a free dinner. He would present there at that dinner, and then hopefully get some of those people as clients. As soon as I quit my job, that paper he was advertising in went bankrupt and so all of his leads just stopped. That was the only source of advertising that was working for him. So then that turned into a whole thing of, "Hey, Ryan, call on all these leads we weren't able to get in touch with." Here I was smiling and dialing, calling leads that were up to 12 months old and who obviously couldn't even remember having responded. It was like, "Oh yeah, by the way, about eight months ago you responded to this advertisement in the newspaper." People are going, "Who are you? What is this about?" I actually billed two whole dinners on that, but the volume wasn't enough. I wasn't making any money. That whole thing fell apart, so then I decided, "Well, I don't want to get another job." I had about two weeks of money left. My wife didn't work. I had two kids. My second child had just been born one or two months earlier. We lived in a house with a couple of cars. It was like, "Man, what do I do?"

I had been copywriting for the previous company, which was a home schooling company, and it was something I really wanted to do, so I said, "Well, I'm just going to launch my freelance copywriting business." So I did. God provided three clients in that first week or so. The rest, as they say, is history. I continued from there.

BEN SETTLE: A lot of people can't imagine being in that position where you just had a baby, you have another child, and a wife. You have all these responsibilities. You have no job. You have no real secure income. What do you do? What's going through your mind during those two weeks where you have to make something happen?

RYAN HEALY: Well, I guess maybe I have a little bit of a unique personality that when my back is against the wall I tend to go, "All right, this is it. Make it or break it time!" I make lists and I just do a whole bunch of stuff and things seem to happen. Not everything I do works, but some things I do work and then that's enough. Then there's also this kind of strange calmness that comes over me where it's like, "Man, I am so out of my element." It's like you get to that point where you recognize, "I have to do something, but it's not me. It's God who's got to pull me out of this." To me it's almost, like I said, a strangely calming experience where you're putting your faith in God that you're doing the right thing and that He's going to help you get to wherever you need to be.

BEN SETTLE: I'm just wondering, you felt pretty strongly about not going out and just getting another job. Is that something that you felt God didn't want you to do?

RYAN HEALY: Yes, I don't think I was supposed to get another job. I definitely don't think that was for me. That's not to say it's not right for somebody else, but I felt strongly that I was supposed to be in business for myself. In fact, God will sometimes speak to you and you'll be thinking to yourself, "Did He really just say that?" The example I want to give is that before I quit my job, when I got this bonus money, I had talked to my wife about it. I knew when bonus time was hitting. I waited until I got my bonus, and that's when I quit my job, because I figured the bonus money would give me a couple months to try to work things out and get a business going. Before I quit my job I had this master plan. I was going to be a financial planner and everything like that. I was interested in that for the income potential. My heart was really wanting to be a writer. I've always wanted to be a writer, but I was just too chicken to quit my job and go be a writer because I had no connections. I had nothing. On the financial planning side, I had this guy who was willing to mentor me and help me and give me an opportunity to make some money with him and all this. I thought, "This is the logical choice. There's a plan there. There's a source of income." It does not make any logical sense to just quit my job and just go try to be a freelance copywriter, but in my heart that's what I wanted to do. So I told Stephanie, my wife, I said, "Wouldn't that be funny if this whole financial planner thing was just a red herring that God threw out there just to get me to quit my job? Wouldn't that be funny?"

BEN SETTLE: Sounds like that's the case.

RYAN HEALY: That's exactly what it was. God knew me. He knew that I wouldn't just do it, because I try to be responsible and provide for my family and stuff like that. He knew that I would feel irresponsible quitting my job just to pursue this thing, especially since I had all these other things in my history that never worked out. I'd been burned. Like I could go to my wife and say, "Hey Steph, here's what I'm going to do. I'm going to quit my job and then I'm just going to do this thing which I have no idea how to do." She wasn't going to go for that. That's what it was.

BEN SETTLE: What kind of writer did you originally want to be? Was it a copywriter or just a writer in general?

RYAN HEALY: It was back in eighth grade when I became inspired to be a writer. I was walking down the hall in my middle school one day, and all of a sudden the thought came into my head just as clear as day. "I'm going to be a writer." I just knew it. I don't know, sometimes you just know things. At the time I imagined I would write novels, books, and things like that. I was really into reading books and still am. In high school I took all the AP English classes and read a bunch of literature. In fact, I still love to read literature. I try to do that on a regular basis. At least go through a few classics a year. That's kind of what I imagined myself doing. I did pursue journalism in high school and at the community college where I took a year of college, but I knew I wasn't going to pursue journalism as a career because the pay was so bad. I did it more for the experience than anything else.

BEN SETTLE: You mentioned that you just kind of knew it. I'm just curious of your experiences, it's pretty rare for God to appear to us as a burning bush. How do you think He speaks to us? Do you think it's just like a feeling in our gut or like a thought planted in our mind? What do you think about that?

RYAN HEALY: I think when God talks to us He puts a thought in our head that we can sense that maybe it didn't come from ourselves. Sometimes when I'm thinking, it's really clear what are my thoughts because they tend to be me-focused and carnal in nature and all that stuff. But sometimes God puts these thoughts in your head and you're kind of like, "Where did that come from? I wonder if He's serious." It's not an audible voice that you hear, but it's just a thought. Now, one way that you can know for sure that God is talking to you is the law of the double witness. That is all things will be confirmed by two or more witnesses. God can also talk other ways. He can talk through an email that a friend sends you or something like that.

BEN SETTLE: He can use a donkey if He wants to.

RYAN HEALY: He could use a donkey even! He could use an ass! Where I was going with that is let's say that God puts a thought in your head that maybe you should quit your job. You're going, "Well, that's weird. Okay, let me sit on that for a little while." Then your mom calls you up or a friend calls you up and says, "Hey, I just quit my job!" or "I was thinking, when are you going to quit your job and do that thing you've always wanted to do?" Now you have a second witness. So you had the thought in your head that seemed out of place. Then you have something else that was outside of your control where God sent somebody to tell you something. Then maybe there's a third thing. Maybe you see the same day there's an article in the paper about some guy who quit his job and made a business and became successful in business. Sometimes God works that way. He sends the message from multiple people and multiple sources so that you know it's from Him, right? What are the chances of you hearing the same message from two, three, four, different sources in a very short time period? Pretty slim, I think.

BEN SETTLE: I think you're right. For this book, one of the interviews is with Matt Gillogly, and he had a very similar experience. He was going through a rough time. He went from making $150,000 a month to zero. He was in a really weird spot in his life and he kept getting people coming to him out of the blue that he didn't even know, saying things that kind of pointed him in the direction that he ended up going, which was to serve

Christian entrepreneurs, which he still does now. He was talking about a very specific verse in Deuteronomy. He said it just kept coming up all of a sudden out of the weirdest places. "Okay, obviously someone's trying to tell me something."

RYAN HEALY: Right. "Okay. I get it." I've actually even tested God a few times, seeking confirmation. This doesn't always work, but if you feel led to do this, then maybe it's something you should try. I'll be seeking confirmation on something because I don't know the answer. It's like, "Well, I think I'm supposed to do this, but I don't know the answer." Just go to your Bible and let it fall open where it may and read the first thing. See what it says. More than once I've been pleasantly surprised to find that the exact verse I was reading about was a confirmation or had to do with the issue I was dealing with. That may sound weird and a little bit out there, but if you believe that God is sovereign over all things and that He's in control of everything, then it makes perfect sense.

BEN SETTLE: It does, and I'm actually looking something up right now that I think you'll get a kick out of. It's something Maxwell Sackheim wrote. He's talking about a copywriting formula to attract, interest, convince, and induce action, which is kind of like the AIDA formula. Here's what he wrote in an essay:

"As part payment to the advertising business, I decided to write a book about my advertising experiences. Naturally, I kept putting it off, until one night before dropping off to sleep I picked up my bedside copy of the Holy Bible and turned the pages at random.

"My eyes alighted on this sentence, 'Judas went out and hanged himself.' I didn't think that was very inspiring, so I closed the Book and opened it again only to read, 'Go thou and do likewise.'

"Well, that disturbed me even more, so I tried again and came across this sentence, 'What thou doest, do quickly.'

"Then instead of hanging myself quickly, I chanced to turn to Numbers, chapter 24, verse 14, where I found a reference to advertising.

"There Balaam, the prophet, is recorded as having said to Balak, king of Moab, 'I will advertise thee what this people shall do to my people in the latter days.'

"I am not capable of translating that into modern language, but according to my references, Balaam was resisted by the ass he rode, for which the ass was smitten three times while the angel of Jehovah stood in the way of its progress."

It's kind of interesting that challenges actually are maybe what are supposed to happen. That's kind of what I sense about it. If it was just handed to us, maybe we wouldn't even do it right.

RYAN HEALY: That's why it always requires wisdom when you encounter trouble or opposition. Is God telling you to go another direction or has God genuinely given you that direction and you're supposed to push through it? I guess the only way you can know that is through prayer and discernment.

BEN SETTLE: It's interesting you bring up wisdom, because when I was talking to Terry Dean for this book, he was very big on this. The big mistake he said he made when he was struggling was that he kept praying for money. Then he finally figured out to pray for wisdom. About a week later is when he bought his first computer and started his online business.

RYAN HEALY: That's really cool. Early on, seeking wisdom has always been very important to me, so I can relate to that.

BEN SETTLE: Is that something you prayed for originally?

RYAN HEALY: I've been praying for wisdom since I was a kid – wisdom and patience. My prayer for patience was in response to seeing my dad's temper a few times, and I thought to myself, "You know, I don't want to be like that, so God please give me patience." I don't recall what originally inspired me to start praying for wisdom. It might have been my grandfather. I didn't get to talk to my grandfather, either of them, very much because they lived out of state and I only saw them once every five years or so. My grandfather on my mom's side said, "If there's one thing I can tell you to do that would change your life, it would be read one Proverb a day. There are 31 Proverbs. You read one a day, and if it's a 30–day month, you read two on the last day. Then you just do it again the next month." He said, "Do that over and over again, and things are going to go well for you." That's where my interest in Proverbs came from. I've read the book of Proverbs more than any other book in the Bible. The people reading this or listening to this probably know that the Proverbs were mostly written by King Solomon, who's considered the wisest man of all time. Solomon was the person where God said, "I'll grant you anything if you ask for it. So what do you ask for?" And Solomon said, "Give me wisdom." When Solomon said, "Give me wisdom," the Lord responded by saying, "Since you did not ask for money and wealth and fame and you asked for wisdom instead, therefore I will add all these other things to you." You know, the money, wealth, fame, etc.

BEN SETTLE: How much better would this world be if, instead of going out there preaching, "Give me money and you'll be blessed financially by God," you'd hear more of that. Nobody ever talks about that story.

RYAN HEALY: Right. When I was a kid and I came across that, I was like, "Well, shoot. Of course, I should pray for wisdom."

BEN SETTLE: It's funny. I love that story in the Bible about Solomon, and just all those stories are so neat, like in the first book of Kings when he's trying to solve the argument. "Well, saw the child in half and each one of you take a half." The only one who really cares about the child is obviously the real parent.

RYAN HEALY: Yeah, that was brilliant. The mother who was making the false claim was like, "Yeah, do it! Saw the kid in half!"

BEN SETTLE: Not to coin the cliché on wisdom and that, but it's true, that whole mindset. It's kind of like that book with *Obvious Adams*. Have you ever read that?

RYAN HEALY: I've not read it yet. I'm ashamed, but I haven't.

BEN SETTLE: I'll send you a digital copy of it, if you want it. I've probably read it 20 or 30 times. It's not very long. It's a little pamphlet. I put it in the glove compartment, so whenever I'm at the store or something with my wife and I don't go in, I just read that. It's not like I'm this diligent student or anything. It's more of an entertainment thing. It's all about looking at the obvious in things. The guy who sent it to me was Gary Bencivenga. I sent him a testimonial and I guess he just liked it and he says, "I want to send you this gift." He said David Ogilvy, who he used to work for, told all his people to read this a few times over here. I can kind of see why. It's all about that. It's not the same as sawing your child in half and finding out who the real parent is, but it's all these obvious solutions to things. I can't recommend it enough.

RYAN HEALY: In some ways that reminds me of Occam's razor. The simplest explanation is usually the correct explanation.

BEN SETTLE: It makes sense. In almost every case it sure seems to be.

RYAN HEALY: Except for some other cases, which I have mentioned now.

BEN SETTLE: You talked about Proverbs and you read a Proverb every day. What's your favorite Proverb, if you can think of one? Is there one that maybe sticks out for a Christian business owner in particular?

RYAN HEALY: One that I've quoted on my blog before is this one. I actually wrote this one down before our call. I'm not very good at remembering the reference. I can remember the verses, but the references sometimes I forget. So I actually looked this up beforehand. It's Proverbs 22:29. It says, "Do you see a man skilled in his work? He will serve before kings. He will not serve before obscure men." That's one of my favorites just because I think it applies very much to entrepreneurs and businessmen and businesswomen. If you're diligent and you're continuously improving your skills, then God will give you those opportunities. He will bring those people into your life. Our perspective says, "I attracted him," right? "I got really good and I attracted him into my life," whereas we could also look at it from the perspective of, "I got really good. God saw what I was doing and He brought me this guy."

BEN SETTLE: I think that's a lot more accurate. That's definitely been the case for you then, right? I'm just thinking recently when you did that radioactive blog post. Doing basically what I believe God would want someone to do, if you had that information that you had and you shared it, you probably saved people money and helped people identify bad things going on.

RYAN HEALY: It definitely got a lot of exposure and some business contacts through that. I guess one example would be Mark Allen, whom you know. I've been hopping on his radio show a few different times, about three or four times now.

BEN SETTLE: He loves copywriters.

RYAN HEALY: He's a good guy. I've been joining him and helping with some quick website critiques and things like that that we do on the phone. That, of course, opens the door to get another audience that I didn't have before. These things tend to spider out. They take on a life of their own and just continue to grow. Rarely has it happened where I did one thing and then, boom, it was a grand slam. That sometimes happens after you've been in business for quite a while, but generally what happens is you do a whole bunch of things consistently over time, and a whole bunch of little things happen consistently over time, and those begin to snowball and add up to something bigger. That's kind of how I look at it.

BEN SETTLE: You get base hits and you manufacture runs. You might hit a grand slam or a home run, but it's doing the little things right constantly, day in and day out.

RYAN HEALY: Yes, exactly. An example of that, this week is a little bit unusual, but this is the second recorded call I've done today and I have yet another one tomorrow. It's just making the time to do those things that help to grow your business.

BEN SETTLE: That's a good way to look at it. I'm curious. Have you been a Christian your whole life or were you converted later in life?

RYAN HEALY: I was four, so not quite my whole life, but still pretty young. I was raised in a Christian family. I was the oldest of five. When I was four years old, I think I just had one brother, maybe a second brother on the way. I was at the dinner table and my mom and dad said, "Ryan, do you want to say the prayer?" I said, "Sure." I don't know what I said. At first I probably said, "Thanks for the food," and then I said, "Jesus, please come into my heart." Of course, my mom was, "Ryan, what did you say?" I said, "Jesus, come into my life." She was emotional and all that stuff. I don't know why I said that, I just did. I've been a Christian ever since that time. Not to say I haven't had my ups and downs. I have. I remember a period of time when I was seven or eight when I was unsure. I was like, "Did I really become a Christian? When I did this, did I lose my salvation?" I was thinking these thoughts at seven and eight years old. I kept asking Jesus back into my heart every day because I was afraid that He was going to leave.

BEN SETTLE: Now, I know a subject close to your heart is debt. You have a blog about that. You've shared many of your stories publicly about that. What have you learned about debt that you would like to impart to the rest of us?

RYAN HEALY: There's one practical thing I think that everybody should be doing who has debt, and that is you should be tracking your debt every month. What I have is a spreadsheet that lists out each of my debts individually. It lists out the payment. It lists out the interest rate. Based on the balance and the interest rate, I just kind of assign a number – 1, 2, 3, 4, etc. – and that's the order in which I'm supposed to pay off the debt. What I do is every month I update those balances so I can see whether my debt is going up or if it's going down. What happens when people get into debt is they tend to want to stick their head in the sand and ignore the problem. They might be getting calls from collection agencies or whatever, and they don't want to answer the phone. They don't want to open the mail. They don't want to look at their bills because it's such a big problem. They think that there's no way they could ever overcome it. You're going to feel a lot of relief if you just write it down. Just see how much you owe in total. It's a little bit scary at first, but once you know, you know. You can't be afraid of the unknown anymore because you know it. It's not unknown. After that, like I said, on a monthly basis, update those numbers. Watch whether it's going up or down, and just that simple act of writing it down is going to force you to be accountable. You're going to look at that and go, "Oh, my gosh! Our debt went up. We can't do this." You're going to talk to your wife or your spouse and say, "Okay, look, we really need to get control of our spending because our debt's going up. We can't be doing this. We have to get it to come down." Then you look for ways to trim expenses or grow your income or a combination of those things to start steering the ship in the right direction. That one thing was a huge help to me, because for a long time it was like I didn't know. I just had some debts and I just made the payments and I had no idea whether it was going up or down every month. As soon as you know, that's when you can finally do something about it.

BEN SETTLE: I remember it didn't dawn on me, the kind of trouble I was in, because I used to be in pretty bad debt. Thank God I'm not at the moment. I hope I never will be again, because it was the worst. I remember it was 2002 and I was working at this place duplicating videos. That's what my job was. It was a fun job actually. Nightingale Conant tapes. We duplicated this *Debt Into Wealth* program by John Cummuta. It was a good product. I actually used some of the tips to get things paid off, but more importantly than that, he really makes you realize what kind of trouble you're in. There's no sticking your head in the sand after watching that thing. He really lays it on you. The way he put it – and I think this is kind of apt for what we're talking about with Christian businesses – he goes, "I know this is kind of depressing. I know that you don't want to hear this, but I'm like the Southern Baptist preacher. I've got to get you lost before I can get you saved." Like a good problem/agitation/solution sales letter.

RYAN HEALY: That's funny.

BEN SETTLE: You're great at drawing business lessons right out of the scriptures. You're one of the best I've seen at it. How do you go about doing that when you're reading your Bible exactly? Are you consciously looking for lessons that you can teach to others or does it just kind of come to you when you sit down to write a blog post?

RYAN HEALY: Usually it just kind of comes to me as I'm getting ready to write a blog post or something. I'll sit down, and something I've read recently will trigger a thought, or sometimes a thought will happen as I'm reading the Bible and I'll go, "Oh, I should write about that." I'm a pen and paper kind of guy. I've got a spiral notebook that I write ideas down in. Sometimes I'll take notes underneath my to-do list. It'll say Blog Post Ideas, "Write a post about this verse." Sometimes I do it like that. My audience is not specifically Christian business owners, so what I try to do is I try to write to my audience most of the time and then kind of drip on them a little bit with Bible references and things like that. I know that if I just try to beat them over the head with Bible verses they would all unsubscribe and leave, at least a lot of them would. This way I can still kind of subtly and consistently maybe persuade them of some things. That's kind of my goal.

BEN SETTLE: I'd like to go off on that just for a second. I'm curious about what your thoughts are. Do you think Christian business owners should be shy talking about their faith and Jesus? You seem to have struck a nice balance with that, but what about someone who doesn't know? They're afraid to say anything because they think everyone's going to leave. Do you have any advice for someone like that?

RYAN HEALY: I suppose it depends on what kind of business you're in. I don't see any reason to necessarily hide the fact that you're a Christian or a believer. If it comes up naturally, by all means talk about it. On the flip side, I personally am not fond of ads in the Yellow Pages where it has a fish sign, or putting a fish sign in your retail window. That's just me, because it almost feels like you're using Christianity to sell people. That's just my own preference.

BEN SETTLE: It's like if someone just comes out of nowhere with, "I'm a Christian" with no context they're trying to get something from you and it's awkward.

RYAN HEALY: Here's an example, because I've gone back and forth on this issue a few times. I use Twitter and Facebook, and I think you do, too. On Facebook I asked everybody, "Do you want me updating you on business stuff, or would you rather me not?" Everybody who replied was like, "Yeah, leave the business stuff out of it." What I realized is everybody on

Facebook who was reading my stuff was primarily friends and family, so I unfriended anybody who I hadn't met before or at least talked to on the phone before, so I just got rid of all my business contacts on Facebook. Now, on my Facebook profile, I'm not shy about it at all. It says I'm a father and a follower of Jesus etc. On my Twitter profile, that's a much more public "out there" profile and for a while the first thing my little bio said was, "Follower of Jesus." I don't think that's necessarily a problem, but I use Twitter primarily for business purposes. I'm updating people on business, copywriting and ads and a few personal things thrown in. After a while I got to thinking, "Well, is that doing a disservice here, because if somebody just hits my profile and they're not a believer and then the first thing they read is "Follower of Jesus," that's going to turn them off and I'm not going to really ever have an opportunity to connect with them. I removed that from my public business profile. Even though it's true and I'm not ashamed of it at all, I just thought that maybe I'd have a better chance of connecting with people and building a relationship first before I come at them and say, "By the way, I'm a follower of Jesus."

BEN SETTLE: Some people liken things like Twitter and social media – and in my opinion the analogy isn't perfect but it does fit – that it's kind of like a social gathering and you're just meeting people. Are you going to wear a name tag that says this, or are you going to tell everybody first thing, "Hey, I'm a Christian," or "Hey, I'm Jewish," or whatever religion. It doesn't matter. "I'm an atheist." Maybe for some people that makes sense. I know there are some people who kind of build their business around certain markets and that's fine. That makes perfect sense.

RYAN HEALY: It would be like having one of those, "Hello, my name is . . . " tags. You'd be like, "Hello, my name is Ryan and I'm a son of God." [laughing]

BEN SETTLE: "I'm a follower of Jesus, a book lover, I read classics, I'm a husband." I don't know. It's interesting to ask people this question, because I think a lot of people wonder about it. They don't want to come off as someone who's just trying to get something using the religion. But at the same time they don't want to hide who they are either and they're kind of in that in-between spot.

RYAN HEALY: I think the real important thing, as you mentioned earlier, is just context. If there's a context for it, then great. Be open about it. But if there's a lack of context, then don't necessarily be up front with that. Talk about it if the opportunity comes up.

BEN SETTLE: A lot of it comes through your actions. I interviewed Greg Perry for this book, too. He's a good friend of mine and he was telling me about this. I'm ashamed to say that I've never eaten at Chick Fil A, but the way he makes it sound it's like I really want to go visit one of these places. It's a Christian-run business and the people there behave like the best customer service you'll ever get apparently. They will bend over backwards to make you happy and just to make your life easier. He goes, "That sticks out in a world full of people who hate Christians as the world gets more anti-Christian in some areas." That place will stick out even more, like a sore thumb, because they're not just talking the talk, they're walking the walk. I thought that was interesting.

RYAN HEALY: I admire some things about Chick Fil A, although I have to say early on when I was getting started in blogging, my very first blog was a health blog, and Chick Fil A, at least the last time I checked, was heavily seasoned with MSG, which is not really good for you.

BEN SETTLE: Well, it is fast food. I wouldn't go there for a healthy meal necessarily. If it's 10 p.m. and you need something to eat and the kids are hungry and you have that or McDonalds, it might be a good choice. I don't know. I've never been there. I just thought it was interesting that there's a Christian-run business that can at least stand out and be servants and show it.

RYAN HEALY: Yeah, they're servants. They also, I think, are still closed on Sundays.

BEN SETTLE: He was saying that. They're closed on Sundays, they're very family oriented and just set that example. You almost don't even have to ask if they're a Christian-run business. It's just obvious. It's that whole Fonzi thing. Fonzi's cool. You just know it. He doesn't have to go around saying he's cool. He doesn't have to go around and wear a name tag saying he's cool. Everyone just knows it because of his actions, and that's kind of like Christians. Anyway, the next thing I wanted to ask you is, what has God's Word taught you about adding foresight? How have you used this knowledge to help build your business?

RYAN HEALY: There are a couple of scriptures that I pulled up. Let me flip back to Proverbs again. Good ol' Proverbs. Proverbs says something about everything I think.

BEN SETTLE: I have a feeling you're going to be consulting Proverbs a lot in this call.

RYAN HEALY: Yeah, I am. This is Proverbs 6:6–11 and this one has always motivated me quite a bit. "Go to the ant, you sluggard. Consider its ways and be wise. It has no commander, no overseer or ruler. Yet it stores its provisions in summer and gathers its food at harvest. "How long will you lie there, you sluggard? When will you get up from your sleep? A little sleep, a little slumber, a little folding of the hands to rest, and poverty will come on you like a bandit and scarcity like an armed man." You've probably heard of *4-Hour Workweek* before – this idea that you can work four hours a week and make a ton of money – and I think there's maybe a kernel of truth there. My sources tell me that Mr. Ferriss worked actually quite a bit more than that when he was building his business.

BEN SETTLE: And from what I understand still does.

RYAN HEALY: I think he still does. The promise is appealing, but I think the reality of it is that success in business takes hard work. You asked specifically about foresight, and in Proverbs it talks about the ant being self-motivated, has no commander, no overseer, which is similar to me. I don't have a boss telling me what to do, so it's up to me to go out and, figuratively speaking, gather up the food for the winter. There are dry spells I've had in my business. I wish that there were no dry spells sometimes. That would make it a lot easier, but you have to prepare for those times. An employee gets paid every two weeks usually. In my case, I may get paid a whole bunch of money at once and then not get paid anything for six to eight weeks. You just never know. I think it's important to always be kind of diligent, looking at where the next client is going to come from, saving your money, not just blowing it all when you get a bunch of money in. You need to kind of keep a tab on your expenses and all that stuff. Another one about having foresight, this one may seem a little bit backwards and this one's not from Proverbs. It's from Ecclesiastes. Ecclesiastes 11:1 says, "Cast your bread on the surface of the waters, for you will find it after many days." I like this verse because when I remind myself that if I'm adding value, if I'm doing things that add value, I don't necessarily need to get paid today for the value that I create today. Sometimes that value is going to come back in the form of money or a deal or something else down days later. This verse says, ". . . after many days." I found that to be true. You might do something for somebody, and a year later he sends you a referral. That referral becomes a client and generates a lot of money for you. I've had that happen. I try to remember just always be creating value for people, whether it's people on your list or your clients or your prospects or just colleagues, like you, Ben. Then stuff will happen.

Getting back to the previous verse, because I don't think I finished that thought, he says, "A little sleep, a little slumber, a little folding of the hands to rest, and poverty will come on you like a bandit and scarcity like an armed man." This is one reason why I consistently work five days a week, 40 hours a week, eight hours a day. That fluctuates up and down a little bit, depending on the week, but generally speaking, I work a full work week. I actually think that's biblical – not necessarily the number of hours – but I feel like it's biblical to work and to work hard. God has given us work as part of what we do.

BEN SETTLE: I think you're right. He set a day aside for us to rest, not that we're supposed to anymore slavishly follow it, the Sabbath was made for man, not man made for the Sabbath. He knows our flesh bodies better than we'll ever know it. Taking that five days, and it could be six days, but whatever, it's important just to have a little rest, but we are supposed to work, right? Isn't that the whole point?

RYAN HEALY: Absolutely. Here's what I would really love. I think we should be working five or six days a week. I don't see a problem with six days a week, although culturally that's not as acceptable these days, especially if you're married. My sixth day of work is helping take care of the kids, how's that?

BEN SETTLE: People can define work, too. They always think it's going to a job, but work is whatever you're doing, as long as you're not laying around playing video games or something.

RYAN HEALY: That's true. The other day I was weeding in my yard and stuff. That's pretty hard work.

BEN SETTLE: That's work, man.

RYAN HEALY: So I would advocate that, and I would advocate that every seventh year we get the whole year off. That's what I'd like.

BEN SETTLE: I wish they'd go back to the year of Jubilee.

RYAN HEALY: I know. The Jubilee is awesome. That's every 49 years, but then you get a rest year every seven years.

BEN SETTLE: Let's talk about that, and this goes back to the debt thing, but I remember you wrote a really good blog post about this on your debt blog, how we should do that, the year of Jubilee. It seems like even the Israelites didn't really follow it that much. It's barely ever talked about.

RYAN HEALY: They didn't follow it, and because of that God sent them into bondage and they had to pay for those jubilee years and all of those rest years in bondage. If you see the time that the Israelites went into bondage, they had to pay back that debt by not keeping that year. God forced them to keep the year by sending them into bondage.

BEN SETTLE: When you've been cheated or lied to in business, what scripture do you look to for comfort and instruction?

RYAN HEALY: One of them is Romans 8:28, which most of the people reading this probably know, but it says, "And we know that all things work together for good to those who love God, to those who are called according to His purpose." Whenever that happens, I always think there's a reason. I know that God is ultimately going to work it out for my good, so that gives me comfort. Then I also look at it and I think this is an opportunity for me to exercise forgiveness – love your enemies and forgive your enemies and all that stuff. It's all good and well to talk about it in a church setting, but when it happens, it's not as easy as it sounds. I look at it and say, "I'm upset, but this is an opportunity for me to forgive."

BEN SETTLE: A lot of times you can turn those emotions into good, too. It's like you have an extra energy now that you didn't have before.

RYAN HEALY: Yeah, it's a freeing experience. Overall it's a difficult thing to do, but I think it's really positive ultimately. There's this other verse I can't remember, a parable that talks about a guy who owed a debt that essentially could never be repaid in an entire lifetime. It was like the equivalent of millions of dollars.

BEN SETTLE: Like the United States, basically.

RYAN HEALY: Yeah, basically like the United States. He goes to his master and he says, "Master, I can't repay this. Please have mercy on me," and the master says, "All right, I'll have mercy on you. Your debts are forgiven. You're free," and he goes off celebrating. Then somebody comes up to him and says, "Hey, I owe you $100 and I can't repay it," and the guy flips out. "Hey, pay my $100!" and he's beating the guy and trying to get his $100, after he just had millions of dollars forgiven. So what does the other master do to him? The other master comes back to him and says, "Hey, you won't forgive this guy his little petty debt when I just forgave you all this money? Now guess what – now you're going to have to pay it all back." I think that's how it is. Anyway, the lesson being this client rips me off or whatever. It's painful in the moment, but you know what? God has forgiven me a whole lot more, so I ought to extend some grace and mercy and forgive this client for what they've done to me, especially considering what God has done for me, and there's no way I could ever repay that.

BEN SETTLE: Has that happened to you a lot of times, where you've gotten cheated really bad? Or is that a once in a great while type thing?

RYAN HEALY: I can think of four clear examples where I was ripped off thousands of dollars.

BEN SETTLE: Do you still associate with those people anymore?

RYAN HEALY: No.

BEN SETTLE: Have you been reading Ray Edwards' book on this that he's been putting on the internet?

RYAN HEALY: I think I read the first chapter. It was really good.

BEN SETTLE: Yeah, he's really taken this to a whole new level.

RYAN HEALY: Yeah, it's great stuff. I think it's a great message, to forgive.

BEN SETTLE: What does the Bible say about exceeding other people's expectations, especially when we would rather not put in the extra effort, and how would you use this principle to grow your business?

RYAN HEALY: The verse that comes to mind is Matthew 5:41. Jesus is speaking here. I think this is part of the Sermon on the Mount. This little piece of it is within a couple other things. It says, "Whoever forces you to go one mile, go with him two." The context here is that during the time that Jesus lived, a Roman soldier could conscript you in a sense. He could come up to you and say, "Hey, carry my pack," and if he did that, you were required by law to carry his pack for one mile. Understanding what Jesus meant by that, it was within the context of the time that He lived and it was basically saying, "Hey, if a Roman soldier comes and forces you by law to carry his gear for a mile, carry it two miles." In our situation, we're actually entering into a business relationship, so it's not like we're being forced into that business relationship, but once we're in the business relationship, sometimes clients can ask unreasonable things and can be unreasonable. We're all human, so I guess we're all unreasonable at one time or another. I generally try to do my best to over–deliver, to exceed expectations, and to just do my best. I've been involved in one situation recently – and I'm just being honest here – where we had a contract and the client came back to me and asked me to do something that was completely outside of the contract. It was like a totally new project. This was a case where I kind of put my foot down and I said, "Look, this is what I agreed to. I'm happy to work on this project and make it right and make some changes, etc." Without going into too much detail, that's where it's at and I'm still torn about that because of this verse, actually. "Whoever forces you to go one mile, go with them two." In a business context where my labor is paying the bills, it's like I can't really take two to three weeks out of my schedule and just do this brand new project for this client, because then I wouldn't be able to pay my bills. So I'm in this kind of paradox. I think legally and contractually I've done the right thing, but have I done the right thing biblically? I don't know.

BEN SETTLE: I think you have done the right thing. There's a verse that says a man who doesn't provide for his family is worse than an unbeliever, so if you're doing something for him free when you should be doing something that would pay the bills… to me there's no moral problem at all, especially if you fulfilled what you said you were going to do. I don't know if that makes you feel any better or not.

RYAN HEALY: It does to a degree. With my personality, I want to be on good terms with all of my clients all of the time. I know that's unrealistic and it's actually impossible. It would be nice if there was never ever any kind of conflict between a client and a contractor. I feel like I've done pretty well over the years. There have been very, very, very few situations where something didn't work out quite like I expected. I guess another example would be if you had a retail store and somebody came in and said, "Hey, give this to me for free," and you're like, "Here, take two!" You wouldn't be in business for very long. You'd be bankrupt in a matter of hours.

BEN SETTLE: And you wouldn't be able to feed your family, and you'd be worse than an unbeliever. You've said that in your view business is not so much about the survival of the fittest. Why do you look at it that way, when practically everybody in business does, non-Christians especially?

RYAN HEALY: First of all, the whole idea of the survival of the fittest springs out of evolution. It comes from an evolutionary perspective, and I disagree with the evolutionary perspective, so I don't agree with this whole idea of survival of the fittest. Even in that phrase – survival of the fittest – let's define what fittest means. What does that really mean? You've seen businesses where maybe they had a better product, but they failed.

BEN SETTLE: Happens all the time.

RYAN HEALY: It happens all the time. So we'd have to define what that actually even means, but that's kind of a side thing I guess. I personally believe more in Adam Smith's invisible hand when he was writing about economics. I actually haven't read *Wealth of Nations*. I've just read a few things about Adam Smith, but he wrote about how economies work and how free markets work and things like that, but ultimately he said there was an invisible hand guiding the activities of men. He was clear in his writing that when he said an invisible hand, he was talking about the invisible hand of God. When you read the scriptures, there's a verse in the scriptures – I think it's in Genesis – and it says, "This dude was the father of all who farmed, and this dude was the father of all who tend sheep."

BEN SETTLE: I think that's Genesis 4, Cain's line.

RYAN HEALY: Yeah, it's pretty early on in scripture. I read that once and I was like, "What?" Maybe one of them was the father of all who make music.

BEN SETTLE: Yeah, the harp and the cymbal or something like that.

RYAN HEALY: You see some scriptures like that in the Bible and you go, "That is really fascinating, isn't it." It's my personal belief that God puts people into certain businesses. If He gives you the desire to be a car mechanic or somebody who builds homes or to be an accountant or a writer, or whatever the case may be, I feel like God is orchestrating that. He knew you before you were born. So business isn't so much about survival of the fittest. It's are you doing what God wants you to do? Are you walking in God's favor? There are a couple of verses from Proverbs. One here is Proverbs 20:24, "A man's steps are directed by the Lord. How then can anyone understand his own way?" If you've ever been confused about what you're doing, you might want to talk to God about that.

BEN SETTLE: Which I think a lot of people can say. I think everyone's been there at least once.

RYAN HEALY: Yeah, there are days where I've thought, "I'm going to do this, this, and this today," and I get to the end of the day and everything is totally not what I expected.

BEN SETTLE: I've got a quote for you for that. You'll love this. You know C.S. Lewis?

RYAN HEALY: Yeah.

BEN SETTLE: His stepson – a very, very interesting guy; I don't know if you've ever heard him or anything – he's running the Narnia movies and he did an interview with somebody last year. He said, "Our plans are what we get up and we plan to do today. All the interruptions of the day are God's plans." I thought, "That's very true!"

RYAN HEALY: It is true! You look at that and you just go, "Man, I am so not in control." This verse in Proverbs 21:30 is one chapter later says, "There is no wisdom, no insight, no plan that can succeed against the Lord." In other words, the Lord will prevail over everybody. That's why I say it's not so much about survival of the fittest, but are you doing what God wants you to do? If you're doing what God wants you to do, I believe that He's going to bless you in what you're doing. But if you're doing something that God doesn't want you to be doing, He's going to redirect you or not make it work out.

There's a story from my friend, Chuck. He lives down in Phoenix, AZ and he tells this story where God had him start a business for awhile. I forget what the business was, but people would call him up on the business line and that's how he got business. God said, "Go into business," and so he did. That phone line rang every single day. Every single day he would get business. This is a true story. Chuck told this and I've known Chuck for a long time and he's a great guy. One day God said, "Close down your business," and so Chuck went, "Okay." He told his wife, "I think God told me that I need to shut down my business and it's time to do something else." So he did exactly what God told him to do. He sold the business to this other guy. Chuck goes on and he's going to find out, "What does God want me to do now." I don't know how much time passed, whether it was a couple months or a year or something like that. Chuck ended up running into the guy that he sold to somehow, or the guy called him, and the guy told Chuck, "Chuck, I swear on my life, this phone has not rung a single time since I bought the business." When God wants you to do something and you're doing it, then it's going to work. But when He tells you to do something else, you should probably do something else.

BEN SETTLE: Instead of survival of the fittest, it's survival of the wisest.

RYAN HEALY: Yeah, right, survival of the wisest. I can get behind that.

BEN SETTLE: What biblical advice do you have for Christian business owners in the freelance or commissioned sales business for when money gets tight and when they don't even know when or where their next paycheck will come from?

RYAN HEALY: My advice first would be to pray. Next is just to acknowledge who writes your paycheck. I think I originally encountered this idea on Terry Dean's blog from a long time ago, and it was actually a post talking about debt. He was asking the question, "Who writes your paycheck, God or MasterCard?" I thought, "Huh, that makes a lot of sense." I think it's really important to acknowledge where wealth and money comes from. It comes from God. It's His provision, so acknowledge Him as the guy who writes your paycheck. Don't be seeking after other men to bail you out and stuff like that. That may be part of the answer, it may be part of the direction God gives you – "Hey, go talk to this guy and ask him for a loan." I don't know, but ultimately it comes down to God is the one who provides for you, so always keep that in mind. I remember very, very specifically there was a time in my freelance copywriting career, I think it was February, and I had run out of money. I didn't have any money left and I didn't have any projects on the table or anything. On the one hand it was kind of nice because I didn't have any work to do necessarily. I didn't have any deadlines to meet.

BEN SETTLE: Yeah, a little break.

RYAN HEALY: Oh man, talk about stressful though, because I'm the only one who earns money in my family. Well, that's not entirely true. My wife sells a little bit of jewelry sometimes, but that obviously doesn't pay the bills. I went to bed that night, and I think it was a Sunday night, and I said, "Lord, I'm out of money. I've done everything I can to find another client. I don't know what else to do. I'm totally at a dead end. Lord, please help me out here. Please send me something." I went to bed, I woke up in the morning, and the first thing in the morning a client who I hadn't talked to in like six months called me up and was like, "Hey Ryan, I've got a project for you." I had the check by the end of the week. I was like, "Wow! Thank you, God. That was a nice quick turnaround on that one." [laughing]

BEN SETTLE: What does the Bible say to Christian business owners about planning?

RYAN HEALY: We talked about the ants and the sluggards, and also how God directs our steps. There's one other verse that I thought kind of applied here. That's Proverbs 24:27. It says, "Finish your outdoor work and get your fields ready. After that, build your house." I think a lot of us go about it backwards. We're like, "Hey, let's buy a big house and get a big fat mortgage! Oh, now how are we going to pay for it?" This verse is basically saying you want to plant your fields and get all that stuff taken care of, then go build your house. It's pretty simple and straightforward. I don't think it requires a lot of explanation.

BEN SETTLE: No, but it's a very important lesson, because everybody mostly does it opposite, even Christians – especially maybe Christians. Isn't that what the whole debt thing is about?

RYAN HEALY: Yeah, essentially. It's one reason why we're a nation that lives on debt. I've contributed to it, so I'm just as guilty as anybody, regretfully.

BEN SETTLE: You're not alone. It's like 80-90% of Americans are in some kind of debt, and that's scary.

RYAN HEALY: That's a huge number, somewhat unavoidable since our nation is built on debt from the beginning.

BEN SETTLE: Even if you try to stay out of debt, I'm finding sometimes it's really hard to make that payment some months. For example, at tax time you get hit with a tax bill, and normally you pay your credit card balances no problem, but holy cow! We've been trying to play catch up for two months now.

RYAN HEALY: I totally relate to that. January through May is such a difficult time, at least for me, because I have to pay a huge whack of taxes in January, then I have to pay an additional whack of it in April, and then it takes me all the way through May until I finally feel like, "Okay, I'm starting to get recovered now."

BEN SETTLE: That's exactly it. I'm just treading water, then next month I should be back ahead, God willing. But really, it's bad planning on my part. Honestly, I can't blame anyone but myself. There were expenses that I did early this year when I didn't think the tax load would be so high, and I should have waited.

RYAN HEALY: It's the same with me. It's a planning issue, but it's difficult no matter what to pay your taxes.

BEN SETTLE: It is, but we made it worse. We have health insurance, but we had to change it because we use a natural doctor and it doesn't really cover anything anyway. So we decided to go to the dentist and the doctor and all this stuff in April, get the dog checked up, blood tests… we're talking a few thousand dollars in expenses that could have been put off at least a little bit longer, but I didn't think about it. It was really bad planning. It's like a lesson you can only learn the hard way, it seems. Here's another question: A lot of Christian business owners seek money and success. Why is this a big mistake?

RYAN HEALY: We talked a little bit earlier about the importance of seeking wisdom instead of wealth. I think wisdom should be a much higher priority obviously than seeking money, but there are some other reasons to not seek money first. Here's another one from Solomon. Proverbs 23:4 – "Do not wear yourself out to get rich. Have the wisdom to show restraint. Cast but a glance at riches and they are gone, for they will surely sprout wings and fly off to the sky like an eagle." Now consider the source. You're talking about the richest guy who ever lived. I find it interesting that he says, "Cast a glance at riches and they're gone." In other words, money is temporary. It's here one day and gone the next. It's not something that you can really put your trust in or anything like that, and you shouldn't. In Proverbs 30: 8,9 – I love this one, by the way; I think this is really good for business owners – it says, "Keep falsehood and lies far from me. Give me neither poverty nor riches, but give me only my daily bread. Otherwise I may have too much and disown you and say, 'Who is the Lord?' or I may become poor and steal and so dishonor the name of my God." I think that's such a great verse. In the Lord's Prayer we say, "Give us this day our daily bread," and here's one where Solomon was agreeing with that. "Give me only my daily bread," because if you have too much money it's easy to pound your chest and become prideful and say, "Hey, look at all the great things I've done. I don't need God," and that's clearly not good. On the other hand if you become poor and get forced into a situation where you're doing something dishonest, that would dishonor God. I just think that's a great verse to keep at the forefront of your mind.

BEN SETTLE: That is a good verse. That's very good. This is really good stuff you're quoting. These are real practical things. We're not asking anybody to become a pauper or wear a burlap sack or live in a cave. It's true, it all comes back to that. If you start getting too successful you can believe your own PR if you don't have that balance.

RYAN HEALY: And I'm not sure there's much advantage to being rich anyway. If you have enough food to eat every day and you have money to pay your bills, does it get any better than that? You're worried about losing it, you're worried about, "How do I protect my money from the government?" In my experience, I've met some wealthy people and yeah, they didn't have to "work" eight hours a day, but you know what they spend their days doing? Meeting with accountants and CPAs and figuring out how to keep more of their money. To me, I'm thinking, "Well shoot, I'd rather be middle class and able to actually do the work that I enjoy doing rather than be fabulously wealthy and doing the work that I hate," which is meeting with CPAs and accountants and dealing with government crap. That to me is stressful. I don't want that. But if you're rich, I guarantee you're going to be spending a lot of time doing that.

BEN SETTLE: You know Paul Hartunian? He was saying this once on a teleconference call. He basically said, "The reality is most people don't need to make more than $2–3 million. Any more than that is probably overkill for the average person." Not that they shouldn't try for more if they want it, but if they want to have a free life, be free on the earth and not have to have a lot of problems and not be servant to other things, like you're saying, like to the government and the accountants and the IRS – because now you're really on the radar – but you just kind of want to be able to do what you want to do, whatever work you want to do, you'll never need more than a couple million dollars.

RYAN HEALY: I would agree with that – not that I've ever experienced it – but yeah, I'd much rather have a little more flexibility and be actually doing something that I love. That would be my preference, to have my daily bread, as the verse says, and be able to have some time with my family and do the work I love. That's awesome. There's a verse in Ecclesiastes I remember reading in middle school that just struck me, like "What?" It's Ecclesiastes 9:9. "Enjoy life with your wife whom you love all the days of this meaningless life that God has given you under the sun all your meaningless days, for this is your lot in life and in your toilsome labor under the sun. Whatever your hand finds to do, do it with all your might, for the grave where you are going there is neither working nor planting nor knowledge nor wisdom." Basically what I get from that is enjoy life with your wife, and whatever your hand finds to do, do it with all your might. So what do you have? You've got your family and your work. I put a little more positive spin on it maybe than Solomon does. I think maybe I'm a little more optimistic than he was.

BEN SETTLE: Why is it so important for Christian business owners to have the heart of a servant?

RYAN HEALY: I think to really serve your market well you need to have the heart of a servant. You have to want to serve, and you have to want to go beyond the call of duty, so to speak.

Imagine going to a restaurant and you sit down at a table and your server comes over and everything that she does for you is done begrudgingly. Are you going to be thankful about that? You're going to feel disrespected. You're going to feel like, "Man, let's get out of here. Let's go to a different restaurant." But if she serves you gladly and is happy to refill your water or bring you something that you need, some extra napkins or whatever, you're going to feel respected and loved and you'll probably want to come back. I just think that it's a good way to run a business, to really want to serve your market. I think that if you are going into a market just for the money, like back when I was setting up my vending machines just because of the money, that's not a great recipe for success. Sure, vending can be a good business, but I should have seen the warning signs, because I don't drink soda. Yeah, I like sugar, but I try to avoid it. I'm not really fond of junk food. I think it's unhealthy and it's causing a lot of people to be obese, and here I was trying to go into a vending business. It wasn't something I could get passionate about and go, "Oh man, I just really want to serve people who are hungry at 3 pm. I just really want to give people a Coke."

BEN SETTLE: "I want to rot their teeth out. They've got to have the rotten teeth or I can't live with myself." [laughing]

RYAN HEALY: [laughing] I guess where I was going with that is if you're not passionate about serving your market, it's probably a sign that maybe you shouldn't be in that market. A bad market for me to be in would be the pet market. I know that you're an animal lover, Ben. For me, I'm not so much and I recognize that about myself. If somebody comes to me and they're like, "Hey Ryan, can you write a sales letter to sell this product to pet owners?" I would have to say no. I don't have that mindset, I can't connect with that market, I don't understand it, so I'm just not a good person to serve that market, and that's fine. I don't think there's anything wrong with having pets. It's just recognizing who I am and what my character is. If you have the heart of a servant you're going to go the extra mile, you're going to put in the extra hours when it's required, you're going to be able to do all those things, and I just think it's going to give you an extra edge in business. Besides that, you may never ever come out and say you're a Christian. You may never come out and say anything about Jesus. But people will be able to see the love of Jesus in you, and I think that is important. If you can act out love and be love to people, they're going to see something in you, and who knows where that can lead. Someday they may ask you, "Man, you're always smiling. Why are you always smiling? Or why do you always do this?" and now you have an opportunity to talk about what's behind that.

BEN SETTLE: It's like the Chick-fil-A example – MSG aside – but the servant part. The way Greg explained it to me was a mother had three kids in the car and she was going through the drive-through and it was kind of late. They were closing up, the doors were locked, and they were just about to close the drive-through. She said, "Is there any way I can just eat inside? I'm exhausted. I've been driving all day and my kids are exhausted." Most places would say, "No, too bad," but they opened the door for her out of love. "Come on in." They apparently brought an umbrella out and walked her in, because it was raining. You hear about this stuff and think, "This is almost unbelievable," but that is being a servant.

RYAN HEALY: Yeah, absolutely. Most places would say, "No, too bad, we're closing."

BEN SETTLE: You were talking about the clients that you've been dealing with that try to take advantage of you and add more stuff on there. Had they come to you over the agreed written thing that you'd agreed to and said, "Can you fix this or help this?" that's something you probably would have jumped all over, I'm guessing.

RYAN HEALY: Oh, absolutely. I would have done that right away. In fact, I thought that's what they were going to do. They never included me in the discussions. It only came back later with kind of a bait and switch kind of thing, or that's how it felt to me.

BEN SETTLE: Don't you hate that? Has that happened to you often, or is that just once in awhile – not just getting screwed over, I'm not talking about that, but where clients try to squeeze more out of you than what they asked originally.

RYAN HEALY: Not too often really. I had one client quite awhile ago now. He still has never paid the balance of what he agreed to pay, but he continually tried to do that. He tried to use the contract to negotiate more stuff. Everything's a learning experience. You start to learn, "Oh, I guess I shouldn't have taken this guy at his word. I should have read the contract more closely."

BEN SETTLE: That's a mistake I think everybody makes. Terry Dean has an interesting take on how to do business with someone. I don't know if he's talking about taking clients, but definitely joint venture partners, which in a lot of ways is what a client is. He's like, "I don't do business with anyone who I wouldn't leave my house keys with." Now we can't always apply that in freelancing, because sometimes we don't even know our client till the day before we start the job, but it's a very interesting way to look at it.

RYAN HEALY: Yeah, it is interesting, and I definitely agree with that in principle. If you feel like you trust them enough that you can leave your keys with them, that's awesome. That's an ideal situation. My problem is I'm a little too trusting.

BEN SETTLE: I'm sure you wouldn't leave your keys with a lot of these gurus out there. I was just going by that blog post you wrote. You wouldn't leave the keys with any of them.

RYAN HEALY: Yeah, not with them, but I do tend to be overly trusting with people. It probably depends on your personality, but since I am that way, I do get my keys stolen all the time. [laughing]

BEN SETTLE: Or I lose the house. [laughing]

RYAN HEALY: I lose the house. Have to buy a new house!

BEN SETTLE: How does spiritual warfare affect Christian business owners?

RYAN HEALY: This is a tough question. I will say I believe that spiritual warfare happens. I believe in spiritual warfare. I also believe that in most cases we don't even know when we're engaged in spiritual warfare. Sometimes your spirit is engaged in something and your flesh may not know it. You may sense it a little bit, but you don't really have a clear understanding of what's happening in the spiritual world, and I think that's just because most of us can't hear and see spiritually as well as we would like to. I feel like I've gotten better at identifying things. Like this client I mentioned to you, you said, "Does this happen often?" and I mentioned this client who still hasn't paid me for this project I did. His last name I won't say, but his last name is important because his last name has a meaning. His last name has to do with birth, so when this client came to me, I realized God was telling me something, because of the meaning of his last name. What I got from it was the birth of a new mission. His last name doesn't sound like that at all, so don't try to figure that out, but the bottom line is to me it was the birth of a new mission. That mission for me, I believe, was forgiveness. He was the first client who ripped me off, then I got a string of them that did the same thing. But to me I look at it and it wasn't like, "Oh Ryan, you're a terrible copywriter," or anything like that, it was, "God brought these people to you specifically so you could be involved in the new mission that you have right now." I believe that was obviously a spiritual thing. I believe I was engaged in spiritual warfare in those cases. I prayed for those people and did the best that I could consciously to deal with it.

I'm not so much into the whole Frank Peretti version of spiritual warfare. Frank Peretti wasn't a teacher, he was just a popular Christian author. He wrote *This Present Darkness*. He was the guy who basically made the whole idea of spiritual warfare popular. He wrote *The Oath*, which is another Christian book, and some other stuff. I'm no expert at this and I think it's important to be in tune with what's happening. When weird stuff starts happening in your business or even in your life, I think you do need to go to that next level and say, "Okay, spiritually what's going on here? What do I need to do to deal with this?" There was a time recently in my family where I was recognizing some spiritual warfare going on with my kids. I was like, "Man, this is really strange," so I began to pray about it and talk to my kids, and the problem went away. It was gone. I think there are also seasons of warfare. I don't think it's something that's necessarily just constant. I think that's where Christians go wrong sometimes. They think they're always being attacked, like every day.

BEN SETTLE: Every little thing, like they stub their toe.

RYAN HEALY: "Oh, Satan busted my toe." I don't give Satan that much power really.

BEN SETTLE: I don't either. In fact, I don't understand why anybody would. Gina Parris put it this way. She said too many people make their devil bigger than their God.

RYAN HEALY: Oh, totally.

BEN SETTLE: Just reading through the scriptures it's pretty obvious that if you have the Holy Spirit in you then you can't really be affected by demonic forces, unless you let your guard down and that armor isn't on all the way, which is probably where we all go wrong. We all slip – the faith and all that – things slip. It's like if you take that breastplate off, now you're kind of vulnerable. If you take that helmet off you might be vulnerable there. If you don't have the sword of truth, the Word, how can you fight back? You can't. That's just my own personal view of it. I wouldn't debate anybody on it or anything. God likes to use these war terminologies a lot through the Bible to teach. It just seems to me that if you don't have a full suit of armor on, even in real life, then you're more vulnerable than if you do have the whole suit of armor.

RYAN HEALY: Absolutely. The subject of spiritual warfare fascinates me. You hear some pretty amazing stories about how things happen in the spiritual realm first and then they happen in the physical realm later.

BEN SETTLE: Just go back to the book of Daniel. He was praying and all that. The angel appears and he's fighting the prince of Persia and the other one's fighting the prince of Greece.

This stuff's going on, we just don't see it, like you said. We can take this really deep. There's this scholar named Michael Heiser. He's a Hebrew scholar, one of these really high-level ones. He just loves reading through the Hebrew and studying the context of the idioms and all that. He talks about the divine council, which is mentioned in one of the Psalms, where you see the word *god* with a little g. If you go back to some of these early verses when the separation of the nations was going on in Genesis – and this is his teaching; again, I'm not going to debate this with anyone, I just find it fascinating – the text seemed to say that God was giving up the nations to different angelic beings, I guess is how you'd want to put it. He kept Israel obviously for Himself, to be the light and to show the way. Even when you see wars going on between other nations, that could be two different angelic entities battling, and it's showing up. We see even the enemies of Christianity fighting each other. They're prideful beings, probably. Why wouldn't they? Who knows, this is just all conjecture obviously, but I find it really fascinating on all these different levels.

RYAN HEALY: I certainly believe there are geographic principalities, or principalities who have control over certain regions. One of my friends believes that even today we're fighting the same battle that Daniel fought. There's a verse that says Jesus was crucified from the foundation of the earth. Then there's also the verses that God says, "I am the alpha and the omega. I know the beginning from the end," or even the verses that talk about, "I knew you from before you were born. I knew the number of hairs on your head." That kind of stuff is like, "Wow!"

BEN SETTLE: Ray Edwards and I were talking about this when interviewing him for this book, how a lot of Christians don't even really believe in the supernatural. They're not even really

Christians. They question a lot of the supernatural stuff that happened in the Bible. "That couldn't have happened. Nah, that's just allegorical."

RYAN HEALY: There's actually a group of people, and I forget their names, but they basically have created a version of the Bible where they deleted anything that they thought was impossible or couldn't be true.

BEN SETTLE: Isn't that the Jesus Seminar?

RYAN HEALY: Maybe it is, I don't know. It's really funny because they came up with this Bible that's this really thin book. [laughing]

BEN SETTLE: It's like one page. [laughing]

RYAN HEALY: "This is the only part of the Bible that's true. The rest of it's fake." Well, how did you figure that out?

BEN SETTLE: Ryan, this has been fun. Where can people get more info on you and find out more about what you're up to and what you're doing?

RYAN HEALY: I'll give out my blog, which is www.RyanHealy.com. That's my business blog and I write about business and copywriting and advertising there. Depending on when you're reading this or listening to it, I currently offer a free 39-point copywriting checklist when you opt into my email list, so there's that. Then if you want to know more about my Christian beliefs you can go to a website called www.SecretEvangel.com. Evangel just means 'good news.' It's the root word for evangelism.

BEN SETTLE: I'm going to ask this real quick because someone listening to this might not know what copywriting is. What does that mean and why would they want that free critique?

RYAN HEALY: There's a lot of definitions. It's persuasion in print. It's basically conveying a sales message via the written word. That's what copywriting is. The reason that copywriting is important is because it's your sales message that often determines whether you get a customer or not. When you write an ad, the words that you say have a big influence on whether people buy your product or pay for your service. That's what copywriting is, and the 39-point copywriting checklist just gives you a list of things that you can check for in your own ad or sales letter that you've written. You can say, "Oh, did I include this? Did I include this?" and it'll just help you strengthen that sales letter or ad on your own.

BEN SETTLE: Finally, there's people who are reading this book who are already Christians, obviously, but there may be people reading this who aren't yet Christians. Maybe they've been on the fence. Maybe they are simply curious about Christianity and looking into it and they somehow found this book. What would you say to them?

RYAN HEALY: That is a fantastic question. Personally I think it's pretty simple. You just acknowledge that Jesus is Lord and King of your life and recognize that you're a sinner and that Jesus died for your sins. Then ask Him to forgive you and to come into your life. I think becoming a Christian is as simple as saying, "Hey Jesus, you said all this stuff. Prove it to me. Come into my life and prove it to me," and just let the details work out over time. I don't think it needs to be real complicated.

I would like to share a couple of verses, because a lot of times people who are not Christians have heard things about Christianity that may have turned them off, so I wanted to share a couple of verses which I think are the real good news. Without getting into too much detail, I'll just share these verses from my point of view. One verse is Colossians 1:16 where it says, "All things have been created through Him and for Him." In Colossians 1:19-20 it says, "For it was the Father's good pleasure for all the fullness to dwell in Him and through Him, to reconcile all things to Himself, having made peace through the blood of His cross, through Him I say whether things on earth or things in heaven." In First Timothy 4:10 it says, "For it is this we labor and strive, because we have fixed our hope on the living God, who is the Savior of all men, especially of believers." In Romans 14:11, "For it is written, As I live, every knee shall bow to Me and every tongue shall give praise to God." These are pretty positive things. You have all things were created through God and for God. He says that through Jesus he reconciles all things to Himself. God is the savior of all men. Every knee shall bow. Then Jesus himself before He died said, "And if I am lifted up from the earth will draw all men to Myself." With that I would say if you don't know Jesus, I think you should get to know Him. He's a pretty good guy. No secret handshakes, no church membership – Jesus is not a club or a denomination or a church or a church building. He is who He is.

BEN SETTLE: Thank you very much, Ryan. I really appreciate it.

Christian Business Bonus Tip #5

Following is a Bible-themed article written to my website newsletter subscribers. To join my free mailing list and access 700+ pages of advanced web marketing tips, go to:

www.BenSettle.com

The Bible's Best-Kept Marketing Secret

I KNOW some people are freaking out right now.

"Ben how DARE you! I didn't join your list to learn about the Bible! I want secularized marketing info! What the hell are you doing??? Quit trying to push your beliefs on me!"

If that's you, chill, dude.

Even the most hardcore "fire breathing" atheists I know can use the info below to increase sales (and by a LOT).

So just relax, take a deep breath and let's. get. busy.

Here's the scoop:

Many years ago, a smart Biblical scholar named EW Bullinger wrote a book called "How To Enjoy The Bible".

One of the best parts is this (paraphrased):

> When we come to ask ourselves ... "Where did I learn this?" "How did I get this?" "Who taught this to me?" it is astonishing to find out how much we have imbibed from man, and from traditions; and not the Word of God. All that we have learned...must be tested and proved by the Word of God. Where we find it is true we must learn it over again, from God. And where it will not stand the test of His Word we must be not only content, but thankful to give it up...

And guess what?

This advice is SOLID GOLD when applied to marketing.

Why?

Because, just like with the Bible, there's a lot about marketing that doesn't jibe with typical orthodox "doctrine" (and especially goo-roo doctrine).

Happens all the time, too.

It even happens with the old school marketing geniuses.

There is, for example, something Claude Hopkins emphatically taught that I now profitably do the exact opposite of.

If you test, you've likely seen this phenomena, too:

Where doing the **opposite** of what you're "supposed" to do yields more sales and profits.

Let's face it — every market is different.

Every marketer is different.

Some things may work better for you due to your unique experiences, talents, product and market than they would for me (and vice versa).

Which is why it's vital to test everything.

Yes, even the "set in stone" stuff.

Otherwise, if you stubbornly cling to "rules", and never color outside the lines once in a while, you're almost certainly stepping over the proverbial dollars to pick up pennies.

And that particular marketing "sin" is unforgivable.

Ben Settle

For over 700 pages of advanced web marketing tips and secrets, go to www.BenSettle.com

The Business Of Forgiveness

Interview with Ray Edwards
www.RayEdwards.com

BEN SETTLE: Ray, how did you first get started in business, and what were some of the challenges that you faced along the way?

RAY EDWARDS: The whole story, which I hardly ever really talk about, is that I grew up in an entrepreneurial family, so I was exposed to this culture of being in business for yourself and what that life was like. Normally when I answer this question, I just talk about how I started my copywriting and consulting business, but I was thinking about this before we got on this conversation. I realized that the real story was starting with being a child and growing up around a grandfather who ran two businesses. He actually had an auto shop, where he did tune-ups and rebuilt carburetors, and then when he got done with a car job, he would use that greasy GoJo stuff to clean off his hands. Then he would take two steps up from the garage into his bookkeeping office, where he ran a bookkeeping business and kept books for coal miners in Eastern Kentucky. He would put on his little bookkeeping visor with the green plastic brim, and do books until the next car job came in. He had the freedom to decide when he was going to take days off and when he was going to be closed. I really caught that idea as a child, that this was how you were supposed to live your life. So when I got my first job in the radio business as a disc jockey, I was shocked to discover that there was a schedule that I was expected to keep. I loved radio and I really enjoyed it a lot. I didn't like the 'working for somebody else' part of it, so even while I was in radio I was constantly looking for a way to start my own business and be independent of someone else's schedule and expectations.

I actually tried the Amway business for awhile and I learned a lot. I don't know that I recommend the multi-level business to everyone, because it's definitely got some challenges, and there have been some abuses in that business. Anyone who has ever tried to do a network marketing or multi-level marking business knows what I'm talking about, but I did learn a tremendous amount. I have friends who are still in that business and are doing remarkably well. I think there are great things about it, but I think you have to be a mature, solid, psychological person who knows who you are and who you are spiritually, or you can get yourself into a lot of trouble. Anyway, I was not at that place of spiritual and psychological maturity when I tried it, and while I did not get myself into a lot of trouble, I did get myself into some trouble. From the standpoint of keeping a good balance of family, business, spiritual values and so forth, I got a little bit off track. I was at least mature enough to recognize at the time, "Ah, you know, some things about this are not working out so great." So I opted out of that business. I didn't know this at the time, but I started an information marketing business. I didn't know what it was. I knew that, as a radio personality, I relied on certain sources of information to put together the content for my show every day. I thought, "I'm going to be the guy who puts that information together for other people and charges them for it on a monthly basis." I started what was called a show prep service, where I put together all this information every day. I was doing it for my own show anyway and it was just stuff like This Day in History and Famous Birthdays, and jokes about the current events of the day. Every day, for my own show, I was writing material and I thought, "Well, what if I just syndicated this and wrote it for other people and they paid me for it?"

So I started this show prep service called, of all things – it was a brilliant title, so pause with me now as we reflect on its brilliance – "Radio Show Prep."

BEN SETTLE: Very creative!

RAY EDWARDS: Oh yeah. I was nothing if not creative. I had a website at RadioShowPrep.com and I was trying to think how I took payments. I actually got a merchant account, back when it was hard to do. I got this course from Cory Rudl and there was a place you could go in his course to apply for a merchant account. I think I paid about $600 in application fees. It was just crazy stuff. I made a little bit of money, but I did this for over a year, every day. I had a publishing deadline every day. I was doing a morning radio show, so I would get up at 4 AM, go in, do the radio show, then I had stuff to do around the radio station until 2-3 PM usually. Then I would go home and take a nap, and then I would get up, have dinner with my family, and then I would be back at the computer writing show prep for my show the next day and also for my subscribers. It really got to be a grind. It was killing me. I actually wound up selling that business to someone else for $4,000. It wasn't quite enough to retire on. And then I sold a couple of eBooks. One of them was on "How To Get Out of Debt." That was the one that made the most money, which is weird, because if you think about it, I was selling a product to people who didn't have any money. But the "get out of debt" market is full of people who will pay you money on how to stop paying other people money. It's just a weird thing. And through that, I discovered marketing online and Internet business, if you will – the information marketing business online. I figured out that I was really good at writing copy and I was really good at direct marketing skills, so I started doing that for other people. And that's really how I started my Internet marketing, as a copywriter/consultant/marketing strategist kind of business.

That's how I got started. Looking back at all of this, it seemed to people that I was an overnight success, because what people see is the external story. I was in radio until 2006, and then I started my copywriting business online at that same time. I went from no one ever having heard of me, to suddenly I was the guy who wrote copy for all these big gurus like Armand Morin and the *Chicken Soup for the Soul* guys, Jack Canfield and Mark Victor Hanson, and Alex Mandossian, Jeff Walker, Rich Schefren and Matt Bacak – just about anybody in the Internet marketing community that you can name. I've written quite a bit of copy for Frank Kern and Ed Dale. It's been a crazy ride. People say, "Wow, you went from a nobody, never heard of you in 2005, to by the end of 2006 you've written for everybody and everybody's recommending you. How did you do that?"

The reason I told that long story leading up to that is that really, that is the story of my 'overnight' success – starting from the time I was 14 years old, trying to figure out "How can I be in business for myself?" Overnight success takes decades. That's the message. Thank you very much, have a good evening. The challenges that I got along the way – and this is what got me thinking – were mostly in my head. I read a book recently by a guy named Danny Silk, called *Culture of Honor*. It's really written for people in the church, so it's not really about entrepreneurship. But what I took from it was this great chapter on how we think economically affects how we behave in every other way. Silk makes these distinctions, and I think I've actually modified them somewhat from his book. If you go back and read the book, you're going to go, "How did Ray get that out of that book?" I apologize in advance. There is lower-class thinking. And by the way, this is not about your value as a human being, so don't get your feathers all ruffled, thinking "Well, how come he's calling me low class?" That is not what I'm saying. I'm just saying that economically, lower-class thinking sounds like this:

"Wealth is limited, a few people have all the marbles, and the rest of us suffer. I'm thinking only about today or maybe to my next paycheck and how am I going to pay for my groceries next week.

"I'm only thinking about the immediate circle of people that I'm familiar with – my coworkers, my family, and a few friends. That's all I'm thinking about." It's a very limited view of the world.

Middle-class thinking is a step up from that. The middle class mentality tends to be that hard work produces money. "If I work harder, I make more money. Maybe next year we can build that additional bedroom onto the house or take that vacation or buy that boat." I may be saving for my retirement. My thinking about other people extends beyond my immediate circle. It extends to my neighborhood and my city. Upper-class thinking sounds like this. "Managing other people's hard work produces money. If I can manage a bunch of middle class people to do a good job, I'll be able to produce more money." Consequently, the upper-class mentality tends to produce a higher income, but you're still thinking about income and a paycheck. You're thinking about the 5-year plan and investing for retirement, instead of saving for retirement. Now instead of hoarding money, I have money that's working for me and growing. And I'm thinking about more than just my neighborhood and my city; maybe I'm thinking about the country, the United States of America. I'm thinking about Presidential and Congressional politics and things like that. Most business owners, myself included, get kind of stuck between this middle class and upper class thinking. That's what I was really doing all those years, even in the beginning of my copywriting and consulting business. I was thinking first about doing hard work that produced money. Then I was thinking about managing other people's hard work that would produce money.

But wealthy thinking sounds like this. "Ideas that benefit the most people multiply resources." So suddenly you're thinking about more than just a big paycheck or a big score on a product launch or something like that. You're thinking about ideas benefitting more people, multiplying resources for everybody, not just for me. You're thinking about the next generation and beyond, not just about your immediate friends and family or your kids, or even your city or your country. You're thinking about the next generation on this planet. You're thinking about how you can equip a movement or steward resources so that you leave them bigger than you find them. And you're thinking about God's Kingdom, and how to bring that to the earth, because you're coming from a place of wealth. I'm not talking about just your bank balance. I'm talking about how you think about life, and how you do life. A real transition for me lately that has really made a huge difference in my business is adopting a wealthy mindset. It freaks people out when I talk about this, because I know that a lot of people immediately think, "Oh my gosh, he's gone over to the gospel of prosperity! Jesus loves me and wants me to have a Rolex." That's not what I'm talking about at all. What I am talking about is, if I had this wealthy mindset back when I was in my 20's and I was in that multi-level marketing business, I think I would probably have stuck with it, because I would have seen it differently. So often it's not about the vehicle. It's about how you're driving the vehicle and where you're headed with it.

BEN SETTLE: You mentioned something about being an overnight success. You started when you were 14, but the real success kind of poured on very suddenly. How did that rapid success affect you? It affects some people negatively at first. They become egotistical or whatever. Were you more centered and grounded when it happened?

RAY EDWARDS: Well, I was more centered and grounded. I was not nearly at the place where I am now, in terms of my value system. I had strong values and I was following Jesus at that point. Part of my story that I didn't talk about was just my spiritual journey. I was raised a Christian and when I became a teenager I questioned all of that and I didn't get good answers, so I decided that it was just fairy tales and I turned my back on it. It was only as an adult, after having gone and done all the stuff that the world tells you will satisfy your needs, and realizing that it was all empty. I had money, I had all sorts of adventures in getting my own pleasure through food and sex and various mind-altering substances, and I just tried it basically all. Not every single vice that you could possibly list, but pretty close to the full list. My wife and I had a child, and as he grew older and started asking more questions, we began to think, "We should probably have some sort of value system that we can pass on to this kid." He ended up getting saved and coming home and saying "Hey! I'm saved! How come you guys are not?" or "How come you walked away from all of that?" So to make a long story short, we came back to Christ. Right about the time or shortly before that, I started out with my copywriting and marketing business. I had come back to the Lord in a very real way, and I was more centered. It did throw me for a loop, though – that "sudden success" – because suddenly people were treating me differently. The word "guru" gets thrown around in the Internet marketing and direct marketing world a lot. Guru in its most basic form just means "wise teacher." To be cast in that light by other people can really show up your character – both the good and bad parts. We've all seen people who, as success goes to their head, start thinking that they are a guru and that they have everything figured out. Weird stuff can happen. There's one guru in the self-help business who got so convinced that he had everything all spiritually figured out and that it was all based on him because *he* was the spiritual answer, that he ended up misleading some people in a pretty bad way. People actually got hurt, physically hurt. I'm convinced that, in his heart, he really wanted to help people and do good, but he started believing his own press releases and that leads to some bad outcomes.

I did have my own challenges in dealing with that. I don't think I hurt anyone, but I certainly had to face up to "Just what am I about?" and it led me to exploring what the real foundation of my spiritual and ethical decision making was, what my values really are. It led me to a place where I decided to make a pretty radical decision. I went to ministry school. I know I freaked a lot of people out, because I was part of this high level mastermind group of top internet marketers and we had our mastermind meeting. This is where we all come together and talk about what's happening in our business and what we're about to do and ask what the others think and get their feedback. So all these people are gathered together, and they're great folks, great friends of mine, and they're all talking about how they're going to make their next million or their next $10 million, and I said, "Okay, here's what I'm doing – I'm going to ministry school!" You could have heard a pin drop in that room. Everyone's saying nothing and I said, "Well, I want to keep running my business while I'm in school, but this is what I'm going to do and I just need your feedback in helping me figure out how to do that." It was a big shift. For me that sprung from suddenly having a lot of success and making a lot of money and getting a lot of recognition, and it really got me thinking about what my life was really all about.

I don't want to paint the wrong picture here. I didn't become a multi-dodeca-millionaire. I still have to generate income to pay my way in life and to be able to give and do all the things I want to do. I don't want people to get the wrong impression, but it really forces you to think about what's important in your life. We see people self-destruct, right? They get really wealthy and they go completely off the rails and end up ruining their lives, and that's why – because they didn't see those signals that say "Hey, you need to think about what's important in your life!" or "You're now in a position where you can really get yourself screwed up."

BEN SETTLE: It's interesting when you were telling your story there about how you kind of fell away after your teenage years, but when you had a child, all of a sudden you realized how important it was to have that foundation. There's that Scripture, and I'm the worst when it comes to remembering which Scriptures, but the one where, when you bring up a child the right way and God's way, that they never really fully depart from it. It sounds like you had that lifeline to come back to. Now your own child is going to have that same lifeline when he grows up, and it all started just because you were brought up the right way.

RAY EDWARDS: I totally agree with that, and I think when we accept what the Lord did for us in making the ultimate sacrifice and paving the way for us to be able to spend eternity with Him – when we get 'saved' is the Christian-ese way of saying it – He makes a deposit in us. His Spirit lives inside of us. Even if we completely turn away and start doing bad stuff, He still is there. He's grieved when we do that, but I can look back over the course of my life and see that He protected me and He was making a way for me to come back to Him. It's like the story of Joseph in the Old Testament. His brothers sold him into slavery and told their father that he was dead. Many years later they find out that he is now the leader of Egypt in a time of famine.

When they came to beg for food and relief, they discover that here's their brother and they were terrified that he was going to take vengeance, and he didn't do that. But he said, "What you intended for evil, God intended for good." In other words, He was able to use it for good. I think there's a lot of truth in bringing our kids up in the right way, that God makes a deposit in their life and He always leaves a path open for them to come back home. Some people may be offended by this, but it's kind of like those Motel 6 ads where Tom Bodett says "We'll leave the light on for ya." I think God always leaves the light on for us.

BEN SETTLE: That's a great analogy. You mentioned this School of Supernatural Ministry. What exactly is that and how has that affected your business?

RAY EDWARDS: It's a year-long school, and the curriculum comes out of Bethel Church in Redding, California. That's actually where I am right now. I'm in our motor home here in Redding. We're visiting for just a week and then we're making a three month circuit of the USA.

BEN SETTLE: You're not far from Willow Creek, by the way. With Bigfoot.

RAY EDWARDS: Oh, that's right! I saw that picture of you with Bigfoot.

BEN SETTLE: Just go down 299, you'll find it.

RAY EDWARDS: I'm going to make a note of that, because I'm all about the Bigfoot, man! My wife and I did the ministry school together and we tell people that. They think it's probably all boring seminary work, but it's really training in three realms. There's the intellectual, with the book learning and Bible study and teaching by the instructors of course. Then there's the internal work, which is direct experiences with God. And then there's external work, which is bringing encounters with God to other people.

I'll kind of set up the framework for this before I talk about how it's affected my business, because it really has had a concrete effect on my business, and a good one. Jesus commanded us in Matthew 28: "All authority in heaven and on earth has been given to Me. Therefore go and make disciples of all nations, baptizing them in the name of the Father and of the Son and of the Holy Spirit, and teaching them to obey everything I have commanded you." The first thing to notice is that the church over time kind of modified that mission statement to say, "Go and make disciples *in* all nations." Right? We sort of decided somewhere along the way that, well, we can't make disciples *of* all nations, because that would be everybody, so we might as well make it *in* all nations. But that's not what it says. It says "disciples *of* all nations." That's a bigger mission than I think many of us grew up believing the church had been given. And in Matthew 10, Jesus is sending out his disciples. I believe that includes us, if we're his disciples. This is what he tells them to do: "Heal the sick, raise the dead, cleanse those who have leprosy, drive out demons." You see, this stuff makes the church uncomfortable, because that sounds weird. Cast out demons? Surely you jest! But Jesus wasn't joking. He also said, "Freely you have received; freely give." "Go into all the world and preach the gospel to every creature. He who believes and is baptized will be saved; but he who does not believe will be condemned." Now, this is Jesus talking. He says, "And these signs will follow those who believe: In My name they will cast out demons; they will speak with new tongues; they will take up serpents; and if they drink anything deadly, it will by no means hurt them; they will lay hands on the sick, and they will recover." He doesn't say, "These signs will accompany only the apostles," or "These signs will accompany the special people that are professional religious guys." He says, "And these signs will follow those who believe. They will lay hands on the sick, and they will recover."

He also says, in this same passage in Matthew 10 where He is talking to His disciples, "I am sending you out like sheep among wolves. Therefore be as shrewd as snakes and as innocent as doves." I think it makes us uncomfortable that Jesus – gentle Jesus – said we should be as shrewd as serpents and as innocent as doves. That word shrewd can be wise, crafty, or clever, and I think it speaks to us in the marketplace, as business people. I think that what Jesus is saying is, "I'm sending you out in the world and I am calling you to be as shrewd as serpents." He's not saying we should have the same moral values as serpents; he's just saying be as clever as they are. Learn their ways and be as wise as they are in those ways, and at the same time be as innocent as doves. Doves being innocent, what do they do? Well, the dove in the New Testament symbolizes the Holy Spirit, who is all about love, comfort, and instructing us in the way of truth, and it leads us straight back to the mission that He gave to us as His disciples: to heal the sick, raise the dead, and to destroy the works of the devil, in essence. When I look at my business that way, it makes me examine business practices differently. I'll tell you the result, and we can talk about how this all comes together if you want to, because I've given it a lot of devoted thought. The result for our business has been that I went from working 60–80 hours a week in my business, before my wife and I started this school, to working 20 hours a week, because I had to. Frankly, I stopped doing all the things that I had been doing that I felt were required to promote myself, because I couldn't do them. I couldn't travel to conferences and speak, promote myself and network, and meet people and so forth. I just had to trust that

God would take care of us.

Honestly, Ben, I figured that what this meant was that our income was going to go way down and we were just going to have to have faith that God would take care of us with a low income. What happened was really interesting. What happened was our income actually increased. I worked less, made more money, and became more discerning about what business I was willing to take on. You would think that this would destroy your business, that it would decrease your revenue and profits, eat into your credibility and exposure in the marketplace – but the opposite of all that happened. I believe it happened because God has a very different plan for business people than what we've been taught, especially in the church! When I say 'the church,' I mean the organization that we typically think of as the church. I make a distinction between the worldly manifestation of that and what really is the church, which is the Body of Christ on earth. That may be a deeper topic than we want to get into right now. But I really think that there's a spiritual war taking place and that the front lines of that spiritual war are actually in the marketplace, in the business world.

BEN SETTLE: What are some examples of that? When someone hears 'spiritual warfare,' what does that mean? Is that just mental or are there really spiritual forces attacking you? How does that work?

RAY EDWARDS: It's all of the above. It is mental and it is spiritual forces attacking us. Did you see the movie, "The Usual Suspects"?

BEN SETTLE: I did, yes.

RAY EDWARDS: There's a character in the movie named Verbal, and Verbal says in the movie, "The greatest trick the devil ever pulled was convincing the world he didn't exist." I think that's so startlingly true, even in the church. Especially in the church, because the American church in particular has this sort of sanitized Christianity wherein we don't talk about the devil very much. We think of it as, "Well, that's sort of a medieval idea. You don't really believe there's a devil, right?" It's like this little red guy with a pitchfork running around and poking people, or sitting on their shoulder, telling them to do bad things. That's kind of an ancient idea, right? When we talk about the devil in the modern American church, we're usually talking about a malevolent force of evil that sort of subtly influences us, but that's not what we're taught in Scripture. If we take the Bible seriously, then we have to take a different view of the devil. I believe the first trick the devil perpetrated on the church was to rob her of her power. Jesus said He had all authority. So if Jesus has all authority, how much does that leave for the devil? It leaves none. If one person has all authority, then someone else has none. But the church has decided that the power of the Gospel died in the first century, and so she has adopted a position of powerlessness. And this comes directly back to the spiritual warfare and how it relates to business questions.

Bear with me for just a moment as we kind of walk through this. The church cannot, as a whole, show the world a Gospel of power. Yet, we owe the world a Gospel of power, because Jesus commanded us to give it one. He told us to heal the sick, raise the dead, and cast out demons, and that makes us uncomfortable, because it's kind of freaky – like, "Raise the dead? That can't really be for us today, can it?" And yet, all you have to do is a little Google search on the term 'resurrection,' and you'll find that all over the world there are reports of this very thing taking place.

BEN SETTLE: In his book, *Megashift*, Jim Rutz documents a whole bunch of those.

RAY EDWARDS: Exactly! Now, it doesn't happen so often in America, and I believe that's because in the church we've created a culture of unbelief. There's a guy that I really respect and he has a saying: "The Holy Spirit in America is trapped in the body of unbelieving believers."

BEN SETTLE: Very interesting.

RAY EDWARDS: We say we believe, but if you sit down with most mainstream Christians and say, "When you say you believe, do you also believe that Christians can heal the sick, raise the dead and cast out demons?" and the response you'll get is, "Well, I don't believe THAT! That's not the way it works now!" Well, that's because the reason that they're able to believe that, and what most of them don't know, is that there's a history in the church that has led to that position. The history is one where the church itself, the church leaders, decided that they would construct a doctrine that would explain why they were powerless, why miracles don't happen, why they don't really heal the sick, raise the dead, or cast out demons. A Gospel where Christians can do those sorts of things – through the power of the Holy Spirit, because it's God that's doing the thing, it's not us, and I want to be clear about that – that kind of Gospel, that heals the sick, casts out demons, raises the dead – changes people so completely that it can only be described as being born again. That is a Gospel that people cannot deny. But what the world sees is a church that is very little different from the world itself, in any way that matters. The American church has the same divorce rate as the American populace at large. It has about the same health as the American populace at large, and in fact the quality of marriage and relationships in the church, in some studies, looks worse than the world at large. In terms of charitable giving, the church looks worse than the world at large in America. Jesus said that the world would know us by our love. That's what He said, and that certain signs would follow those who believe. Yet the world identifies Christians as people who hate gays, hate Democrats, and who definitely do not love one another, because we spend all of our time in the church arguing over doctrines.

BEN SETTLE: With all those different denominations, it's terrible.

RAY EDWARDS: Right. What does the word 'denomination' mean? It means 'divided nation.' Think about that. I mean, that's not how Jesus said people would know us. And as for healing the sick, forget it. The church has actually created a theology to explain why that doesn't happen. They call it cessationism. They say that all those miracles, all those that they call 'sign gifts,' ceased in the first century. They were just to establish the New Testament. Well, that's really handy, except it doesn't say that anywhere in the Bible. Go ahead. I looked it up. It's not in there. You can check it out yourself.

BEN SETTLE: Just going back to when the church merged with Rome, they watered everything down – things that didn't even make sense. They're trying to force things to fit some kind of so-called 'realism' instead of what actually happened.

RAY EDWARDS: Exactly right, and yet there has always been a remnant. God's people always have a remnant, a small group of people who are faithful. And there have always been those who practice what Jesus actually taught. If you're reading this and you're thinking, "Well, this kind of sounds weird!" what I would urge you to do is not listen to me – just go and read the Bible. Don't read a study Bible with someone else's notes stuck in it that put across a certain point of view. Just read the Bible itself and see what Jesus actually taught. All around the world, Christians are returning to their first love, Jesus Christ. They are healing the sick and even raising the dead. You said it yourself. There's a book called *Megashift* by Jim Rutz. Jim and I are friends. He has much more documentation about this than is even in his book, about miracles that are happening all over the globe, even in America. And if you think, "Well, why doesn't it happen in America?" it's because we have this culture of unbelief. In the Gospel of Luke it says that when Jesus went to his home town, he couldn't perform any great miracles there because of the unbelief – Jesus Himself. He could heal a few sick people, but he couldn't do any great works because of the unbelief. I believe this is the same thing we see here in America. There is a movie also, called *Finger of God,* which you can Google. I urge you, if you're interested in this stuff, to get a copy of this DVD. It's a documentary that shows in America all the miracles and signs and wonders that are happening in the community of believing Christians. Maybe it won't convince you of anything, but it will change the way you think about these things for sure.

The second trick that the devil has performed is like the first. The devil has convinced Christians that money is evil, so we're all conflicted about it. Now, when you break money down to its most basic definition, it's really just an exchange of value. It's not paper or gold. It's just an exchange of value. It's me saying to you, Ben, "Hey, you have something that I value and I would like to have it. And I have something that you value, so why don't we trade? We'll exchange value." Another way of looking at that is that it's a way of me influencing you. I'm influencing you to do something for me or to give me something, and you're influencing me to do the same. Money really is influence in the natural world. But we get all conflicted because we believe that money is the root of all evil, because we think that's what the Bible says. But that's not what the Bible says. The Bible says that the *love* of money is the root of all evil, but that's not what we hear. Don't get confused here, because a lot of people think that the Catholic Church has a ton of wealth and some denominations have a lot of money, so I'm about to tell you that the church has no economic power. You might be tempted to say, "Well, Ray, that's not accurate." On the whole, when I talk about the church, I'm talking about the Body of Christ – all the believers, all the people who identify themselves as Christians. They have very little economic power as a whole, because they've given it up, because they believe that the love of money is the root of all evil. It's like they're driving with one foot on the gas and one foot on the brake all the time. They get a little success and they feel guilty, because money is the root of all evil, so I shouldn't have this money, so I feel guilty about it. That disables them in their Christian walk, because now they feel like they're sinning, but they still want to have the nice house and the nice car, so their connection with their Creator is cut off. So the church has no economic power. They have no influence. And because they have no influence, the church has really given up its authority in every sphere of society – in the sphere of family, economics, entertainment media, government, arts, science – even religion.

We've come to a point where we just have ceded all the power and authority that we have in all of those realms, and one of the biggest tools of influence in all of those realms is finances. Money. Influence. So the devil has rendered the church, as a body of people, powerless in the supernatural realm, because they can't bring a demonstration of the Gospel's power. They can't heal the sick, raise the dead, cast out demons – they can't do any of that, and they're powerless in the natural realm as well. Money is influence, but the church has made the engine of influence into an instrument of evil, so what this means is that the front lines of the spiritual battle is not in the hands of the clergy. It's not in the hands of the professional religious guys. Jesus said that these signs, remember, would follow believers. So that means it's the job of every believer to bring signs and wonders, to heal the sick, to bring the Gospel of power that changes people's lives. And it means that we need Christians who can be like modern-day Josephs. Joseph was brought into Pharaoh's house as a slave and he rose to a position of influence. He became a leader in the nation of Egypt, but he didn't buy into Pharaoh's pagan religion. He was faithful to God and therefore he rose to great power in the land, because he could be trusted with that great power and influence, and he could be counted on to accomplish God's will. So our job, as Christian business people, is not to just be "successful." For most Christian business people, what this really means is that they're not living out the gospel in a real, full way. They're not seeing a gospel of power in their lives.

Let me just camp on that for a minute. I have friends and I have family who identify themselves as believers. They're my brothers and sisters in the Lord and I love them. And yet, I hurt for them, I ache for them because I see them in pain. I see them anxious and worried. And what are they anxious and worried about? All kinds of stuff that they don't have to be worried about, because Jesus told them, "Don't be anxious about anything, but in everything, through prayer and supplication with thanksgiving, make your requests known to God and He will guard your heart and mind in Christ Jesus." He doesn't say "Hey, beloved, if you don't want to worry about stuff, don't worry about it. Here's a suggestion about what to do." He says, "Don't worry about anything." Why is it, then, that Christians are stressed out and freaked out, just like the world is freaked out? Why is it that they don't feel that they have any power over their circumstances, just like the world doesn't feel like they have any power over their circumstances? What does it say when a modern day Christian, who has a good income and a good house and a family and lives in America, the greatest country on the face of the earth with the most prosperity on the face of the earth, and yet that Christian is overweight, stressed out, has heart disease, anxiety and depression disorder? How can that be, when Christians in the first century were willing to be eaten alive by lions while singing hymns as it was happening? Something is different. The something is the Gospel of power in your life. When you have the kind of spirit in you that those first century Christians had, those martyrs had, you are very clear in what your values are. You're not all caught up in a guilt complex about, "Well, I don't know if I should be successful or not, because I'm just not sure, and I need to take Xanax to deal with all these conflicts that I have within myself!"

No, it's much worse than God calling you to be successful as a Christian in America. I believe He's calling you to break the spirit of poverty over your life and to claim your territory for God, that he destined you to claim and to create massive wealth. Not so that you can have five Rolls Royces and ten Rolex watches and live a life of conspicuous consumption, but so that you can sow into the Kingdom of God. Create massive wealth so that you can be a good steward of that wealth, just like Joseph was, and you can wield influence for the Kingdom of God. You've been given a command by your Lord, if you are a believing Christian, to pray a certain way: "Our Father, who art in Heaven, Hallowed be Thy Name. Thy Kingdom come, Thine Will be done, on Earth as it is in Heaven." And we say that just like I've just said it, in a singsong way of repeating phrases. But when you break it down, what does it mean for God's will to be done on Earth as it is in Heaven? It means a whole different sort of world than we see around us right now. If we're bringing Heaven to earth in that prayer that Jesus wants us to pray every day, that is a spiritual battle. It's a spiritual battle and we're claiming territory for our King, King Jesus. And we have to guard our hearts at all times, so that we're not given over to the ways that the devil will attack us, as successful business owners and creators of massive wealth, because he will attack us. So that is the battle. The battle is guarding your heart so that you can do your duty in bringing heaven to earth, as a Christian business person.

BEN SETTLE: You know what's interesting about this when you're talking about that? In the New Testament, there are a few instances where the devil tempts Jesus and he tells Jesus, "You see all the kingdoms of the earth? I could give this to you" because temporarily, he's kind of the prince of the air. It's his to give right now. It just seems to me like, especially in a country where you have a lot of capitalism or commerce going on, that he would be attacking those sectors quite a bit, as opposed to other countries where there is perhaps a lot of poverty. I'm just going by stories I've heard, that spiritual warfare takes a different face. I'll give you an example. I don't know if it was Calcutta, but it was one of those weird kinds of pagan nations over there in Africa. It's not uncommon for people to see very weird and strange things. Over here, we don't think any of that exists, so he attacks us in other ways.

RAY EDWARDS: Yes, absolutely.

BEN SETTLE: I'm thinking of this example which is really bizarre, but I'm just going to say it. It could have been made up, who knows, but there are stories in one village where kids are being visited by something that tells them to go sleep in the graveyard. We hear this and it's weird, because these kids are actually going to sleep in the graveyard. There's weird evil spirit stuff over there, you know? But over here we wouldn't see that. Instead we're being told that none of that stuff exists, which is almost a worse attack, because now you don't even know it. Like you said, the church is kind of blind to all of this. They're more worried about having their adjustable rate mortgage instead of what's really going on.

RAY EDWARDS: Absolutely, and I think that in these other countries where there is less of a culture of unbelief, we see some of the more weird manifestations and we see them more often than we do in the United States. But they still happen in the United States, I believe. I would like to be clear about that. The devil, this Satan, the Angel of Light at one time, Lucifer, he really only has one tactic. He lies. The Bible says he is the father of lies. He was a liar and a murderer from the beginning. What does he lie about? He lies about who we are and he lies about our identity. It was his very first method of attack. If you think about it, in the Bible in the Garden of Eden, what was the tactic that he used with Eve? When he tempted her, he said, "Has God really said that you would die if you eat the fruit from the tree of the knowledge of good and evil? Has he really said that you would die?" Contained within that question is the planting of the seed of a lie. The lie is that we're something different than what God has told us and have we really heard from God? So he lies about who we are and he lies about whose we are.

If you go back to that story that you were talking about, with Jesus being tempted in the wilderness, there are a couple of interesting things about that. Jesus went into the wilderness for 40 days. He fasted and He was in the desert for 40 days and then it says He was hungry. So that's kind of mysterious in itself, because I think I would have been hungry long before the 40 days was up. But the first thing the devil does is to say to Jesus, "If you are the Son of God, why don't you turn these stones into bread?" Now think about this. If you go back and read that passage, what happened right before Jesus went into the desert? He was baptized and the Holy Spirit descended on Him in the form of a dove, and a voice came from heaven and said, "This is My Son, in Whom I am well pleased." Boom, Jesus goes into the wilderness for 40 days and the devil says, "If you are the Son of God..." Jesus' identity is publicly confirmed by God speaking from the heavens and He is led by the Spirit into the desert for 40 days, and the devil comes to Him and the first thing he says is, "Well, if you *are* the Son of God..." He's calling into question Jesus' identity and he's calling into question what God said – right out of the gate! It's the same tactic he had from the very beginning, and the reason is that he hates us. You have to remember this. Satan is not this nameless, faceless force that is like a force of nature. He's a person and he hates human beings because we are what he wanted to be. What did Lucifer want? He wanted to be like God, and we are created in God's image, and God lives in us if we are believers.

Lucifer is now trapped on this planet of seven billion representations of what he is not and never will be, but he wanted most of all. So he is definitely devoted to destruction. Once he's driven a wedge into your identity of who you are and what God says, we give in to sin because we forget who we are. We give in to sin, and what happens when we sin? We cut off our conduit, we cut off our communion with God. It doesn't mean we're not saved anymore. If we're a believer we cannot be snatched out of His hand. I believe that because I think that's what the Bible teaches and it's pretty clear, but we can cut off our relationship. It's like if you're married and you do something wrong to your spouse in some way. You're still married, but you're not talking. Anyone who's married and has ever experienced that chill that comes into the room when you've goofed up and done something wrong, you know what I'm talking about. The communication lines are cut off. That communion is not there. So we cut off our conduit to God and then we become vulnerable to Satan's temptations and the things that he presents to us. Again, he's not creative. He just has the same old routine that he runs all the time.

Someone other than me, I don't know who came up with this, but they said there are really three Gs that Satan tempts us with: Gold, Glory, and Girls/Guys. It breaks down like this. We start becoming successful in our business, or we're not successful in our business, and the first temptation is gold. That's where we let that love of money creep in and we do things out of greed, avarice or stealing. We shave a little bit off a deal, we do a dishonest deal, we lie, we cheat, or we do something that damages someone else and we know what we're doing when we do it. There are all kinds of ways that the love of money or the love of gold can lead us to do things that are sinful, and they deepen that separation that we have from our communion with God. The second G is glory. That just means that we're not giving credit to God. We take the credit for ourselves and we start to believe our own press releases, like we were talking about earlier, instead of giving credit where credit is due and saying and confessing publicly, "All the success that I have comes from God." That's what Joseph did. He confessed that he got all of his success from God. That's what David did, and what Daniel did. Glory is very seductive, though, because we love to be glorified. And then the third G is Girls (or Guys) and that's where we're sexually tempted to do something that's out of covenant. We defy God's will for our most sacred covenant. We defile our bodies, we defile the bodies of others, and we do it by breaking covenant. It doesn't mean just infidelity or premarital sex. It also takes the form of lust and pornography. People think that Jesus came and we're not under the 600 and some-odd laws of the old covenant, so we have it easier now because everything's forgiven. That's not true. The grace and forgiveness that Jesus brings actually puts us under a higher standard, a much tougher rule, and that's the rule of love and grace. For instance, he says that we know that we're not supposed to commit adultery, but if we look at a young woman with lust in our heart, we've committed adultery with her already. Which is tougher, not committing adultery or not lusting?

BEN SETTLE: Right, especially when your flesh is always telling you, "Hey, look at this! Look at that! Do this! Do that!"

RAY EDWARDS: Exactly. And so if you're a person who looks at pornography – let's be really transparent here – people don't just look at pornography. They're usually doing something while they're looking at the pornography. So you're not just lusting, you're committing an act to consummate that lust in your flesh. You may have never actually had an affair with another person outside your marriage, but if you've indulged in pornography, then you've fallen to the temptation of girls, or guys, or whatever it is that you get your satisfaction from looking at and participating in. Those temptations we become vulnerable to, once we have started listening to the lies of the devil about who we are and about who God is and what His destiny is for us. And why does he do it? He does it because he hates us. If you're a believing Christian and have belief in a gospel of power and God makes a difference in your life, and God's making a difference in your business, and you are taking ground for the Kingdom, you're showing people that through Kingdom principles you're prospering, just like the Bible says you will. I'm not preaching a prosperity gospel, where Jesus is going to buy you a Rolex. I'm saying that if you're a good steward of God's presents and your relationship with God, and you follow His commandments and you're taking ground for the Kingdom, you will be rewarded with prosperity. The Bible says you will. So when that happens, of course, the test is whether you will steward that wealth in the right way for the Kingdom and not for your own selfish pleasures. Satan will tempt you and when you're in that position, he's going to come at you harder, with more spiritual warfare. So what you're going to find, in both my opinion and my experience, is more opportunities for sin, whether it's in the area of gold, greed or glory. You're going to find more opportunities to sin in the area of glory where you say, "Yep, I'm pretty great. Look at me, what I did!" You're going to find more opportunities for sin in the area of sexual violations of God's law. You have got to be on your guard, because these are the areas where spiritual warfare will be brought right to you, right on the frontline.

BEN SETTLE: It's interesting. There's a study Bible, I don't know if you've ever seen it or not, called the Companion Bible by E.W. Bullinger. He did the editing of it. He has an appendix in the back, I think it's Appendix 19, and he talks about how you don't look for the serpent, or the devil, in the areas of crime in the pages of the newspaper, and immorality and all that. You look for them in the pulpit, in the professor's chair, and now I think we could add the business sphere too. Everything you've been saying has added up to that. I interviewed Gina Parris for this book, too. She's an Internet marketer and she does coaching and other things. She brought something up that was very interesting. She was saying how when you have the Holy Spirit in you, the devil is scared of you because you have the Holy Spirit. It's almost like people have been making the devil bigger than their God. It's interesting how if you don't have the Holy Spirit in your heart, you are open to all these things you've been talking about, big time.

RAY EDWARDS: Absolutely. That's one of the sad things about the state of American Christianity. It's changing by the way – I am convinced that it's changing – but so many Christians have a big giant devil and a little tiny God. Part of it springs from this belief that the devil is in charge and all we can do is hold on until we die or until Jesus comes back, and it's something that some people have labeled rapture mentality. It's like the theology of those *Left Behind* novels. By the way, I want to be clear on this. There are a lot of different views about how things will end, and the end times, and what the Book of Revelation means, and the Left Behind camp, and there are a lot of different ideas about all of it. I don't mean to demean anyone. I don't pretend that I have all of the answers. Tim LaHaye and Jerry Jenkins, who wrote the *Left Behind* series, are my brothers and I love them. They're smart, wise, funny, talented guys. I just believe that when we start subscribing to this idea that the devil is in charge and that things are just going to get worse and worse until it all burns, I don't think that's what we're commanded to do. I think we're commanded to disciple the nations, to heal the sick, to raise the dead, to feed the hungry, to take care of the poor and the widows and orphans.

That all sounds like what Jesus told us to pray in that prayer, when we say, "Your Will be done, on earth as it is in Heaven." The prayer doesn't say, "Your Will be done on earth as it is in Heaven, someday, after we suffer for many, many centuries." The Bible is clear that we will suffer persecution, but hear what I just said – it says we will suffer persecution. It doesn't say that the devil is going to run rampant over the earth and have total power over us. Jesus said that He had been given the keys of death and hell. He had been given the keys of the Kingdom. It's His! He says He has been given all authority. That means that

Satan has how much authority? None. He has no authority, so we shouldn't have a great big devil and a little bitty God. We should have a great big God who empowers us to do what he commands us to do: destroy the works of the devil.

BEN SETTLE: To switch gears a little bit, you're writing a book on forgiveness. How did that come about?

RAY EDWARDS: Well, I had to live it first. I experienced a betrayal, which I talk about. I'm writing the book online, actually. This has been an interesting exercise all in itself and I'll maybe talk about that a little bit later if you want. The genesis of it was that I uncovered this betrayal that happened a number of years ago. As you're hearing me talk about it right now, I'm going to make one thing clear. I have disguised the details of the betrayal, because it's important to me that the people who did what they did to me are not exposed. Outing them or exposing them to judgment by other people, or embarrassing or humiliating them in any way would completely go against my beliefs about what forgiveness is all about and what we're commanded to do in terms of forgiveness. I say all of that just because if you know me or you're familiar with me, or you're reading and you're trying to figure out who it was or what they did, you're not going to be able to figure it out, I promise you. Nonetheless, it is a true thing that happened, and even though I changed the details around so that you wouldn't be able to figure out who I'm talking about, it's a true story.

I discovered years later that these individuals had betrayed me. They were in a position of real trust with me and they robbed me. They stole from me and they did it in a very big way. What they did was illegal and I was really hurt. I thought we were friends. We had remained friends over all those years. To find out what they had done and how they had carried on for years in the face of all of that and just continued to pretend that nothing had changed, that nothing was wrong, that we still had that same quality of relationship that we had before they betrayed me, it was really a shock to my system. I actually said that I forgave them. But the truth of it was I was being eaten alive by these feelings that I was having, because it really wounded me in terms of whether I felt like I could trust people, and how it was possible that I thought I knew people and I didn't really know them at all. We've probably all had that experience where we've heard that such and such a person committed some act, and our first response in many cases is to say, "Well that's not possible! That person could never do that!" This was a case where I would have said that person could never have done what you just described, and yet from their own lips I got the confession, "Well, yes, I did it." It was just devastating to me. I was experiencing all sorts of emotional fallout from this. My wife, in her wisdom as I was talking to her about this, said, "You know, you have to forgive them." And I said, "Well, I have forgiven them." And she said, "No, no you haven't! Because if you had, you still wouldn't be having all of these feelings and you wouldn't be hanging onto all of these emotions that you're having. And until you let this go, you're going to be enslaved by it." That led me down a path of really digging into what forgiveness really means. What are we doing when we forgive? I had gone along all my Christian life with this idea that forgiving was a nice thing that we were supposed to do.

I started reading what the Bible actually says about it and I found a shocking difference between what I perceived that the Bible said and what the Bible actually says, which I found is often the case. What the Bible actually says is that you don't have a choice. If you're a believer, you are commanded to forgive. Jesus set the example, and He set the bar impossibly high when he was talking about forgiveness on one occasion. I love Peter, because he gives me hope for myself. He was just a big mouth, always letting his mouth get him in trouble.

BEN SETTLE: As imperfect as the rest of us!

RAY EDWARDS: Absolutely. He pops up and says, "Lord, how many times shall I forgive my brother or sister who sins against me? Up to seven times?" And Jesus says – and I have this picture in my head that He's laughing when He says it – "I tell you, not seven times, but seventy-seven times." What He meant by that was, that kind of phrasing in those days was an illustration of as many times as they wrong you. That's how many times you forgive them. You forgive them infinitely. And then Jesus lived that out. He was beaten, spit on, and humiliated. He was ridiculed, mocked and physically tortured. He was killed in the most brutal way that existed at the time that He was walking, alive in a human body on this planet, and what He said while hanging from that cross was, "Father, forgive them, for they do not know what they are doing." He commands us to forgive in His Word. In the Lord's Prayer, as we were talking about earlier, it says, "Forgive us our sins, as we forgive those who have sinned against us." That seems pretty clear. It actually says in Scripture that if we don't forgive people who wrong us, our Father in Heaven will not forgive us. Well, that's pretty tough! What's up with that? What's up with it – and I don't want to get into a huge theological discussion about can you lose your salvation, because I don't believe you can – but what I do believe is that the Bible is clear about in heaven we will be held accountable for what we did on earth, even as believers. And some will be rewarded, and others will not be rewarded.

Jesus tells us, and most people are familiar with this passage, where He says, "Do not store up for yourselves treasures on earth, where moths and vermin destroy, and where thieves break in and steal." What they often don't hear quoted is the next sentence, which says, "But store up for yourselves treasures in heaven." So what is treasure in heaven? I mean, He said to do it, so it must be real, right? What is it? It's rewards, and those rewards stem from following Jesus' commandments, and one of those commandments is to forgive. I think that through my journey of forgiveness, I really studied this out and I came to the realization that I believe for me and I believe for others as well, that one of the chief ways that our conduit or communion with God, with the Holy Spirit, with experiencing God's presence in our lives – one of the chief ways that gets blocked is through unforgiveness. Some people call it 'offense.' It doesn't have to be a huge betrayal like the one that I experienced when those people stole from me. It can be as simple as you were offended by the way you were treated or spoken to by your pastor, or because the church chose the green carpet for the lobby instead of the brown carpet that you wanted. I say that kind of facetiously, and we chuckle, but I think the reason that we're laughing is because we know it's true. Churches split over stuff like this. I think this is one of the top problems in the church. It's one of the top ways that we get cut off from communion with God, and so we stop doing what God commands us to do.

Think about how that happens. If Satan can get us to question our identity and not understand who we are and not understand Whose we are, then we're not going to exhibit the fruit of being disciples of Jesus, because He said, "Here's how they'll know you're following me, by your love for one another." If we love one another, we don't harbor unforgiveness in our hearts. I just felt this call from God to share what I had learned about forgiveness and to share it in the form of a book that I'm writing. I'm doing the scariest thing a writer can do: I'm writing the chapters live as I go and putting them on the web and asking people for feedback. That'll toughen you up!

BEN SETTLE: What do you mean exactly when you say "radical and unrelenting forgiveness"?

RAY EDWARDS: Apparently it means that the first thing I need to do is pick words that are easier to say, because that's a bit of a tongue twister – "radical and unrelenting." It means forgiving like Jesus forgave. It means not trying to do what the church has done over the centuries, which is to explain away the tough parts of the Bible. We don't want to deal with the fact that Jesus said to heal the sick, raise the dead and cast out demons, because that just sounds weird. We don't want to deal with the fact that Jesus says, "Forgive your enemies and pray for those who despitefully use you, and bless the people who curse you." We say that, and it sounds nice, but when you break it down, what does that look like, if I bless the people that curse me? Well, people that curse you are not just casual people that you have a little bit of a tiff with at work. They're cursing you! It means they hate you. And Jesus says you're supposed to bless them. You're supposed to pray for them. Radical and unrelenting forgiveness means not trying to explain away the Sermon on the Mount, where Jesus says, "If anyone slaps you on the right cheek, turn to them the other cheek also." In that culture, slapping someone on the cheek was more than just being physically struck by another person. It was an ultimate sign of disrespect. It's how you treated a slave.

BEN SETTLE: That's very interesting, for anyone who thinks that means you don't protect yourself if someone attacks you.

RAY EDWARDS: It's a complete insult. What I believe the Lord was saying when He said "turn the other cheek to him," was be humble enough to not have your ego invested in them insulting you and treating you badly. Jesus said, "If anyone wants to sue you and take your shirt, hand over your coat as well. And if they ask you to go one mile and carry a burden, go the extra mile." In that culture, again, this was a way of being disrespected, of being treated like you were subservient in some way. The Roman soldiers had the legal right to ask any of their subjects, such as the Jews, which was who Jesus was talking to, to carry their burdens for them for a mile. Jesus was saying, "You're required by the law to carry the burden for a mile, but go an extra mile. Carry it for the second mile." It means letting people off the hook for having done you wrong. We are forgiven by Jesus. He paid the price for every sin we ever committed, because God is a loving God who doesn't want to hurt or punish anyone. But He's also a just God and He cannot let sin go unpunished. So He has a conundrum: what does He do with us sinful creatures, whom He loves and doesn't want to punish. There has to be a payment for sin. Why? I don't know, because I'm not God and I didn't set the system up. That's a mistake that we make. We're like, "Well, God, if You just explain to me why all this stuff works the way it does, I would be okay with it." Like He needs us to ratify his decisions. He's not just a big one of us; He's other than us and so He set this system up and there has to be a payment for sin. Jesus paid the price for every sin you committed or ever will commit, and every sin I've committed or ever will commit. We treasure that.

I treasure the fact that I'm forgiven. Every evil, despicable, horrible thing that I've done, every teeny, tiny little transgression that I've done, every sin that I've ever committed, every sin that I will ever commit, Jesus has paid for because He loves me and because He gave Himself for me. I love that! I'm overwhelmed. I'm blown away. I'm completely undone by that. And then I realize that He says to me in His word that I need to have that same spirit of forgiveness for everybody else. And that wrecks me. How do you do that?

To me it's like what Jesus said when He said to His disciples, "It is easier for a camel to go through the eye of a needle than for someone who is rich to enter the kingdom of God." Again, the church has tried to explain that passage away. I'm sure you've probably heard the story that "In the ancient city of Jerusalem there was a gate that was called The Eye of The Needle and a camel was too tall to pass through it, so it had to get down on its knees and crawl through the gate. And that's what that means, that a rich man's got to get on his knees." That's a great story, except for the fact that it's not true. There never was such a gate. Camels did not get on their knees to go through the gate. That's completely made up. What Jesus meant was that it's easier for a big, giant animal like a camel to pass through the tiny hole in the eye of a needle than it is for a rich person to get into heaven. That's what He meant. He said what He meant, and He means what He says. He's like that – He's God. What also doesn't get quoted is what the disciples said to Him next. They were completely blown away. They didn't have the New Testament, all they had was the Old Testament, and their theology was that if you were in God's will, God would prosper you. He would make you rich, like He did for Abraham. That's what they believed, because that's what their Book taught them. When Jesus said that, it's like He unraveled everything they believed about how you got blessed by God. So they said to Him, "Well, then who can be saved, if that's true?" They were in despair. And Jesus said, "With man, this is impossible. But with God, all things are possible." I believe it's the same way with forgiveness. It's impossible for me to let go of the hurts and wrongs that have been done to me. It's impossible on my own strength, but through the power of the Spirit that lives inside me...

Again we come back to that powerful Gospel that actually makes a difference in your life, that affects the way you live, that affects your ability to deal with the problems that come your way, and through that power I can let people completely off the hook, just like Jesus lets me off the hook and just like I want Him to let me off the hook. Not only that, I can bless them, like He told me to do. I can look at those people who stole from me and I can let them off the hook. I can pray to God and say, "God, they stole from me and I forgive them. I ask You, Lord, please forgive them as well. They didn't know what they were doing. They didn't know the impact that it would really have. They were misled and misguided and I want you to bless them.

"I want you to bless them financially. They stole from me financially and I want you to bless them financially, way out of proportion, not only like they never sinned, but like they did something good. That's what I want you to do for them, God, because that's what I would want you to do for me."

Radical, unrelenting forgiveness doesn't mean that consequences don't still exist. If someone committed murder, for example, and they were forgiven by one of the victim's family, or by the entire victim's family, just forgiven, they would still probably suffer the consequences of the legal system. Forgiveness doesn't mean escaping consequences. In many cases the consequences won't still exist, because you'll have the power and the authority to release them from the consequences. But forgiveness does mean that vengeance is not our business.

In the church we have all kinds of sneaky ways to get around that. I would do this: "God, so and so really did me wrong there, but I forgive him and I just turn him over to You, God," which was actually my code language for saying, "God, You go get him and You kick his butt good. You really mess him up for what he did to me. I know You will, because you're a good God and you'll make it right." That's not forgiveness. When the Lord says, "Vengeance is Mine," what He's saying is, "I will deal with it. It's none of your business." Jesus said that if you come to the temple to make your sacrifice – and of course we don't make temple sacrifices anymore but we do worship, we do make sacrifice, we worship our Lord as believing Christians – but Jesus said if you have something against your brother, such as unforgiveness in your heart, you are to leave your sacrifice and go and make things right with your brother before you come back before God. Wow! Like I said, we have done a marvelous job of watering down and explaining away the parts of the Word of God that we don't like or that we think are too hard. We first disempowered the Gospel and we said, "We don't heal the sick anymore, that was only for the first apostles, and we don't raise the dead and we don't do all that stuff. We're just basically waiting for the rapture and things are really going to go to hell in a hand basket between now and then. So, anybody else want to be a Christian with us?"

BEN SETTLE: One of the questions I was going to ask you've pretty much answered, but even someone now who has been wronged a lot, like you, or maybe violently and physically attacked or raped or something – how do they deal with this? Let's put it this way. If someone has been to the point of being on the verge of insanity because of this, do you recommend just giving it all to God, praying about it and do some serious reading of the Scriptures on these things? I know that there are people who would hear this and say, "Well, he doesn't know exactly what I've been through!" They're probably wondering, "What Scriptures? What can I do?" What can they do, other than just hear this? I'm not sure if I'm asking the question correctly.

RAY EDWARDS: I think you are. I believe that I understand what you're asking me. I have not suffered every injustice that it is possible to suffer, but I have suffered, I think, most categories. I think I do have an understanding. I've suffered violence at the hands of those that I should have been able to trust. I've suffered betrayal and I know those feelings of, "You don't understand what I've been through." I know that feeling and I want to be clear about something. I did not have this epiphany, this spiritual moment, where I said, "Oh! I must forgive everyone! And I have! And now everything is sweetness and light!" This is something that I still have to work at. I have kind of worked out a process that works for me, of some very specific steps that I've gone through, and I'm writing about these on the blog and in the book. Before I get into the steps, let me just say this. The dangerous thing about unforgiveness is that it leads to victim thinking. Victim thinking is where you have this wound that, whether you admit it or not, you nurse and you kind of get part of your identity from it. "I'm a victim of…" whatever it is. "I'm a victim of abuse, I'm a victim of gender discrimination, and I'm a victim of my spouse cheating on me. I was raped, I was physically assaulted. I was stolen from."

I'm not saying that those things didn't happen and that you weren't a victim at one time. But a key distinction to make is, is that thing that you're a victim of, happening right now? For most people the answer is no. It's happened in the past, whether it was last week or last decade, or 50 years ago when you were a child. The question is, are you still holding onto it somehow? Because it's not happening right now, so how is it that it's affecting you? It's not a reality in your present life. Now for someone that is a victim of abuse right now, for example, then my advice is that you need to get out of that situation, and that is a whole different discussion, so we're not talking about that. But what I am talking about is that victim thinking, this whole mentality of "Woe is me, this happened to me, you don't understand how it feels," and nursing it and thinking about it and stewing over it, and even in a lot of cases, going through therapy for years about it. Depending on the therapist you choose to work with, you might be getting someone who helps you deal with it and move on with your life, or you might be getting someone who just helps you to continue wallowing in the pigsty. The latter is a lot more common than the former. This is what I found in my experience and in talking with other people and reading what other people have had to say about this subject. There is a fear that I believe is at the heart of this victim thinking, this holding on to a victim identity. "I was a victim of abuse," or "My husband cheated on me and I've been betrayed," or "My husband divorced me and left me for his secretary," or "Left me with the kids," – whatever the case may be.

Hanging on to that becomes part of your identity, and there's a fear that if you let go of that, somehow you will be a) unprotected and b) the person will get away with what they did. Well, here's the first thing. You can't protect yourself, so you might as well stop trying. I don't mean to scare you, but none of us can protect ourselves. It's so common that it's a proverb. You know the guy who ate healthy all of his life, was a runner, was trim, was never out of shape a day in his life and ended up teaching the nation about aerobics? His name was Jim Fixx. He was a champion of jogging and he died – jogging, of a heart attack. I'm certainly not criticizing Jim Fixx or anyone else who's into health. I'm just saying that we can do all the right things to protect ourselves, and then we're not protected because we live in a world that, let's face it, is not heaven. It's not perfect. The Bible says death will be the last enemy to be defeated, not the first one. My point is that you just can't protect yourself. You have to trust that God will protect you and that He has purposed how things will happen, and that He can turn things to His purpose. You just have to trust His wisdom. That's been my experience.

The other thing is that vengeance is not ours, so being worried that if we don't hold onto the resentment and keep thinking about it and talking about it and telling other people about it, or whatever we're doing to hold onto that resentment, fear, anger or hurt – which are all disguises that unforgiveness wears, by the way – then we feel like they're getting away with it. First of all, they got away with it. They did it, whatever it was. They did it and it's done and there's nothing you can do to undo it. So get over that part. Second, it's not our job to exact the penalty or price for that, and we've already talked about that so I won't spend a lot of time going into it. But here's a question that I've found very useful to ask yourself: What would happen if I let go of this, just for a moment? What would happen? I like that phrase, "just for a moment," because it means that you can have it back if you want it, if you really want your unforgiveness back. But let's just try and think and experiment through this. Whatever happened to you, if you let go of being unforgiving about it, or being afraid, resentful, afraid or debilitated by it – whatever form it takes for you – if you let go of that even for just a moment, what would happen? What I discovered, when I really asked that question and thought about the answer, was that nothing bad happens, because the only thing that happens, happens inside me. And I become free from all those emotions that I was just mentioning – fear, anger, resentment, guilt, hurt – I'm free from all of that if I just let go of it, even just for a moment. When you ask that question, "What would happen if I let go of it, even for just a moment?" it sort of opens up the possibility that maybe you could let go of it, and when you get to that point, there are a few steps. I'll just go through them quickly.

First, feel the feelings that you're feeling. Don't deny the fact that you're angry, hurt, scared, resentful, and guilty – whatever the emotion is that you're feeling. Just feel it and acknowledge it. When I first found out about these people who did me wrong, I wrote them a letter. I never sent it to them. It was 10 pages long when I first wrote it and it was filled with some of the most graphic language I've ever used, because I was very angry at them. But I knew when I wrote it that I would never show it to them, and as soon as I wrote it I felt lighter, because I got it out of my system, and then I destroyed the letter. I didn't just destroy it and then keep a copy on my hard drive. I completely destroyed it so that even I can never get it back. Then I wrote it again, and guess what? This time it was only 5 pages long and it didn't contain nearly the level of vivid language that the first version contained. I went through a few versions of the letter and I destroyed each one. Each one got shorter and each one got less emotionally charged. The last letter, which I can just about quote verbatim, said, "Dear Mr. X and Dear Mr. Y, What you did to me really, really, really hurt me. Please don't do it again. I forgive you. Love, Ray." I destroyed that one too, because it was for me. It's for yourself that you do this, it's not for the other person. You don't need the other person to participate. If they're dead, it doesn't matter to your process of forgiveness. If they're not interested in being forgiven, it doesn't matter to your process of forgiveness. Forgiveness does not require the participation of the other individual.

So you feel the feelings that you're feeling. You get them out of your system. That's Step 1. Step 2 is you ask yourself, "Is it possible, is it just possible…" – you don't even have to commit to doing it – "that I could let this go?" The answer is going to be eventually, if you're honest with yourself, yeah, it's possible. It may not be likely, but it's possible. Once you've been able to answer yes, it's possible, the next question is, "Would I be willing to let it go just for a moment?" The key to that is I'm not asking you to let it go – I'm saying ask yourself would you be willing to, and just for a moment. Most people who are wallowing in unforgiveness just don't want to let it go. I'm saying could you let it go for a moment? You can always have it back. You can have back all of the pain and the heartache and the anger and the frustration and the fear and the self-depreciation – you could have that all back in a minute or two, but would you be willing to let go of it for just a moment? Would you be willing to do that? And by the way, your answer may be no, and if it is, fine. Come back to these questions later and try them again. Write a few more versions of your letter, would be my advice.

The next question, once you've decided, "Yes, I'd be willing to let it go just for a moment," the question is when? When would you be willing to do that? That's just an invitation to do it now. It's not a judgment, it's not an order, it's just an invitation. You're just inviting yourself to say, "Okay, I'm going to let go it now just for a few moments." When you can do that, when you get to that space where you say, "Yup, I'll do it now," and you let go of it just for a moment, you're going to feel a release of all that anxiety and all those emotions. For me it was like a flood of the presence of the Holy Spirit, and I think that's the most important thing that any Christian can cultivate in their life, is that real ever-present experience of God Himself within us. I don't mean just thinking a nice thought about it, I mean feeling it physically in your body. When you get to that point where you've released it and you feel that presence of the Spirit, that's the point at which you can pray for that person. You can pray that God will forgive them like you forgave them, and that God would bless them in the very area where they hurt you. If they stole from you, then you bless them in terms of prosperity. If they physically hurt you, then bless them with physical health. If they hurt you in terms of relationship, then bless them in their relationships.

Then the final step is a really important one, and I believe that you need to forgive yourself. I'm not saying that anything that happened was your fault, although in some cases that might be true, and you'll know if it is. In most cases, what I'm talking about is forgiving yourself for being unforgiving, because we know that the Lord commands us to forgive, and we know that when you reach a certain point you're going to realize, "Wow, by holding onto that the way that I was, I was actually doing something wrong. I was damaging myself, I was damaging my connection with my Creator, and I was taking myself off-task. "God has an assignment for me, and instead of concentrating on my assignment I was looking in the mirror saying, 'Oh, you poor pitiful creature.' I was engaging in self-pity."

So forgive yourself, and I believe it's important to do it out loud. As goofy as it sounds, I think it's important to maybe just look in the mirror and say, "Hey Ray, I forgive you for that. Look, you're a human being and you're not perfect, and I forgive you. Jesus forgave you and I pray that you're blessed." If you can go through those steps, I believe that you will find when you can honestly pray for the person who hurt you, and pray that they can be blessed, you can pray for their forgiveness, and you can pray for your own forgiveness, you're going to feel such a release from the clutches of unforgiveness that it's going to be an experience that will be hard to describe in words, that you're going to be so glad that you did it.

BEN SETTLE: We're going to switch gears again a little bit here. In your business career I'm assuming that you've read many books and have bought many courses and attended many seminars. You're like all info marketers. Your bookshelf is probably lined with all kinds of very expensive, in some cases, products from gurus and non-gurus alike. But what things have you learned from the Bible itself about business that you can never find in those other self-help books and business books and all the other how-to books and products?

RAY EDWARDS: The first thing that I would say is I have a hard time separating out categories of our behavior and living in the scripture, because it's all part of one whole piece for me. For business people, it's not just about business, it's about what our relationship is with God. Your first priority as a Christian, I believe, is your relationship with your Creator. We hear that language so much that I think maybe it lost its meaning for many of us, because if pressed, I think most people would be in a bind to explain what they meant by a relationship with God. What I mean is being in such communication with God that you feel that you know His heart on any given subject. You feel that you can ask Him for His help, or you can ask Him for wisdom, or you can ask Him for help with a decision, and you expect to know that you're going to get it. That being said, I feel that things that I have learned from the Bible that I could never find in another how-to book or self-help book, the first one is what I was just talking about. Self-help as a title is pretty revealing, because I don't want to help myself. I've tried and I don't like the job that I did. What I like is having God's help. When you align yourself with the truth that is in God, then life starts doing remarkable things all around you. It responds to the voice of its Creator.

Being in business, I believe, is a sacred commission. One of the things that has really been pivotal for me in this last year being in ministry school is finally reaching a point where I feel that I've seen through the artificial veil between the sacred and the secular. Before I started school I had some really respected friends of mine – you would know their names, probably; very famous individuals – and they made a comment to me. They're like, "You should keep that religion stuff off your blog, because religion and business don't mix." That kind of threw me for a loop, and then during the course of the last year I realized not only do I not agree with that, I completely disagree with it. If your relationship with your Creator doesn't permeate everything that you do, you don't have a relationship with your Creator. You have an imaginary friend.

BEN SETTLE: That's an interesting way of putting it.

RAY EDWARDS: I believe that the purpose of amassing great wealth is to sow it back into the Kingdom. I have a goal that my wife and I have agreed on, and that is we want to reach a point where we become what Rick Warren calls reverse tithers, where we give away 90% of everything we bring in and we only keep 10%. That doesn't mean that we have an intention of living in a cardboard box under a bridge somewhere. It means that we believe we're going to live comfortably – not opulently, but comfortably – and we're going to be able to give great amounts of wealth for the purpose of growing God's Kingdom – glorifying God, not glorifying ourselves. That may take the form of taking a vacation too, by the way.

This is kind of a sidebar and I'll get back to your main question here in a second – but I was listening to somebody that I respect a lot, a guy named Bill Johnson, and he was talking about a vacation that he had taken. I think someone made a comment about it being something of an opulent vacation, and he said, "You know, tell that to the cab driver who got paid a fare because we took that vacation, the airline pilot and the crew of the aircraft that got paid because we took a vacation…" – and I may be misquoting him, and if I am in any way that's a disservice, then I just admit to it and repent for it right now, but I thought his point was well taken. When you go and take that vacation, the crew of that cruise ship or that five-star hotel that you stay in, or that two-star hotel that you stay at – they wouldn't have a paycheck to be able to go take care of their kids and to tithe to their church if you weren't sowing that money back into the economy. So giving to the Kingdom is about tithing and offerings, yes, and it's also about sowing the seed that you've been given back into the ground, if you think of the economy as ground, so that others can benefit from your wealth. Proverbs talks about the man being cursed who won't sell his grain, because the bakers need it to make bread. Wow, think about that for a second.

Other things that I've learned that I believe tie into this theme of business and the Kingdom, if you will, is in the book of Amos the Lord says, "Behold, the days are coming when the plow man will overtake the reaper." What does that mean? Who is the plow man? He's the guy who's out there laboring in the field, tilling the soil to bring in the harvest. It just means that the whole economy is going to get turned upside down. That verse goes on to say that the treader of grapes will overtake him who sows the seed. The one who's treading the grapes is enjoying the fruits of the harvest. The harvest came from the one who sowed the seed, but it says the treader of grapes is going to overtake him who sows the seed. It's saying that the day is coming when people are going to be reaping rewards that are ahead of schedule – ahead of the work that they did to produce the rewards. Now I'm not going to build a whole theology around that right here, but I'm going to tell you I think that's intriguing. It makes you think about what we believe we know about hard work. I've learned that any goal that I set needs to include submission to God. In the book of James it says, "What you ought to say is, 'If the Lord wants us to, we shall live and do this or that,' otherwise you'll be bragging about your own plans, and such self-confidence never pleases God." What does that say to all the self-help gurus who say, "If you can believe it and conceive it, you can achieve it!"

BEN SETTLE: Let's not forget that Napoleon Hill died broke.

RAY EDWARDS: Yeah, exactly. He died a pauper! They don't tell that part of the story.

BEN SETTLE: No, from the stage that doesn't sound too good.

RAY EDWARDS: In Proverbs it says that we should trust in God rather than ourselves for guidance. This goes counter to everything that people in the self-help or the business field teach. Proverbs 3 says, "If you want favor with both God and man, and a reputation for good judgment and common sense, then trust the Lord completely. Don't ever trust yourself. He will direct you and crown your efforts with success." How about that! By the way, some people will say, "Well, that's Old Testament. We're under the new covenant." Yeah, we are, but Jesus said, "I didn't come to destroy the law, I came to fulfill it. Until the end of the age not one jot nor tittle will pass away" – in other words, not one dot of the i or cross of the t will pass away.

BEN SETTLE: The Old Testament is examples for us today. I don't know why anybody would ignore it. There's so much good wisdom in there. It boggles the mind why anybody would not want to read it. It's like saying, "Don't read Proverbs. It's the Old Testament."

RAY EDWARDS: Yeah. All that collective wisdom of God about the principles of how life works, don't read that. One of the key verses when I'm thinking about business success or doing business as a Christian is in the book of Joshua. Joshua 1:8

says, "Do not let this book of the law depart from your mouth. Meditate on it day and night so that you may be careful to do everything written in it. Then you will become prosperous and successful." Hello? That's pretty clear. It's not like, "We must figure out what this means. We must study this carefully to make sure we understand what it means." It means what it says and it says what it means. "Don't let the book of the law depart from your mouth. Meditate on it day and night so that you may be careful to do everything written in it. Then you will be prosperous and successful." That sounds pretty good to me.

BEN SETTLE: We touched upon this a little bit earlier, but what advice do you have for Christians who feel guilty about making money and maybe even selling. They just feel guilty about it. That seems to be a big problem right now I think.

RAY EDWARDS: It is a big problem for a lot of people, but here's the thing. It's not an issue of money, it's an issue of your heart. It's not the money, but it's the love of money. The Bible is full of passages where it instructs the rich to take care of the poor. How can you do that if you don't have money? If we all decided that money was evil and we don't need to have any, then we would be 100% without any money whatsoever. How could we help anybody? When you board an aircraft and they're giving you the safety drill – you've probably heard this example before – the instructions they give you are, "If the oxygen mask drops down, secure your own mask first and then help the person next to you if they need assistance." The reason they tell you that is if you don't secure your own mask, you'll be dead and you ain't helping anybody. I think that's the first thing to understand, that it's not the money, it's the love of money that's the problem. And why do we love money? It's really comes back to those three G's. We think that money will let us pile up gold or significance for ourselves for glory, or it will get us self–

pleasing stuff like sex. I've said this before. The devil really doesn't have any new tricks. He's just got the same old routine that he trots out everywhere he goes. So how do we deal with that?

The first thing I think is important to do is read what the Bible actually has to say about this issue, not what other people have to say. There are guys out there who will peddle to you the gospel of the Rolex, saying that if you just love Jesus He'll send you some Rolexes, and I don't think that's the message. There's people out there who will peddle to you the message of poverty, and I definitely don't think that's the message. People talk about, "I don't want any of that health and wealth gospel!" Well, okay, but I don't want any of that sickness and poverty gospel. Somewhere there's got to be some truth, and the truth will set you free. A wise, wise person said that. I think the thing to do is to cultivate the presence of God in your life. Jesus said that the Holy Spirit would guide us in all truth, and I have learned over the course of the last year or so to really take that literally. I ask the Holy Spirit for guidance about everything. What I recommend doing is get into the Word. God put His mind into a book for us for a reason, so He could speak to us about what's on His mind. So I think the first place to start is in the Word, and see for yourself what it says about these things. Don't take my word for it, don't take someone else's word for it. Read it for yourself, and when you're reading it, when you run into something that puzzles you or you don't understand or it's not clear to you, simply ask the Holy Spirit. I would suggest get yourself a little journal or a big journal, whatever you prefer. Just get some kind of permanent record. Only you're going to read it. Nobody else will read it. When you hit on some scripture or some question that you don't know the answer to, write the question in the journal and just pray. It doesn't have to be elaborate. There's no magic prayer. Just say, "Holy Spirit, I don't understand what this means. Could you show me the answer to this."

Maybe it'll come in that instant, maybe it'll come later that day, maybe it'll come that week through your Bible reading or through something that somebody else says, but when you get the answer, go write it down underneath the question and that will become a valuable spiritual journey for you. That leads me to my next suggestion, which is to get into a community of believing believers. What I mean is get around some Christians who believe that the gospel actually makes a difference in your life, that you can expect that God will show up and do the things that He says He'll do in His Word. In the course of this last year, my wife and I have seen some amazing things happen. We've seen physical healings before our eyes at our fingertips. We've seen back pain healed. We've seen people walk in on crutches and walk out without them. We've seen deaf ears opened up. We've seen people relieved of burdens of depression and anxiety and we've seen miraculous answers to prayer. We've seen God's miraculous financial provision for people and for ourselves, so we know that God shows up and does things. People read the Bible and they say, "Where's this God? Where's this God of Elijah or this God of the Book of Acts?" He's where He always been! He's right here. It's available to you. All you've got to do is ask for it.

BEN SETTLE: A few months ago I started tithing to a very, very small ministry. One of the things they do is , they basically go into these new-age, occultic, and UFO conventions and they set up a booth and start leading people to Christianity. They don't have a lot of money. They have regular jobs right now and they have to fund their own travel and all that. They don't even have a physical church. I was able to give what I could. I wish I could have given a lot more when I did, but it was just a little bit over a few months, and he emailed me back and said, "I just want you to know that those checks you sent helped pay for our travel." They went to one of these occult convention-type things. He goes, "We baptized three people, including one new believer." You're thinking, "Holy cow!" This isn't money that's going to put a new wing on a church. This is helping towards saving someone's soul! And you couldn't do that if you weren't making any money. You couldn't be used by God like that, you know what I mean?

RAY EDWARDS: You illustrate my point so beautifully, and that kind of ministry is happening all over the place. I know people who are doing that very kind of thing. In fact, my wife and I are traveling with my son. We're going to Sedona here pretty soon. Sedona, AZ – for those who don't know – is like the world headquarters of occultic new-age stuff. We're looking forward to being able to interact with people and minister to them there. What's interesting about the new-age folks is that – believe it or not – they're actually more open to the gospel as it's presented in the New Testament, with power – they're more open to that than a lot of Christians are. New-age people and occult people are looking for a real experience of the supernatural. It sounds so bizarre for me to have to say this, but so many people in the American church don't believe in the supernatural.

BEN SETTLE: It's scary, actually.

RAY EDWARDS: That's frightening! It's crazy. But you can go to a new-age convention and say, "Hey, would you like to be healed of that broken bone you have, because I can get that taken care of right now." The church's reaction is, "Oh, you're weird, get away from me." The new-age person's reaction is, "Sure, what are you going to do?" One of our folks who helps teach at our school was talking about this guy they were interacting with.

They said, "You know what? He was only one encounter with God away from changing all of his arguments," and that's the truth. You're right. If you weren't in business and weren't making money, you wouldn't have been able to help those folks with their ministry. Would those souls have been saved? I don't know.

BEN SETTLE: I don't know either. Who knows what impact they will have on somebody else in that community. We just don't know. I don't need to know. God will take care of it, but it's one of those things. You bring up Sedona. The guy I was talking about who, incidentally, is in this book (Guy Malone), what he does – and this is going to sound weird even to someone who's comfortable with weird things – it's him and two other guys. One of the guys has worked with the MUFON, the UFO people that go out and investigate UFOs. Guy Malone was an actual abductee as a kid. He was being visited by these entities, so that's what got him into this. He found God through that. It's amazing how many of them are actually being bound up literally by demonic activity right now, and they are looking to be set free, and yet the church won't listen to them. They have nothing to say about any of this. They just pass them off to psychologists or whatever.

RAY EDWARDS: It really is illustrative of the fact that the church in many places is in a state of being filled up with unbelieving believers. Let me tell you, I've got personal first-hand experience with this. If you can put your hands on somebody and you can see Jesus heal them on the spot, that person is open to the gospel. If you look at what happened in the New Testament, the way evangelism happened in the New Testament was not handing out tracts or preaching hellfire and brimstone and scaring people into the Kingdom. They always performed a miracle. They always healed somebody, and then the crowd gathered and people were like, "What just happened?" Or Jesus healed someone, and that person went and told everybody, "This guy just healed me!" and then the crowds came.

BEN SETTLE: And Jesus even told them not to tell anybody! They still went out and did it.

RAY EDWARDS: Right! So the model for evangelism in the New Testament is you let God perform a sign or a wonder, and that opens people to the gospel. A power encounter with God opens people to hearing what He has to say. One of the first instances that I really saw this in my own life was actually with my wife. I came back to the Lord before my wife did, and she was, quite frankly, not happy that I was going to church and reading the Bible. She sat me down one day and had a talk with me and said, "I don't know what you're doing with all this Bible stuff, but you're scaring me. You're like a different person and I don't like it." At the time when it started, I was suffering from depression – deep, clinical, being treated with drugs depression. Through a series of really bizarre miraculous events, I ended up seeing an actual psychologist, but he was a Christian psychologist. At our first session he's like, "What's the state of your faith?" and I said, "I don't have much," and he said, "Well, you need to get some. Faith comes by hearing, and hearing by the Word, so my prescription for you is you need to read your Bible." He said it in not so pedantic a way as I just said it.

BEN SETTLE: Why can't they all prescribe that?

RAY EDWARDS: Exactly. So the short version of the story is God healed me from my depression. I came off the meds and it was completely gone, just obliterated – something I had lived with all my life. I didn't tell my wife because she didn't want me to come off the meds. She was upset by that idea, because she's like, "I don't want the guy back that I had before you started taking the meds." I stopped taking the meds, and one day she said, "Wow, this is really working. You're a different person." I said, "Well, you want to know the most interesting part? I haven't taken those pills in like three months," and she just stared at me. She said, "What are you doing?" and I said, "You really want to know?" and she said "Yeah." I said, "Jesus healed me of this depression," and that opened the door to my wife coming back to the Lord. It wasn't the only thing that happened, but what I'm saying is those power encounters are the real demonstration of God's power in our lives. Imagine giving the gospel message to somebody who just got healed of something, or who saw someone get healed of something. They're open. They're like, "How did you do that?"

"Well, it was Jesus."

"What do you mean? Tell me about that! I've never heard about that Jesus."

That's a whole different story than saying to somebody, "Hey, have you thought about where you're going to go when you die?" Try that opening sometime and see how that works out for you.

BEN SETTLE: It's very interesting. You and I are copywriters, but it's almost like the whole proof demonstration to prove your case.

RAY EDWARDS: Absolutely! Hey, copywriters just stole that idea from Jesus.

BEN SETTLE: Man, we could have a whole other three-hour conversation just on that.

RAY EDWARDS: Well, I think I've given ample evidence that I can have a three-hour conversation about anything.

BEN SETTLE: That's what I like about you. Speaking of that, we were just talking about selling and copywriting. You're a professional copywriter, and for some of the folks reading this, what does that mean – a copywriter?

RAY EDWARDS: The simplest way of defining it is you're a typing salesman. You're just writing a message that persuades people to buy what you're selling. In my view, that's what a copywriter is and does.

BEN SETTLE: So basically you're still a salesman – you're just doing it with words instead of vocally.

RAY EDWARDS: Right, exactly.

BEN SETTLE: This is where we get into one of those fine lines, so where is that line in selling and persuasion? We've talked about this in the past – the difference between persuasion and manipulation – but I never heard your side of the story on that. Where is that line where it goes from something that's completely in line biblically, to where it's just off the charts and we shouldn't be doing it, even if other people are saying it's okay?

RAY EDWARDS: Like so many things, the Bible doesn't give us a neat set of rules when it comes to money. It would be really cool if the Bible just said, "Do not have a house bigger than 1500 square feet. Do not have more than one car. Do not make more than $100,000 a year," but it doesn't give any kind of rules like that. It's more about principles and relationship with God. What the Bible does speak to is the heart of God, about how we should treat our brothers and our sisters, and how we should treat our neighbors. I used to have a much more complex answer to this question that you just asked me, as you know, but my answer has become more and more simplified. My answer now is pretty much summed up by Matthew 22:36–40. The people came to Jesus and said, "Teacher, what's the greatest commandment in the Law?" and this is what Jesus said. He said, "Love the Lord your God with all your heart and with all your soul and with all your mind. This is the first and greatest commandment, and the second is like it. Love your neighbor as yourself. All the law and the prophets hang on these two commandments." Now, that was Jesus talking, so I think I can pretty well rely on His analysis of that scripture, because Jesus is perfect theology. He's perfect theology in body. If I run every sales presentation through the filter of, "Okay, if I love the Lord my God with all my heart, with all my soul, and all my mind, is there anything in here I would not say, that I think would be displeasing to Him?" You know what, if you're a believer, the Holy Spirit will immediately identify for you what those things are. You'll know.

In proper American church we refer to the still, small voice. "Oh, it's the still, small voice speaking within you," and there's value to that. I don't mean to mock that, but wouldn't it be great if God provided a way that He could speak to us internally and we could know exactly what He's thinking and feeling about a subject? He does. It's called the Holy Spirit. Paul wrote that He would instruct us in all truth and He would enlighten the eyes of our heart. So what does that mean? It means in situations like what we're talking about, when we're doing a sales presentation, the Holy Spirit will show us what is and what is not correct. The second commandment is to love my neighbor as myself. If I love my neighbor as myself, would I say this to them in this sales presentation? Again, you will know! There's a difference between powerfully and persuasively presenting the points of your proposal, and manipulatively constructing an argument designed to get people to do something that may or may not be in their best interest, and we all know in our heart what that difference is, especially if we're believers and we've got the God of the universe to show us and instruct us in all truth.

BEN SETTLE: What Biblical stories have had the most profound effect on the way you sell and market your products and services?

RAY EDWARDS: I thought about this and I came up with a bunch of stories and I'm like, "Oh, this is not supposed to be a six-hour interview." Probably the one that springs to the top of the list for me is the story of the Good Samaritan. It's in the Gospel of Luke. Most people probably know this story, but I'll just recount it briefly. It's a parable that Jesus told about the Good Samaritan, and in this story a Jewish traveler is robbed and beaten. He's left lying half-dead by the road, and various people pass by. A priest and then a Levite pass by, and they both avoid the man. Finally a Samaritan comes by. Now what you have to remember is that Jews and Samaritans despised each other. They hated each other, but the Samaritan helped the injured Jew. Jesus told this parable in response to the question of who your neighbor was, so that dovetails back to what we were just talking about. Showing a Samaritan as the good guy in the story would have been shocking and scandalous to the audience, but it illustrates how we're supposed to conduct ourselves. It's not lost on me that the Samaritan must have been a business person, because he had money to help the injured Jew. How did he get the money? He was traveling and he had money. He must have been a business person. The people who ignored the injured man were the professional religious guys. Think about that.

BEN SETTLE: That's interesting. They were almost like Romulans and Klingons.

RAY EDWARDS: Never the two shall meet.

BEN SETTLE: This has been a huge amount of awesome information – everything from forgiveness in business, selling, spiritual warfare, everything. I really appreciate it. Where can people find out more about you, the book you're writing, your website, and any URLs you want to give?

RAY EDWARDS: It's simple, www.RayEdwards.com. The book is at www.BreakthroughForgiveness.com.

BEN SETTLE: That sums it all up. Finally, there are people that I'm hoping will be reading this, and obviously Christians will probably be the main people reading it, but I'm pretty sure there will be people on the fence about becoming a Christian. They're interested in it. It's a book about business and Christianity, and maybe they're at that point now where they want to be a Christian. What would you say to them?

RAY EDWARDS: If you are feeling any inclination that maybe this is something that you should do, the first thing I would point out to you is that's God speaking to your heart. Trust that intuition. It's how it happens. Nobody comes to the Father except those who are drawn to Him, so you're being drawn to Him and that's His destiny for you, and there's no reason to wait. Becoming a Christian is not a matter of having to go through some 12-week class or some elaborate training program. It's simply a matter of saying yes to God, your Creator, your Father, your Daddy. If you think it's weird that I call Him Daddy, that's what Jesus called Him. He said we could come to Him and say Abba Father, which means Daddy. That's what that word meant – Abba – in that culture.

I talked earlier about the fact that God is a loving God and He doesn't want anybody to perish, and He's also a God who's perfectly just, so He can't let sin go unpunished. That presented a problem because we do commit sin. God had to solve the problem of sin, and how did He do it? Somebody had to pay the price, so He Himself – through a mystery that we can't even begin to understand – became a human being. We know Him as the Son of God, Jesus Christ, and He took on human flesh. He was fully God, but He gave up all of his God privileges and became a man, a human being. That's important to remember, because all the stuff that Jesus did, He did as a man. All the miracles He performed, He did as a man in right relationship with God through the power of the Holy Spirit – the Spirit of God dwelling inside of Him. That's what each Christian has access to. Jesus Himself said, "All these miraculous things I did – you're going to do even greater stuff than that." He said it. It's in the Bible. I'm not making it up. So if we take it seriously we've got to ask, "Wow, that's pretty cool. How does that happen?" Jesus paid the penalty for our sin. He died and He rose from the dead to show that He had victory over death, and He promised us that all we had to do was believe in Him and accept what He had done, and that we could be like Him in that we could live forever with Him. It's not that we become God or anything weird like that, but that we are accepted into the family. We're adopted into the family of God and we live forever with God and we're totally forgiven.

All you have to do – and it's not a magic prayer – but just say something like this. Just say, "Lord God, thank you for making a way to pay for my sin. I know that I've sinned. I know that I need your help. I accept what you did for me when your son, Jesus Christ, died to pay the penalty for my sin. "I accept that and I want you to be the Lord of my life. I want you to be in charge of my life. Let your Spirit come into me, live through me, and show me how to follow what you want me to do. I accept you and I thank you for saving me like you promised that you would. In Jesus's name, I confess Jesus as the Lord of my life and my Savior."

The Lord means He's in charge. Savior means you recognize that He paid the penalty for your sin, and that allows you to live with him forever when you accept that gift. It's as simple as that. Like I said, it's not a magic prayer. Even if you just listened along with me and you just nodded your head and said, "Yes, I believe all of that. I believe in Jesus. I believe in His sacrifice. I accept it and ask Him to be in charge of my life and come into my life and I'm His," then you are a Christian. The next step after that is to read the Bible and get into a community of believing believers who actually believe the Bible is true. It grieves me that I have to say this part, but there are churches that have the word "Christian" over the door and they don't even believe the Bible is true. That's not the place where you want to hang out. You want to hang out at a place that believes the Bible is true. Be in that community and they will help you grow in your life as a new Christian.

BEN SETTLE: Awesome Ray, thank you.

Christian Business Bonus Tip #6

Following is a Bible-themed article written to my website newsletter subscribers. To join my free mailing list and access 700+ pages of advanced web marketing tips, go to:

www.BenSettle.com

Copywriting Conversations With God

Got this great question about doing copywriting research...

QUESTION: Ben, you talk all the time about the importance of doing research before writing copy. What are some research tips?

That's a very good question. Research is everything — the most important activity of all. Get your research right, and your ads practically write themselves. And there's something I do that (IMHO) gives me an advantage over other copywriters.

It has nothing to do with being "smarter" than anyone.

(I'm not, believe me).

This is actually more of a tactical advantage.

A way I discovered years ago when studying the Bible.

A way YOU can use to research your ads, too — regardless of your spiritual (or lack of spiritual) beliefs.

Listen:

About 10 years ago I studied the Bible all the time.

I had this voracious appetite for it that just wouldn't quit. And one of the reasons why is probably because I spent so much time haunting Bible forums arguing with people, debating and doing all the time-wasting things people do when they learn just enough about a subject to be dangerous to themselves.

Anyway, I found myself getting spanked a lot in debates.

In order to not look like a moron anymore, I decided I better study harder.

And so I followed the lead of what smart Biblical scholars do:

I would read a passage and analyze EVERY single word, metaphor and image associated with it.

For example:

If I saw even an "ordinary" word I'd look it up to see the original Hebrew or Greek meaning. If I read a metaphor about Jesus washing His disciples' feet, I investigated what that actually meant back then to better know the significance of it. And if I ran into an image about locust armies, I looked up facts about how locusts behave, and what they do to their prey to get a better grasp on what that symbology really means.

The point?

This extra effort gave me a FAR more detailed understanding of the Bible I never would have had otherwise.

Now, "fast forward" to today, and that's how I research ads.

I meticulously research every fact about the product, market and author to the tiniest detail.

It's like digging for gold — hard, sweaty, unpleasant work.

But it results in ads that put LOTS more profit in your pocket.

Ben Settle

For over 700 pages of advanced web marketing tips and secrets, go to www.BenSettle.com

Secrets Of A Marketplace Minister

Interview with Terry Dean
www.TerryDean.org

BEN SETTLE: Terry, how did you first get started in business, and what were some of the challenges that you faced along the way?

TERRY DEAN: I first got started in online business by going out and purchasing a computer. That's the funny thing. People used to always talk to me and say, "You probably grew up with computers. You learned computers as you grew up." No, the extent of my ability with computers was using like an old Commodore 64 I had when I was a child. I heard about people succeeding online and I had tried a lot of other things pretty much to make a living before this, such as selling door-to-door or even doing network marketing and things of that nature, and nothing ever seemed to work for me. I heard about the internet and I just said, "This is something I can do," because my big weakness is in selling. That was really where I had my weakest point, in direct one-on-one selling. I thought, "This is a place that I don't have to be live in front of people. I don't have to be a strong salesperson up front with them. I can do this." So I went out and bought a computer and basically taught myself how to use the computer, and then started learning what people were doing online and how I could get started online. At that point in time I purchased a few materials from people out there who taught people about direct marketing. Some of my early materials were by people like Bill Myers or Jay Abraham, which some people might know of or may not know of those names, but they were some of the original people I learned from in doing business online. Basically they were people who did a lot of direct marketing by mail, and I said, "Well, online seems a lot like direct mail, so I'll take what they taught and see how it applies online," and that's where I started building up from, from that point of getting started online.

The big challenge for me really started with that same weakness I told you I had, which was doing sales. That was my weakness in getting started, was in selling, because I had had so many bad experiences with sales people that I saw sales as something that was dirty or something that was dishonest or something that had no integrity. That was a burden I had to overcome and really deal with quite a bit. I went to prayer for it. I studied the Bible for it. I did everything trying to overcome that issue of just not wanting to sell to people, and the eventual revelation I had on that was the fact that if we're really delivering people a good product that's going to help their lives and we're charging a fair price for it, it's in their best interest for us to do the most honest best job of selling to them possible. That was a major challenge for me to overcome, and the funny thing is that's a major challenge that I've seen a lot of other people have had to overcome as well, that issue on selling and seeing it as something dirty or wrong. It's kind of surprising how many people go through that and how much everybody just ignores that issue.

BEN SETTLE: You said you started out in doing network marketing and that sort of thing, selling door-to-door. What was the difference between selling on the internet via computer than when you were doing it face-to-face or belly-to-belly or on the phone? Was there a difference or was it the same? How did that work?

TERRY DEAN: There's a lot of similarities to doing it in person or doing it online, but online I see us as having a major advantage, specifically for people who have the same personality type I do. I'm a very logical, methodical type person. I like to think through something. I like to come up with an idea and mull it over, and I use outlines. I do things of that nature. Online, all of that fits because that means if I put together basically a sales piece online instead of one-on-one selling, I can write it all down. I can go over it again, I can improve on it, I can fix it, I can change the words of what I'm saying, I can go back over and judge every word and make sure every word is giving a good representation for what I'm offering, and it gets rid of a lot of that rejection feeling also. For anybody who's online and runs an email list, you'll have times when you send out an email and people send nasty comments back to you. That does happen. There's not very many that do that, but it eliminates all that fear that you have of one-on-one selling because you don't feel the rejection. If I have 100 people come to my website, and we'll say three people who came to the website bought something, that's a pretty good result. I'm happy if I'm getting 3% conversion on a website selling something in most cases, but that means 97% people rejected me, but you don't feel it. You don't feel that rejection, so you don't have that same difficulty, especially for people who have issues with selling. You don't have the same difficulty of feeling that rejection coming in. It's like you ignore it or don't see it. You may have an email list of 50,000 people. If you send out an email, you might have two or three people who send back comments about how much they don't like you, but that's a very small portion of the overall audience, so you just don't feel the rejection.

And I'll tell you this – if you send out an email to your list, you're always going to get back more good comments from your list than you are the bad ones, so again it kind of gets rid of that feeling of rejection, because you're never face-to-face with them. Even today I think I would still have trouble in direct one-on-

one selling compared to selling online. If somebody calls me on the phone and asks about one of my products, I'm very much just educating them on what the product is. You wouldn't see me very much as a salesperson.

BEN SETTLE: You know what's interesting, and I would love to get your take on this – I don't know if it's just the nature of the internet or what, but it seems to me – and I'm taking this back to an evangelical point of view, as far as evangelizing – you don't see a lot of one-on-one evangelizing either, but you see a lot of Christians on the internet especially, educating people on the internet about Christianity and about God. I don't know about the so-called "conversion rate" would be – no pun intended – but it just seems like you see a lot of that too. This is a great tool for Christians to use, even outside of business, just in their spiritual life.

TERRY DEAN: I think it really is too, because it's going to have the same thing. I don't think I've really thought about that a whole lot either, but in evangelizing people it's pretty intimidating, the rejection there as well, and is a lot easier to do it online. If you've seen my site, even my business site, there's a section on one of the business blogs that says Faith, which is Christian posts. Probably the most aggressive post there is one talking about my hatred of terms like The Universe. If you send me a product or anything that says The Universe in it, I'm just going to throw it away. I'm not even going to look at the rest of what you have to say.

BEN SETTLE: Tuning into the universe.

TERRY DEAN: Yeah, what do they usually say? They're going to say the Universal Power will help us, or something of that nature. If somebody wants me to look at something they say is

Christian, the first thing I'll do to their PDF or whatever they send me is do a search for "universe" and then see how it's being used, to see if it needs to be eliminated, if they have any shot at anything at that point.

On my business site, we're talking about Christianity, about being very bold about Christianity, and I even have a quote on there from C.S. Lewis talking about the fact that you can say that Jesus is either the Son of God or you say He's crazy. You can't say He's a good man or a good teacher, because He didn't leave us that option. That post specifically is the one that's gotten the most comments, and here's the funny thing. With that post, I have never received any hateful emails for it. That might even be a little surprising to people. I've never received any hateful emails. I've received some emails of people trying to correct me about how I'm wrong, but I've never had a hateful nasty email, and I've had tons of people who loved that that was on my site. That was a big connection with people on my list, and a big connection of being bold on the site, with nobody sending negative emails. Are there probably people out there who are upset about what I said? I'm sure there are, but they were just quiet out there. So again that's so much easier of a forum to post that than it would be in a big business meeting, telling everybody that. It would be much more difficult at that point.

Something to think about there – I don't remember exactly which scripture it's in – but it's one of Paul's writings where he's talking about one man waters and another harvests. With that, you could say with online a lot of times we're just watering the field. We plant seeds in people's minds, and they end up being harvested by somebody else, somebody they have a relationship with, somebody around them or something else, but we're just planting the seeds with people online.

BEN SETTLE: That's a really good way to look at it. It's almost like an introverted Christian's playground.

TERRY DEAN: You could say that. I guess that would be a good statement for it, because I'm a very introverted person. I am the opposite of the extrovert personality. That's another reason why online just fits me very, very well. Somebody who's an extrovert online, they can do very well also, but a lot of times what will happen with them is they'll end up getting in contact with people. We'll put them on teleconferences or webinars where they get to be talking to people. Pretty much the more we get them talking to groups of people, the better they do. Then you have people like me who are more introverted. I do a lot of my stuff by writing or I do it by interviews that aren't in front of a crowd, but we can still publish in different ways. There's something that fits all of us online.

BEN SETTLE: It's interesting to think about. When you're doing a lot of stuff online like this and you're talking about your faith and all that sort of thing, you're not only planting seeds, but you don't know how many people you're affecting. It's actually kind of exciting to think about that.

TERRY DEAN: It really is, and you don't know who you're affecting at times. I get emails from people sometimes who were just blessed by something. I get emails talking about how something changed their life or how it really benefited them. It's just amazing what effect you can have that you might not ever hear about. We know that in business online, probably whatever we're doing, we only hear from about 10% of what's ever going on online, both good and bad, about your business or anything else. There's probably at least ten times as many people who are having that kind of experience that you never hear from. It's just amazing who we could be touching and could be reaching that we never hear about.

BEN SETTLE: When you were just getting started with the first computer and everything, were you a Christian before that?

TERRY DEAN: Yeah, I was. At the time when I was just getting started, I was running a house church out of my house. I always felt that I was called to be in ministry. People who've heard my story on the internet side of things hear me talk about being a college dropout and delivering pizzas and that sort of thing. The college that I dropped out of was a Bible college, and I was delivering pizzas just to try to make a living while we were starting up the house church. I started online trying to find a way to financially keep afloat so I could do this ministry that I really felt called to. I don't know how deep you want to go into this, but I think there's a lot of people who try to go into what we call full-time ministry – pastors, evangelists, teachers – who might not be called to that, because that's what I felt I was. I was never called to be a pastor, but that's what I was told that I needed to do, because I felt a calling on my life, not knowing that there were so many ways that we could share our faith outside of the church. The reality is, evangelism doesn't take place in a church. Evangelizing takes place outside, and if you look back through the book of Acts, you'll see that the majority of ministry was taking place at the temple and in the marketplace. I'm going to slap a big misbelief most of us have. We raise people up in what we call full-time ministry as higher than anybody who's not in ministry on their calling, but the reality is that every one of us is called to do something. God has a specific plan for us, and it is no more Christian and it is no higher faith for someone to be in the ministry than it is in any other calling that God might have for them.

BEN SETTLE: That has been a major theme in this book. Whatever you're supposed to be doing, whatever you're called to be doing, it's no less important. Being in business can be just as impactful as being a pastor of a church. In fact, you don't see a lot of unbelievers in church, like you're saying, so you could say you have more influence when you're not inside the church and doing things outside the church. That's very interesting.

TERRY DEAN: I heard a minister when I was younger who said that if somebody isn't in full-time ministry, their ministry must not be worth much. I don't know who else might have heard pastors who said that kind of thing, but that's one of the things I heard when I was young, and they couldn't be more wrong. It would have been very nice of somebody to slap that person in the head at the time for what they could be messing up for people. Probably the strongest minister in the New Testament – if we take Jesus out, because He's not fully human, He's God in the flesh – but probably the one who's done the most is Paul. Paul, by our definition today, was not in full-time ministry because he was a tent maker, yet he accomplished more and wrote more than anybody else, and he wasn't in full-time ministry. I actually heard that statement several times from different ministers, that if somebody wasn't in full-time ministry, their ministry must not be much. They need to be hit in the head with a Bible for believing that.

BEN SETTLE: It's interesting that when you look at all the people that God chose to do certain things throughout the Bible, how many of them were actually in positions of religious leadership? Very few.

TERRY DEAN: They were usually rejected by the religious leadership, and of course Jesus was our example, so if we followed His example that means that we should all be murdered by the religious leadership.

BEN SETTLE: If you think about that, God chose Joseph and Mary to raise Jesus, and Mary to have Jesus, and neither of them were in religious leadership. They were very ordinary people.

TERRY DEAN: And Jesus was not in religious leadership, if you look at Him. Think about it this way. Jesus lived 30 years first as a son and then as a carpenter, before 3–1/2 years in what people would call full-time ministry, so which one had the priority in his life? It's almost 10-to-1.

BEN SETTLE: It's very interesting to hear this, because a lot of Christians that I know – and I don't know if this represents a lot of Christians overall, but just a lot that I know – in business they almost feel like they're not doing enough, like they should be doing something else, and they just don't understand. "Should I be going over to Burma and living in a tent?" instead of doing their business.

TERRY DEAN: This is a huge story for me, and that's because in 2004 when I sold my internet business, I took a break from the internet and you know what I tried to do at that point in time? I tried to go and do ministry again, and you know what, I wasn't happy doing ministry. It wasn't my calling to do it, no matter how much I tried it. I just used the term there again. I called it "doing ministry," but I tried to go out and speak at different churches. I did speak at churches. Actually I spoke quite a bit, but that wasn't the calling that God had for me. Yet even after being in business for a long time, I basically fell into that belief system again. That's how much it roots into our mind.

BEN SETTLE: Things that we're taught as children can just stick in there, and it's really hard to get it out sometimes.

TERRY DEAN: It really is hard to get it out, so this is a change of mindset. There are people who are called to be a pastor of a church. There are people reading who that might be their call. There are other people reading this who are called to run a business. There might be others who are called to help someone else with their business and not run their own business as an entrepreneur. We have to really seek God's guidance for our own lives and what position is right for us. I have a Christian book on financial freedom, and one of the things I tell people in there is don't look just at my story of the internet, but find whatever God's plan for you is. You've got to find what direction He wants, what your skills are, and what He has for you so you can follow that, and not just try to follow in somebody else's footsteps and do what someone else has done. God has a unique plan for all of us. If He gave it to us on a complete roadmap, like everything that we were going to do from today till the end of our life, we wouldn't need Him anymore to help us, so He doesn't do that. It's one step at a time and it's basically slow leading, slow guidance, and it's just in time but never ahead of time.

BEN SETTLE: In the people that you've coached and talked to and worked with, have you found that a lot of them ended up doing things that they didn't want to do, kind of like what happened to you. You found out that being in ministry wasn't your thing. Isn't that part of a process? You may not know what you're supposed to be doing until you've done a bunch of things you're not supposed to be doing.

TERRY DEAN: Pretty much. You know what I like to say? It would really be nice if God would guide us and just speak to us audibly and tell us what to do, but He never does that. I like to say God's guidance is a lot like our conscience. If you're doing something and you shouldn't be doing that, we're talking about sin here, your conscience will tell you no. When you're trying different things and you're going the wrong direction, you'll get a very similar feeling, although it's usually not as strong, but it's inside of you, and you can get that same stop sign. It's almost like God doesn't really tell us where to go, but He does tell us no. He has a stop sign and He tells us when we're going in the wrong direction. I do like what I've heard one minister say. He pastored a 5,000-person church when I heard him say this. He said, "God never told me to start this church, but He hasn't stopped me yet. He hasn't told me to stop yet, so I'm going to keep right on doing it until He tells me otherwise." A lot of times that's exactly what we do. We go out and take action. We do something, and unless we start feeling that stop sign inside of us, then we keep doing it until we do, until we find the right direction and the good way to go. There's another passage of scripture where Paul wanted to go preach in one area. He said he was going to go here, but then it said the Spirit forbade him. So he said, "Okay, then we're going to go here," and he took off to go there. He said the Spirit suffered him not. It wouldn't let him go there. You notice at that point in time the Spirit hadn't told him what to do, but Paul was an action person. He said, "I'm going to go here," and God said, "No." "Then I'm going to go over here," and God said "No." Can you see how that's totally different than the concept we have, where we're like all sitting around waiting for God to tell us what to do? Paul was going to go until God told him to stop. That's the attitude we should have too.

BEN SETTLE: It would be nice if we all had a burning bush telling us, "Go back to Egypt," or whatever.

TERRY DEAN: But that's not how it works. We all do have God working inside of our conscience, and we all can feel the stop sign if we're open to it.

BEN SETTLE: Were you brought up as a Christian pretty much your whole life, or were you converted later in life, or how did that work?

TERRY DEAN: My mother was a Christian, so I was brought up as a Christian. I was taken to church all the time. As many people who grew up in church, I basically left being a Christian for a while until I was 18. At the time I was going to a Christian school, even though I wasn't Christian, coming up on 18. Being the rebellious person I was at the time, I actually asked to preach at their chapel on Friday so that I could make a mockery of it. I got up to preach and make a mockery of it, and that's when I gave my heart to the Lord, from my own speaking, along with a bunch of other people there.

BEN SETTLE: Man, that's incredible! You wanted to go up there and do something goofy, just to do your thing, then you ended up coming to Jesus, and a bunch of other people hearing it did too. Did they know what you were trying to do?

TERRY DEAN: They probably did, because that's just how I was. I can't say for sure who would have known and who wouldn't have known. We had a revival with an unsaved preacher. [laughing]

BEN SETTLE: That's awesome, man! There's got to be a blog post in that story somewhere.

TERRY DEAN: So I came to the Lord again then, and that's where that one concept messed me up again, thinking, "Well, I have a passion for God now. I want to be in the ministry." Up till that point I had wanted to go to a business school, but instead I changed and went into Bible college so I could be in full-time ministry, even though that wasn't the plan God had for me.

BEN SETTLE: Do you think that since your mom was a Christian and you were kind of brought up that way, that that had something to do with you coming back to it when you were 18, during that day?

TERRY DEAN: I'm sure it did, because that meant that there were always Christian books around. I have to give you another qualification of my personality at the time. I was an extremely arrogant person, so I would study some of the books my mom had around about the Bible. When I was a rebellious teenager I could never read the Bible directly. I just couldn't do it, but I could read people's books about the Bible. I did that for the purpose of arguing with what I called "stupid Christians," who didn't know the Bible very well and I knew it better than them.

BEN SETTLE: Isn't that kind of what happened to C.S. Lewis? I think that happens a lot actually. They start out atheist and they want to prove Christians wrong, and then they read the New Testament. A lot of times it's just the New Testament, they don't even read the whole Bible, and they're like, "Huh, this makes sense," and there they are.

TERRY DEAN: Actually, reading the Bible made me feel convicted, so I didn't do that. I read other people's books about the Bible, but even then you've got some of the same effects from it. The answer there is it definitely had an effect. It definitely was a part of me, because even at that point when I wasn't a Christian I still would have said I knew the Bible better than the average Christian did.

BEN SETTLE: That is a really good way to approach things. Even Christians today, a lot of them are afraid to read about the things that are attacking the faith. For example, there's a blogger that I like to read. He calls himself Vox Day, and he'll read all the atheist books. He'll read Hitchens, Dawkins – I forget all their names – but he'll read all their books. He doesn't even read Christian stuff. And then he wrote a book called *The Irrational Atheist* and it was just tearing their arguments apart one by one, because you can't effectively debate somebody like that unless you know their position better than they do. Of course it worked the opposite with you.

TERRY DEAN: It worked the opposite, and here's the sad thing. A lot of people who might have grown up in church, you probably heard a lot of wrong things. That's part of the reason I started to get other people's books. I was like, "Let's find out what people who really study the Bible say about these things, instead of these stupid people around me that just want to say what they've always known."

BEN SETTLE: Do you find that to be the same phenomenon in business today with marketing especially, that people are hearing something and it's not necessarily something that works or has worked for anybody, but somebody's just out there saying it and they haven't actually tested it?

TERRY DEAN: Yes, and you and I both know this to be true. In internet marketing just like anything else, if someone wants to believe that all they have to do is buy this product and they'll instantly be successful, then that's what they keep looking for and they keep being scammed, because that does not exist. It's easier to describe if we took it over to like the weight loss market. There's a lot of pills that have been marketed as, "Hey, you take this magical pill and you'll lose weight." In internet marketing we have the same thing. A lot of people sell the "magical pill." They call it something else, but they sell the "magical pill," that if you take this pill, now you'll be successful, and people want to believe that, because every one of us has that issue of wanting to get by with being lazy. We're the person that wants the easy answer. We want the easiest solution and we don't want to have to go through the work to do it. There's even the magic pill in Christianity. The magic pill in Christianity is, "Hey, you just give your heart to the Lord and you're now saved and you don't ever have to do anything else again."

BEN SETTLE: Yeah, and some people even take that to think they can just go out and do whatever they want – bad destructive things to themselves and others.

TERRY DEAN: Yeah, and that it won't affect anything, because it's the magical pill of forgiveness. With that you can say in our market Christians have given business people a bad name. I think it was John Carlton who said it before – who's not a Christian in any way, shape, or form – but he said in one of his products that I originally learned copywriting from him that he's only been ripped off in copywriting two times – one of them was a Christian. He said, "That Christian must believe that God forgives him for ripping off copywriters."

BEN SETTLE: You're right, unfortunately. A red flag always goes up these days for me, I've just seen it so many times, where they just come out and say they're a Christian without any context, and it doesn't even make sense in the conversation. They're just up to something.

TERRY DEAN: Yeah, they are up to something. The best example for me is I was at a conference – and this is one that will get me into trouble when the person hears this, but who cares anyway, they already don't like me – but I was in this conference and one of the speakers at the conference got up, and the first thing he started saying was how he was up in his hotel room praying for them, that he could really change their life. Then in the next 45 minutes he went through showing all the stuff he owns, then his big sales pitch for his product offer. Then after speaking, he was back speaking to other speakers outside of the room, and I was kind of like sitting off to the side hearing them talk about this, he and a couple other people were making fun of the people in the room and how they were getting them to run up there in their walkers and everything else to buy their stuff that they'll probably never be able to use. That makes me hate our market. It makes me really hate what goes on in our market. I've had the experience that almost anybody who wears God on their sleeve is about to rip you off. It's almost like the moment I hear somebody who brings up that they're a Christian or that they love God – actually, it's kind of nice here, because the funny thing is today saying that you pray or that you worship God, that's popular, but saying anything about Jesus is not popular. There's kind of a dividing line today that's kind of making it a little bit easier. The moment they start mentioning God, they usually won't ever bring up Jesus in their mention of God, because that would not get them as many sales and they wouldn't be able to rip off as many people. There's kind of this little dividing line there.

That was something that actually kept me from wanting to put anything on my blog or say anything about Christianity myself, was how many times I'd seen people do that. Basically they'd just bring it up and they'd use it as a way to scam people. There's a lot of people who've done that. "Hey, I'm a good Christian person." What's that got to do with anything or whatever else as a way to deceive people? I have a friend in marketing who's an agnostic. He doesn't know whether there's a God or not, but I have more faith in his integrity than the majority of Christians I know in business, including the people who say they're a Christian. As a matter of fact, I'm thinking of somebody else who I know and has been a friend who constantly talks about his Christianity, and I guarantee you that this agnostic has more integrity than him.

BEN SETTLE: That's scary. It's sad.

TERRY DEAN: It is scary, because this agnostic person, I would have faith in anything he told me. I'll say this. If I had to stake my reputation on anybody's integrity as a marketer it would be him, and that's an agnostic person, not a Christian person. It's scary when you think about it. Did he gain my trust by talking about being a Christian? Obviously not. He gained my trust by how he acted all the time. Here's a good way to judge someone by whether they're going to treat you right in business or not. This is kind of funny, especially if they sell business materials or something, is watch to see if they ever talk about ethical dilemmas. We know that in business, ethical dilemmas do come up. What I mean by that is you have something that's not real clear what the right direction is, so you almost ask other people. We don't have a clear law about it or how we should go about something, and you'll see that the people who really seem to stand on their faith, the people who really seem to have integrity, are people who have those ethical dilemmas at some point in time. I'll give you an example of one that I discussed with a coaching client. What if you have a contract and you are a JV partner to somebody who you find out is mistreating the customer? You have a responsibility to the customer, but you also have a legal responsibility to that person. That's not an easy answer in most cases.

BEN SETTLE: That happens a lot, too.

TERRY DEAN: That happens a lot and it's not an easy answer. So if someone just has an easy simple answer to questions like that, a lot of times I don't trust them anymore. The real reality is, no matter which direction you take or what you do, it wasn't easy to make a decision in that process about exactly what you can do about this issue. Sometimes it just means you have to take a loss and do that on the deal altogether. Maybe just hand the JV partner everything that was involved and walk away yourself from the deal completely, which is the action they ended up taking. You'll see that a real Christian, someone who really has faith in their business, has those ethical dilemmas at some point in time, so I'm suspicious of anybody who does not.

BEN SETTLE: That's a very interesting way, and at least it gives you a nice guidepost when somebody's throwing the word *God* around. I remember seeing that a lot when I was in network marketing. You'd see speakers always talking about God. In one case the guy was sleazing people left and right.

TERRY DEAN: You write ad copy for clients a lot. I write ads for my own products a lot. One of the ethical dilemmas I have with copywriting is I always end up going back to my copy and making sure every single word is true. Sometimes it's a judgment call. We have our solid truth of what's true, but am I at any point in time misrepresenting anything? That's a judgment call time too.

BEN SETTLE: Yeah it is. In that case, the first thing is, if you're going to say anything that's going to actually going to hurt somebody – in other words, if you wouldn't tell it to your own mom or your own father, I always find that to be a good guidepost. At least that way you know that you're doing it for the right reasons. You're not going to scream at your parents in all caps.

TERRY DEAN: Well, I hope not!

BEN SETTLE: I remember hearing your story a long time ago. In fact, you were one of the first people I even ever heard about internet marketing from, by the way. I remember you telling the story that you were doing pizza delivery, you were struggling, you were in debt quite a bit, you and your wife – at that time did you find your faith ever wavering, or did that help carry you through those hard times, or what happened with that?

TERRY DEAN: I had a lot of mistrust and issues that came up then, and that's because I believed a lot of what we call the prosperity gospel, which you could almost call a "give to get" message. You give money away and God's going to multiply it back to you. Some of the preachers are really good at that message. "God's going to give it back to you 30, 60, 100 fold! You can't out give God!" And I found during that period that you could. [laughing] If you give your rent payment when you committed in a contract that you're giving it to the homeowner, then you have an issue here because you've already promised the money to someone else, so there's actually an integrity there also. I had a lot of problems at that point in time, and I mentioned that the one revelation I had there was from James chapter 1. Anybody can go read through James chapter 1, verse 8. Read the other scriptures around it. Always read your verses in context. The easiest way to be deceived by preachers is when they just quote one verse and they don't read everything around it. Always read everything around it and what's going on. In James 1:8 it says that if we pray for wisdom, basically the message is that God will not hold back. He will give you as much wisdom as you want. That was like another revelation to me of not praying for money anymore, and that's how I wrote it down when I got there. "We're not going to pray for money ever again. We're going to pray for wisdom, because wisdom also brings money." The nice thing was that changed how we prayed, and that was only probably a couple of weeks before I bought the computer, so there was a complete connection here of what went on.

I'll have to tell you this, too. At that point in time we were always giving. We were always praying for God to miraculously get us out of our situation, but we never had any miracle gift. Nobody's ever walked up to me and handed me a check, that I know of or remember. Nobody's walked up to me and given me a check, "Hey, this is from God to bless you." The funny thing is, we have done that for other people at times. I remember there was one time I was at the Christian book store and I just felt like giving the lady next to me $100, so I pulled it out of my wallet and gave her $100. She burst out crying because she said she couldn't have paid her rent that month. That has happened, but I've never had anybody do that for me. I'm much happier about what did happen, because living in the blessing of God is better than having to wait for a miracle. If we had to have that, would you rather have $100 to give someone else or would you rather be the person who needs the $100? It's a much better feeling to be the person who has the money, and that's what wisdom can do for you. That's why I tell everybody that they need to pray for wisdom, because wisdom is the right application of knowledge. We can give you knowledge. You can study your Bible and get knowledge, but wisdom is how you apply that to your life and how it fits your life personally. You pray for God to give you wisdom about how the Bible fits your life and what your personal direction is, and for Him to lead you and guide you into what He has for you. That's something I always tell everybody, whenever we discuss this subject. They need to stop praying for money, because money's not your problem. Start praying for wisdom, because that will solve the money issue and many other issues in your life. It's like anything else going on. Instead of just praying that God takes you out of this situation, ask God to give you wisdom. In many cases what ends up happening is He gives you wisdom so you can get yourself out of the situation, but it came from Him.

BEN SETTLE: It's just like the story of Solomon. He could have gotten gold and all that, and he chose wisdom. He didn't make wise choices later in his life, but at least he prayed for the right thing.

TERRY DEAN: He prayed for wisdom and he got all the gold. No one has been as rich as Solomon was, and that was from him praying for wisdom, praying for the right action. We have the same calling from this. If you pray for wisdom, that's going to cause you to take the right action in your life, because that's what wisdom is. It's applying the Bible to your life specifically. It's going to cause you to take those right actions and it's going to lead you into the life that God really has for you. It doesn't mean it's always easy, but it does mean that's the direction He has for you and it's much better than going any other path. That's why I tell people to pray for wisdom instead. I'll throw this one in here for anybody who wants to go back and study that scripture that everybody quotes – God's going to heap back onto you 30, 60, or 100 fold. Again, read the passages around it. What you'll find is being talked about there is not money, it's judging other people or forgiving other people. Obviously I still believe God has prosperity for us. I don't believe we should be broke. I don't believe that God wants you to be broke and not being able to pay your bills, so obviously I do believe in prosperity, but I believe that the prosperity comes from you following what God has for you, and it doesn't always necessarily mean money. You go back to that specific scripture that they always use and base their giving off of. It's all about judging others, and that if you judge other people, God's going to heap that back onto you 30, 60 or 100 fold. Once you understand what that means, you don't like judging other people very much.

BEN SETTLE: Why do you think so many Christians have a sense of entitlement, and why is this such a big problem? I know that you're real big on teaching against a sense of entitlement.

TERRY DEAN: I think a lot of it has to do with our government systems today. I don't want to get too political, but we'll get a little political here. With our systems of government today, they're basically encouraging people that no matter what you do, no matter how screwed up you are, no matter how dumb you are, we'll still all take care of you. But we go back to the Bible, and the Bible actually says that he that doesn't work shouldn't eat. That's a much harder statement. He that doesn't work shouldn't eat. There's an old saying out there that a liberal is someone who wants to give other people's money, because we all should give to the poor. And here's what's interesting about giving to the poor. I've found that when I directly have given to the poor – because I've helped people, I've given people money, I'm talking about specific individuals that I've given money to – almost every time I've done it, I've screwed up. What I mean by that is I gave to the wrong person, I gave to someone who didn't really appreciate it, didn't use it the way they said, and then came back for more. I've found that I do not have wisdom in that area whatsoever, so in any large giving I don't do it directly to people. Any large giving I give to specific ministers I do know who feed the poor and things like that, that I know do have a lot of wisdom in that area and they know how to give to the right people. You know what he told me? One of the best ways he judged who he could best help in their life with finances was a person that he wanted to give to was always somebody embarrassed about taking it. He said that unless the person's embarrassed about taking what he had to give them, usually there was something wrong in the issue. What he meant by that is that the people he found that were best to give money too, like buy groceries for and buy food for and help, was the man who lost his job and he can't feed his family right now. I supplied this minister with a lot of money over the years, so he gives me all kinds of reports of how he uses it. For example, he said one family he bought like $500 worth of Christmas presents for this family, and the mother was so embarrassed and not wanting to take it. The reason he helped this family was because she had been sick, so she couldn't get presents for the family, so he brought it to them. With the people with a sense of entitlement it's almost like, "Well, that's what I expect from you."

Here's another thing he told me to look for. There's a group of professional beggars that go to different churches that will come to the church and ask for money, and then when you tell them that you're not going to give them any, they tell you what a horrible Christian you are and then they'll go to the next church to get money. What he's telling them – and this has eliminated almost all of them, they don't even come to him anymore – is he says, "The Bible says if you don't work, you don't eat. So I will buy you lunch after you sweep the floor," and they leave. If you don't think that's a sense of entitlement and shows you kind of the attitude that we have today, we're definitely missing something. If that person was really hungry, they shouldn't have a problem going and sweeping the floor for the next 20 minutes or half an hour. They shouldn't, should they? Or they're too high and mighty for that when they're asking for charity. That's a problem. We have that attitude because we have a government that basically says, "We're going to take care of you, no matter what you do, no matter how you screw up, no matter whether you save for retirement or not, no matter whether you lose your job because you didn't show up."

You go some places and people are surprised in a recession when a whole bunch of people get fired. Now, there's a lot of people who might have got fired through no fault of their own because their company just dropped people, but you know who's going to go first in those companies? It's going to be the people who didn't show up and didn't do more than what was required of them. That's who they're going to get rid of first. Especially in the small companies, the ones who don't have as many politics in them as corporations, on the small business side, the managers and the owners do eventually know who's doing more than what they're required to do, and they do not want to let them go, the people who are doing more than what they're required to. A lot of times I've seen businesses drive themselves into the ground because they refused to get rid of anybody, because they care about their employees in those cases. Again, we know that's not on the big corporate side, but on the small business side I've seen them do that.

Here's what I want people to think about here. Your bosses are not your supplier. God is your supplier, and He is watching all the time. He is watching everything that you do at your job, and whether you do what you're supposed to or not. I think a lot of times, people who are employees might put in their 15 minutes of work today when they're supposed to be working 8 hours, then they end up wondering why God doesn't supply them at other places, like God owes them something or people owe them something. They don't look at what's really in the Bible and what God has promised us and what He's told us to do. For example, if you spend a lot of time in Proverbs you hear God talking a lot about the prostitute, you hear a lot of Him talking about the lazy person, and you hear a lot of talk about the person who's doing violence and shedding blood. You hear a lot about that. There's so many references to that laziness and the fact that God doesn't supply for us if we're lazy, if we're not doing the actions that we're supposed to. We end up having such a sense of entitlement in the church that it holds everybody back, thinking that they're going to succeed without any work.

Here's where it hurts people who start an internet business, who go in and try to start an internet business. This sense of entitlement hurts them because I've seen people who believe, "Well, I'm a Christian and I'm praying, so it's all going to work out, no matter what I do." It's really weird and I hate to say this, but I think on average, of the people I've coached and I've talked to, I think more Christians get scammed online than the average person. If we said that 60% of people online are getting scammed, I'd say it's 70% of Christians that are getting scammed – I don't know what the numbers are – and the reason is they have that sense of entitlement, so those little magic pill solutions for some reason make even more sense to them. They're saying, "Well, I'm blessed by God, so if anybody can do this, it's probably going to work for me too." Little do they know that it never worked for anybody. They're just falling into that same greed message that people are hyping up to them. That sense of entitlement will hurt you in business, because the real reality of business is you're going to work hard, you're going to work long, at first especially, and you're going to build your business. What I love to say is, if you go back to the Bible, it says, "Everything we put our hand to will prosper." The key principle, if you go back to that scripture, if everything we put our hand to prospers, that means you have to be putting your hand to something. If you're not putting your hand to something, there's nothing to prosper. That's true for a lot of Christians. Again, it doesn't apply to everybody, but I've seen a lot of people who wonder why they aren't more successful online than they are, and it's because they never put their hand to anything new.

It goes back to that same thing again. If you want more than what you have, if you want better results than you had before, you have to do something new. I've actually talked to people before, and I think of one specific person I know, a friend – not a business associate, but a friend – who in talking to her she told me this huge plan that she believes God has for her life. I asked her what she was doing to move forward with it. What was she doing right now to move forward with it? Was she buying books about that subject? Was she going to a class about that subject? Had she signed up for a class? You know what the answer was? She was still just praying about it and looking at magazines about the subject. She wasn't doing anything to move forward with it. That was like 15 years ago. Guess how close she is to it today? Still the same spot. I think she's probably given up on it at this point, because she didn't take the action to go that direction. The sad thing is there's a lot of believers with that same attitude. We'll say they're working in a job, but the question is what are they doing more advanced than that?

I remember something a little outside the Christian thing here, but I think it's really representative. I remember Dan Kennedy talking about something before. One of Dan Kennedy's principles was that you shouldn't give people a raise unless they become more valuable to your company. There should be no automatic raise. Unless you become more valuable, you don't get a raise. One of the business people that he trained with, he told the story that she had somebody come and ask when he was going to get his raise, and she told him, "You can, on the principle that you take on more responsibility, and I'm going to have you go to this class first," and he refused to go to the class. I think that's really representative of a lot of people. They want more, they want to grow, but they're not willing to do what's required to get there, which may be turning off the TV, it may be studying and taking action, it may be going and testing something and failing.

I'll say this, that one thing that I had going for me – which is kind of surprising, because I'm an introverted person – is I've been bold enough to be willing to fail. This whole time from starting my business online, since I was one of the early adopters online, I think I failed more online than anybody I know of. I've had more failures than anybody you know probably. That's because I've tested more things over a longer period of time. In the beginning I had no clue what was going to work, so I was testing everything – basically throwing everything at the wall to see what would stick in the very beginning, so I failed more than just about anybody, but I had the boldness to keep going and have those winners. That's something that people have. That's a difference I've seen with people that I've coached that are really successful and the people that are still struggling. I've seen both and I've coached both. The people who are very successful do not take failure personally. They do not take it very personally. They don't get discouraged because of a failure. It's just a way of doing business. They know it's a part of doing business. The person who's a beginner who's still struggling wants to try to get everything lined up to perfection before they get started, because they're going to take it personally. They'll say things like, "If this doesn't work, I don't know what I'm going to do." Now remember, I came from being broke. I came from having no money. People say they're at the bottom of the barrel. I was under the barrel with it sitting on top of me. I came from there. The strategy at the very beginning was, "We'll test a whole bunch of things until we find out what works." And even with all the knowledge we had, the reason we talk about testing is because we don't know everything that's going to work all the time correctly for us.

I've tested a lot of things. I'll test headlines. I'll test, "Hey, if I put a video on this page, will it work better than before?" Sometimes it does, sometimes it doesn't. I test things to this day and I don't have a definitive answer for every single question. It's funny, but when I coach a struggling marketer compared to a more successful one, the successful ones immediately understand, but the struggling ones expect that I would have all the answers and I could give them every answer clearly and never be wrong. I even scold them and try to drill it into them that I'm a successful marketer because I've screwed up more than anybody.

BEN SETTLE: There's the irony of it.

TERRY DEAN: That's the irony of it, that I know a lot of things that don't work. That's kind of an advantage, because that is why they come to me for their coaching, is I can tell them a lot of things that won't work. They'll say, "I'm going to do this," and I'll say, "No you're not. You're not doing that. I did that and that's not going to work," so I can save them a lot of trouble and heartbreak by telling them what's not going to work, but that doesn't mean I always know what will work every time in every situation. I just went off on this whole tangent from our sense of entitlement, didn't I?

BEN SETTLE: It's good stuff. Look, I know people personally who need to hear what you just said, people close to me who are trying to get their business going. They're kind of in that phase where they're praying about it, but there's just not a lot of action going on. I think what you just said, I think a lot of people are going to benefit from that.

TERRY DEAN: That's true for people who are Christians or non-Christians. If you don't take the action, you're not going to get any results. If you don't put your hand to something, God has nothing to prosper. I guess I'm very passionate about that.

BEN SETTLE: I know you're passionate about the next question I have, too, and that is what is your opinion of Christian businesses getting into debt.

TERRY DEAN: I hate debt. I'm not just going to say Christian business. I'm going to tell all Christians I hate debt. Let's put one thing out on the table real clear first. You should never ever go into debt for consumer items. There's no reason to ever go into debt for consumer items. Don't go into debt to go buy that new pair of shoes. Don't ever go into debt to buy whatever you want to buy. The only place that debt would ever make sense is if it was an investment. That's the only place it would ever make sense. I think as Christians we have commands here, and the first one we have to look at is that God says we're supposed to owe no one anything but to love them. At first that scripture would look like that means that we should never have debt for any reason, or it would be sin to be in debt. I don't believe that, because He also told us back in Deuteronomy 28 that one of the blessings of the law – and Jesus fulfilled the law for us so that we could walk in the blessing – but one of the blessings of the law is that we'd be lenders, not debtors. If we are allowed to lend, then it cannot be a sin just to be in debt, because if we're allowed to lend to people, then obviously we would be causing someone else to be sin, which would be wrong if debt was always wrong. But what we do have that is wrong, especially in America – I don't know about other countries – but in America we have an attitude that debt isn't that big of a deal. There's another scripture that says that the borrower is a servant or a slave to the lender. I want you to think about that any time you're going to take a debt for anything. "Now I'm putting myself as a slave to that person or that company." If you take that attitude that you're willingly selling your life as a slave, you'll have a much harsher attitude about debt. You knew I was passionate about this subject because that's the attitude I have. I am your slave if I take a debt.

You want to know how strong this belief is in me? I have a monthly print newsletter. I will not accept yearly subscriptions to the print newsletter. I will not. I'm one of the very few business coaches that bills people by the month, not by the year. I will not bill by the year and will not let people pay by the year. The reason is that I feel if I take your money, I'm now in debt to you. I am not your slave. If I don't like you as a client, this is your last month. That's just the way it works. This is your last month being a client. I've done that before. I've told someone, "We are done. You've paid till the 22nd and you are done. I've cancelled your subscription. I will help you till the 22nd." I've done that before. It's a print newsletter. Hey, if I don't want to do this anymore, I have one more issue I've promised to send everybody. Nobody's paid for more than one issue, so I can be done after my next issue if I want. That's the promise that I've made. That's how far this debt belief of being enslaved is engrained in me. I know especially on the coaching side, it's easier to make money with long-term coaching subscriptions because people don't use them. When they're paying every month they remember, so you actually end up doing more work monthly, but they get more action out of it also. From the profit side from the coach's side, they make more with a long-term subscription, but I will not do it for that commitment.

Now for your business debt, let's talk about that. Have you exhausted every other possible option before you go into debt? Have you sat down and prayed that this the only really viable option for growing your business? In the right case, in the right situation, that might be where you have to go. We have a little bit of a different mentality in online business. With an online business you don't need debt, at least not much at all. I'll tell you how I operate within my business. I do have credit cards. My credit cards are paid off about every week. It's much easier to do business using credit cards, but they get paid off constantly. That's another part of that hatred of debt. Again you can see how much it drills into me.

BEN SETTLE: I think you and I are kindred souls on this. I'm the same way. Once I paid off my last debt, that was it. I tell my wife, "I don't care what the situation is." As soon as something's on that card and I see it on the website, boom, it's gone.

TERRY DEAN: It's gone, it's paid. My business one is actually a PayPal credit card, which I get to see right inside my PayPal account. Whenever I'm logged into my PayPal account, boom, it's paid. They're connected and pretty much every business expense is inside PayPal, which makes it nice and simple there also. With a brick and mortar business offline, if you want to go buy a McDonald's or you want to go buy a big store, you probably are going to go into debt. You're just going to have to, most likely. But with that, I think you should really take the attitude that debt is not a simple small solution, and I'll give you an example of what I think about debt. For a lot of this I'm just giving you examples of my own story, because I think this is one of those cases where it has to come back to your conscience and your wisdom and the answers for your life. When I bought our first home, I did not have the cash for it and had to borrow. I went to the bank and they were going to have a really high rate of interest, so my oldest brother loaned me the money. It wasn't a big a loan because it wasn't a big fancy house. We actually put our mortgage on a 7-year contract. We pay them off within 7 years. None of this 15-or 30-year stuff. We're going to pay it in 7 years. That first year my wife and I both made the commitment that we buy nothing, because we are a slave until this bill is paid, so we don't get anything. We had the minimum of an entertainment budget, maybe $50 for an entertainment budget for those months. We didn't buy anything for the house, we didn't do anything until that debt was paid. We paid off our house in one year because we made a commitment. I think if you take this commitment against debt and the attitude that you will not have it, God puts His power alongside of you to do it. People get in all these debts and they can't pay these debts, and they get a little bit of extra money and they go and spend it at Starbucks. I think that faith without works is dead, so if you believe that God wants to get you out of debt, as I do – I still believe in prosperity and that God wants you out of debt; He doesn't want you to live in debt – that faith has to come with action, which means I'm going to do whatever it takes to get out of debt. Remember, I was there with credit card bills. That meant that when we had those credit card bills and we made that commitment to wisdom also, we didn't buy extra things. We took any extra money that came in and we paid extra on the credit cards to pay them off, the same thing that we did with the house. Then for my second house, the one I live in now, we paid cash for this one. I remember the first thing we ever bought with cash was a couch, and that couch felt so good. It's yours and you're not enslaved to anybody else. It's your couch. A lot of people say they own a house. You don't own your house, the bank owns your house. You stop paying for that house and watch what happens. It ain't yours anymore.

Some people today are walking away. This upsets me. This makes me mad. I'll just throw it right out there for people to think about it. There are people today, because their house is losing value, that are walking away from a loan contract that they committed to pay, and these are people who claim to be Christians. If you can pay your home mortgage, you have no right to walk away, no matter what, because you made a commitment to it. I have a serious problem there. You just walk away because you don't believe in the commitment you made, where the Bible tells us that we swear even to our own hurt. If we said that we're going to do it, we committed that we're going to pay this, then we pay it if we can. Again, we understand that there's situations, and I do believe the U.S. has good laws for bankruptcy and things, because a lot of bankruptcies are caused by medical bills that are so high. Those are good things for people who get into those circumstances, but I'm talking about people who willingly walk away and they could have done something about it. That's happening today and you actually see it on the news all the time, people walking away because they're underwater on whatever it is. Take the attitude that this isn't mine until I've paid for it. This business is not mine until I pay the bank back. I believe that when you make that commitment, when you take the actions that go with that commitment, that's where God's going to bless you and help you to get out of the debt. He can help you move faster. He can prosper you because you're taking action to go along with what He told us to do, and that's what religion is.

BEN SETTLE: You know what's interesting, when you were talking about how maybe a brick and mortar business most likely would have to go into debt, what I didn't realize is one of the options out there is simple investors. There are angel investors and other investors who want to invest money in something. You don't even have to get a loan if you know how to contact them.

TERRY DEAN: That is definitely true. You don't have to get a loan. At that point you get a partner, but then that brings up some partnership issues.

BEN SETTLE: Yeah, it does. I'm just saying as far as staying out of debt, and you probably have a partner who knows what he or she is doing, if they're putting their own money into it, like an angel investor. The only reason I know about this is because I once sold a product on how to buy businesses with no money down. Investors were the secret. They're retired business people who have money and they want to do another venture and they have experience.

TERRY DEAN: They want to have a part of the business, but they don't want to be doing something every day.

BEN SETTLE: Yeah, and they're happy to lend you their experience, like you were saying, "Don't do this. Don't do that." I just thought I'd throw that in there. What advice would you have for Christians, or anybody who'd be reading this, if they're bound up in debt – what advice do you have for them?

TERRY DEAN: I guess I was getting ahead of myself there. Make a commitment that you want to get out of debt, and with that, you make that commitment before God that this money isn't mine. That's the attitude I took. When I was in debt, we took that attitude that we owe these people. From all the money we make, it's not ours, it's theirs. It's their money until we get the debt paid off. I'd taken the loan from my brother for the house. I don't think we did anything that we shouldn't be telling people. We had a full contract mortgage and everything for it. I actually paid a lawyer to draw up the contract to my brother for doing the loan. With that, we paid him off quickly because we said all the money we make is not ours, it's his until we don't have a debt. I think that's the attitude they should take, no matter what level of debt they're in now. "I don't have any money until I pay this off," because the Bible says that if you're in debt you're a slave. Does a slave own anything?

BEN SETTLE: They don't even own themselves.

TERRY DEAN: No, they don't own anything. That means until you're out of debt, you don't get anything. We better be glad that we live in a society where we don't have the debtor's prison, where you get in prison or sold into slavery because of your debt, but I do want you to still think of it as you're in slavery until you're out of debt. It sounds like you have the same attitude as I do about it. That attitude can kind of change your whole perspective when you even think about debt.

BEN SETTLE: It's something to avoid at all costs. It's not good. Just because all the talking heads on the news are saying it's good, it's not. "Oh, you can go spend $150 at Starbucks every month, go ahead," and I'm thinking you can pay something off with that. I'm just thinking of people I know.

TERRY DEAN: With the stats of selling stuff online, you'll actually find that if you use credit cards a lot you spend more money. I make a lot of money. We have no debt, but my wife and I still budget every month a certain amount of cash for entertainment. We take that cash and put it in our wallet and that's what we spend on entertainment that month.

BEN SETTLE: That's smart. That's good. I'm going to start doing that.

TERRY DEAN: The big thing that solves between a husband and wife is now there's no argument about what you're buying or not. I buy whatever I want. If you want to go buy golf clubs, it's not her problem. [laughing]

BEN SETTLE: [laughing] Or you have to save up for the next entertainment budget.

TERRY DEAN: Yes, that's what you do, and also you know what happens when you're actually looking at the cash that's in your wallet? You think a little bit longer about the buying decisions you make. That's something to think about. Our budget is probably higher than what someone listening to this might be at the beginning, but that doesn't really matter. It's not the amount that matters. We started with a much smaller amount, but it's not that. It's just the principle that comes in. It's more the attitude that I have an allowance. That's what I have. It's totally separate from business. I'm just talking personal on that side, and that's what we do. If you actually did that, it would solve a lot of financial problems. A lot of couples have trouble with each other because of finances and how money is spent. Just think about that concept also, how that can help, and how that relates back to our debt issue as well, because it gets you thinking on the concept that, "Here's the money I have to spend. I don't take on debt."

BEN SETTLE: When you were getting out of debt, when you were just starting out and you had all those different debts, did you use things like the debt snowball principle or anything like that?

TERRY DEAN: By the debt snowball principle are you talking about that you just pay off the smallest or pay off the highest interest one?

BEN SETTLE: Yeah, there's some fancy calculations on how to do that. There's many different ways, I think, but that's the basic gist of it – the small ones first and let it snowball.

TERRY DEAN: With our original debt, we had gotten to such a point that we couldn't pay it all off at the beginning. We hired a lawyer to contact the companies for us to get us a lower interest rate, which he did. It's kind of funny, but you'll find that if you actually are in a situation – we screwed up royally with the debts we had gotten into – the lawyer negotiated basically off the interest rate for a bunch of them, on the commitment that we would pay them a certain amount all the time. We paid the entire debt, but we didn't have to pay 40% interest rate while doing it because of that. With that, it became more of a process that we just paid extra, and the way it was designed was it just went to whichever bill was the highest. That's how it was designed when we did our original payments to pay it off in the beginning. With that, I didn't really use a debt snowball system. We just got the best rates possible. Some of them still charged a little bit of interest on it, but it was lower than what their usual rates were. If you want to talk about usury rates, you can call it usury when you see how much credit cards charge when you get behind.

BEN SETTLE: And it grows very fast.

TERRY DEAN: It grows very, very fast. The lawyer basically got them to get rid of that super high rate and we just started paying it off, and so it just kind of paid out to all of them and we paid off the debt. It was actually a process for us. We went through and we paid off all those original debts, then we borrowed to buy our house and we paid that off quickly. It was just step–by–step as we went through the process. As I told you, after getting out of debt, after paying off the house and before we moved up, the first thing we ever bought with just cash was a couch. Then it moved up to where we bought a car with just cash. Then it moved up to we bought a house with cash. We don't need anything else, but you can see it kind of snowballed in that direction too. That's actually a biblical principle as well, because God trusts you with more as you prove you can be faithful in the little.

BEN SETTLE: Why do you think so many Christian business owners are squeamish about making money at all, and what does God say about these things, from your studies of the scriptures?

TERRY DEAN: The first issue I think is some of the same issue I had, which is they don't want to sell things. In a business, if you're squeamish about selling anything you're not going to make any money. It's what you have to do. Nobody makes any money until some money changes hand, so that's one of the first issues. Another issue really comes in that people have this attitude that's similar to the one thinking that people should be in a full-time ministry position as a pastor. They think that somehow you're more holy or you're more spiritual if you're poor. If you're poor, you must be more spiritual. They even have the concept that Jesus had nothing, but here's what I always tell people. Here's the best example of getting rid of the whole concept that Jesus had nothing. Read the scriptures. At the last supper Jesus told Judas that he was going to be the one to betray him. The other disciples sitting around obviously didn't hear him good, because they all thought He told him to go give something to the poor, because he got up and left during the dinner. If that's what they thought, then that must have been a pretty common thing for Jesus to tell Judas to go give to the poor during dinner. If I see someone get up during dinner and immediately leave the room or run out of the room, my first thought usually isn't that they're going to run off and give to the poor, but that's what their first thought was. That means it probably was a pattern. We also know from the scripture that Judas was stealing money from the bag and nobody knew about this. If you read about some of the personalities, people like Peter, I guarantee you that Judas stealing from the bag wouldn't have gone over real well with Peter.

BEN SETTLE: He might have cut an ear off or something.

TERRY DEAN: That wouldn't have worked very well, so Judas was able to steal money from the bag they regularly gave to the poor with, without anybody ever knowing. You know what that tells me? That this bag does not have $20 in it, because if there's $20 in my bag and you steal my $20, I'm going to know about it. If there's $5,000 in my bag and you steal $20, I might think I miscounted it last time I looked at it. If you want to steal money from something, it better be something that has a lot of money in it. It said he regularly stole from the bag, so that meant that there was regularly money in this bag. Jesus was not broke, as some people would say He was. If you look throughout the scriptures, especially if you go to the Old Testament – this was another one I was telling you of my youth when I grew up – I love it when people say, "I'm just like poor old Job." You know what my response to them is? When you study, you find out that Job's trial lasted about nine months. If you are just like poor old Job, then you are the richest person in the world, you went bankrupt and got sick and lost your family over a nine-month period, and then after the nine months was over you're going to be twice as rich as everybody else, because that's what it says about Job. If a Christian is just like poor old Job, they're already the richest person. They're going to lose everything and then they're going to get more of it, within about nine months. I've never seen anybody who has the attitude that they were just like old Job who that happened to.

BEN SETTLE: Do you think part of this mindset, the squeamishness, comes from the scriptures that talk about the rich man and it's hard for them to get into the kingdom of heaven, it would be easier to go through the eye of a needle and that sort of thing?

TERRY DEAN: I think it does have to do with that, and let's think about the rich man you're talking about. The rich man you're talking about was born rich. Have you ever noticed that there's a difference in attitude between the majority of entrepreneurs and their children? Take that representation there, and we talked about entitlement earlier. The children of an entrepreneur, unless they've been raised correctly – and it's even harder for them to raise their kids correctly when they have a ton of money – but unless they're raised correctly, that sense of entitlement is a massive hole in that person. They trust in themselves. They trust in the money. They've always had the money, and they're afraid of ever losing it. The majority of entrepreneurs that I know have the attitude that if they lost their money they could get it back again. It's not as big of a fear for them. It's not as big of an issue for them when you look in that direction. I want to point to one more thing from that scripture about going through the eye of a needle. In that scripture, Jesus also says it's impossible. He said with men it is impossible. I've heard some people translate it as the eye of the needle was some hallway that people had to take off all their baggage to get through.

BEN SETTLE: Yeah, I've heard that too.

TERRY DEAN: It can't be, because He said with men it's impossible, so there's no way possible with men alone that they can do this. Without God's help it's impossible for them ever to do this. But with God, all things are possible. In those situations, the person who's been born with the money, that means they're going to have to really have an encounter with God at some point. They're really going to have to have it. It's also changing our attitudes there and seeing that it's really easier sometimes to walk in the faith when you're desperate and when you're in need than when you have everything. Sometimes it just seems harder, so that's something to keep in mind when we talk about that subject. The other one that I think a lot of Christians have trouble with is the one that says the love of money is the root of all evil. That's one where people don't even read the entire scripture. They read half of it and just say, "Money is the root of all evil."

BEN SETTLE: Yeah, they forget the first part.

TERRY DEAN: Money is a tool. The love of money is the root of all evil, loving money. You can love money even if you have none of it, because that bank robber loves money. He's willing to do whatever it takes to get money. That's the same as the stockbroker who rips off all of his clients so he can get more money. It's the same thing, the love of money. That means that you love money more than people, and will do whatever it takes to get the money, no matter who you have to hurt. That's what that means. Instead of loving your neighbor, you're loving their wallet. That's where you shouldn't be.

BEN SETTLE: That probably goes back to that whole thing about society's entitlement again. They want everybody else's stuff instead of going out and earning it. That can be a real dark rabbit hole for someone to tumble into, I think.

TERRY DEAN: It really can. It can really mess up their sense of direction. I talked about this idea that you have to test a lot of things in business. You have to try a lot of things. If you have that sense of entitlement or you have that attitude, that whole concept is totally foreign to you, to have to test things and things might not always work out. If you test too expensively, you can screw it all up. When I say test, I mean if I have $1,000, I'd like to spend it on ten different tests. I'll spend a little on each one. If I spend my $1,000 and three of them work, I'm going to do more of those three. The other seven didn't, so we push them off to the side and do more of the ones that worked. That's the process we do on the testing. If you have a sense of entitlement, it's like, "I should just do one thing and it either works or it doesn't." We could do a session called "Gambling on God."

BEN SETTLE: Why is success such a bigger test for the Christian business owner's personality and their character than failure is?

TERRY DEAN: The reason is that it's very easy to forget God when you're successful. If you're in debt, you're having trouble paying the bills, then in that situation you really want to pray because you're desperate. You want to pray because you need help. You want to pray because you need a direction to go in. Once you become successful it becomes a problem. When we're a failure it's easy for us to say, "I don't know what caused it. I don't know what happened, but I'm praying for God to get me out of this." When we become a success it's very easy to say, "Look at everything I've done and how successful I am," and just totally forget God, forget praying, forget all the prayers that were before that, forget all the blessings that He gives you. Here's what we really have to do, and this is something I have to remind myself of all the time, because I have the same problem everybody else does. I find it's easier to forget God when you're successful than when you don't have anything. It's easier to think it was your wisdom and your might. Here's what really brings you back, and that's when you have an attitude of gratitude and you make every day a day of thanksgiving, which God told us to do anyway. "In everything, with prayer and supplication with thanksgiving, make your requests known to God." With that, we make every day a day of thanksgiving for everything that He's provided you in your life. Then you're going to find it very hard to be arrogant and walk away from God when you're a thankful person. What I'll end up doing is I'll thank God for the health that I have. It doesn't matter how much money you make or how successful you are if you're sick all the time. So I thank God for my health. I thank God for what He's given me in my life. I thank Him for the wisdom He's given me. I thank Him for the business He's given me. I thank him for the strength and the intelligence He's given. I thank Him for the wife that I have that even when I failed in all that network marketing and everything else, I had a wife who still told me that I could do it. A lot of people talk about the fact that their wife's against them when they're starting a business, or their husband's against them when they're starting a business. I had a wife who told me I could do this.

BEN SETTLE: That's good to have in your corner.

TERRY DEAN: Yes it is, so I'm thankful for the spouse that God provided me. I'm thankful for everything that He's given me in my life. I remind myself of that. I remind myself to have that day of thanksgiving every day, because that's what's going to keep you in the correct direction when you're successful. That's the real issue, that it becomes very easy to be arrogant and prideful and think that you did it all, not looking at every other person. A lot of people say that the entrepreneur was a self-made man or woman, yet nothing like that ever exists, because everybody has an influence on us. There are people around us who have helped us. God has given us the wisdom to do what we do, and all those who have been part of our success all the way through. There's no such thing as a self-made person.

BEN SETTLE: That's a very interesting thing to think about too, because a lot of people might hear you say that and say, "I don't need anybody to help me," but you're not saying the government's helping anybody. You're just saying other people and God have helped people.

TERRY DEAN: The issue that people like me have with government charity isn't the fact that they give. I like having giving people around. I've had people giving to me. They've given me help. I'll guarantee this – if you're moving from Indiana to Florida, you'd like it if somebody would help you. The difference is that when the government helps people they have to steal from other people to do it. A friend and I were discussing it, and we said that if the government ever said that everything we owed in taxes for the year, if we would give twice as much to charity we wouldn't have to give them anything, we would both do it in a second because we could choose the charity. We could choose who it was going to, but twice as much. When you're in the tax brackets we are that's a lot, and we'd be willing to do that. We'd be willing to give twice as much if we didn't have to pay it to the government. It's not a question of helping people or not helping people, it's a question of whether you're being forced to help specific people or not. We believe in helping people. I think it was Ryan Healy who linked over one time to the story of Davy Crockett who spoke to the Senate. He linked in one of his blog posts, saying that Davy Crockett spoke to the Senate. There was some poor lady who needed help and they were asking whether the government should help her. He said that the government should not, because they shouldn't take other people's money, but he'd be willing to give his full check for the entire week if they would do the same to help her, and nobody was willing to do that. They weren't willing to give their own money, but they were willing to give other people's money.

BEN SETTLE: We saw that recently with the health care debate. People are like, "I'm not a jerk. I have no problem getting taxed," and I'm thinking, "Well, why don't you donate to the government then?" I'm talking about people who make a lot of money saying this. I was like, "Why don't you put your money where your mouth is and at least serve as an example."

TERRY DEAN: That's what I always laugh about. We have politicians who go into office and their tax records are open to us. If you look at their tax records, their actual giving percentage-wise is lower than the average American.

BEN SETTLE: I remember that was a big thing with our current vice president Biden, if I remember correctly. It wasn't very much.

TERRY DEAN: I think his was less than $1,000 or something for the year.

BEN SETTLE: But it's easy to give Terry Dean's money. I always find that an interesting conversation.

TERRY DEAN: It's not about not giving, because everybody in their life needs people around you who help, but it's the fact that they have the choice of help. I don't expect that anyone should have to feel like they have to help. I'll give you a guarantee. I know God well enough and I know forgiveness from God. I know what conviction is, so I get convicted when I do something wrong, but I know no guilt because God has delivered me from guilt. So the worst way for anybody to ever try to motivate me to do anything now is guilt. It does not work at all. So if someone asked for help, I may choose to help them. If it's something I feel I can help them with, if it's something that's going to really help them, I will help them. If they try to use guilt or try to push me to do it, it's a guarantee they will get no help whatsoever, because I don't have the guilt in my life that God's delivered me from. That's something that everybody needs to think about. God brings us conviction, which brings a change. He does not bring us guilt. Guilt drives people away from God because it says, "I'm such a dirty rotten person. I did such a wrong thing," and you run from God because you feel guilty. You felt bad about what you did before, but conviction brings you toward God, because you're going to change what you do. That really comes into the same thing if you talk about as you become successful, because that's what we're talking about now. As you become successful, one of the things you will do is you will give more. You will give to charities you believe you can help.

I told you, I just screwed up when I gave individuals cash, so I give through other people. Another benefit of that is now they don't know who's giving to them, so they don't come and bug you for more. They don't know who's doing it, but you can hear the reports from them, from who it was given to. You're going to give more as you grow. Never ever give out of guilt, because that's the wrong motivation. God tells us that we need to give out of love. If you go to I Corinthians 13, Paul told us that if we gave everything, even if we gave our body to be burned, if we gave everything to the poor, it profits us nothing if it's not done out of love. That means if you do it out guilt, if you do it because the missionaries showed you all the starving children, then you're not doing it for the right reasons. You're not doing it out of love, because you care. I'll give people a tip there. If you're ever going to go to a service where they're going to be giving you all kinds of stories and they're going to be telling you why you should give to this, always decide how much you'll give, if you're going to give anything, before you ever get to the meeting. That's a quick tip.

BEN SETTLE: That mindset is interesting too from the prosperity side. People think, "If I just give and give and give, it'll all come back automatically."

TERRY DEAN: If you're not giving out of love, if you're giving to get, that's out of greed. There's a lot of people in the prosperity mindset who give out of greed, not out of love. There's also a change in attitude that when you believe that God has made you successful, He has given you wisdom, giving actually becomes part of the gratitude. It becomes part of that thankfulness that you have towards what He's already given you, instead of you trying to get anything out of it. It's a whole change in attitude there as well, because that is giving out of love, if you're giving out of gratitude for what God has already given to you. If you look at the Bible, you'll see that's exactly the direction that we're constantly told to give – to give out of gratitude and thankfulness, not to give out of any commitment or requirement.

BEN SETTLE: We touched on this a little bit earlier, but we could probably go off on it a little more. Why do you think Christian business owners are afraid to talk about Jesus?

TERRY DEAN: Because in some cases it will cost them business, but I don't need everybody's business. Here's the interesting thing. Here's what you're going to find if you talk about Jesus. I'm not talking about if I'm on your email list, and I'm sure you're probably on my email list. We don't talk about Jesus all the time. That's not what we're saying there. We talk about business, we talk about the subject people sign up for, but if you read through our messages, at some point you'll hear about Jesus because that's part of our life, because we tell you about our lives. That's just going to be in there. It's not like we're going to hide it. We're not going to hide our faith – we're supposed to be that light that shines – but it's not going to be something that always there. It's not like we're always pitching you on it. I'll tell you one of the things I like best is I've spoken at conferences before, and I like it best when you don't say anything at the conference, and somebody asks you afterwards, "You're a Christian, aren't you?" That's when it's best, when they knew it without you having to actually say anything specifically about it. That's what you really want more than anything else. We're willing to talk about Jesus as being a part of our life, and whenever it integrates in as being a part of our life. It's not like we're trying to push or that we're trying to evangelize or that we're trying to be in people's face about it. We just mention it as part of our life, like we do anything else.

If you go to my site you'll see a video of me trying to get my dog to stay down. You'll see that on my site. It's just because I do that kind of weird thing. You'll see pictures of me with Darth Vadar or something. I'm sharing parts of my life, and Jesus is part of my life, so I'm going to share it. I think a lot of people don't do that because they're so afraid that they're going to offend someone and that someone's going to get mad and someone's going to leave. What they don't realize is that's okay, because everybody doesn't need to be my customer. I don't need everyone to be my customer. That again comes back to a little bit of the faith that I do have, and that is that if everything I put my hand to prospers, God's going to bless me with the right customers for me. In marketing and business we should have an attitude that it's not just about finding customers, it's about sorting customers. It's about finding customers and then sorting them to have the ones that should work with me, and then sorting out the customers that I don't want, because I don't want every customer. Some customers are too much hassle.

Here's something that's really funny. I told you one of my best friends is an agnostic. Have you ever noticed that an atheist is usually an agnostic with lots of anger issues? One of the pastors I've had always likes to say that he doesn't believe in atheists. Someone says, "I don't believe in God." He says, "Well, I don't believe in atheists." I think it's really that atheists are agnostics who have lots of anger. Have you ever noticed that somebody who comes after you and tells you that they're an atheist, usually it's because they've had anger issues about it. But the agnostic people are people who are honestly asking questions in most cases, because that's what they're saying is, "I don't know." There are two different attitudes. I've never had someone who's said they're an agnostic get upset about anything, about Jesus or anything else. They just see that as part of who I am. But an atheist would probably not be a very good customer of mine, because at some point in time – because of who I am and how I talk and what I say – I'm going to make them angry because they have those anger issues. They already had the anger issues before they got to me, and I don't want them taking them out on me. I would like to sort them out before they ever become a customer, because there are more than enough customers in this world for me. There's more than enough customers for you, and you don't want them all as customers. You're a copywriter, and as a copywriter there would be a lot of customers you don't want.

BEN SETTLE: I actively fill sales letters with verbiage to turn off the people I don't want. You're exactly right.

TERRY DEAN: We do this all the time. There's customers we do want and there's customers we don't want. Somebody who actively hates God and hates Christianity is not the right customer for me. They just aren't. I don't want them. I have no problem mentioning Jesus in my business at some point, because I don't mind turning those people off. I told you the one issue I do have about mentioning Jesus is the fact that there's been so many scam artists who use God as a crutch, so that's always entering into my mind when I do it, that I do it ethically and correctly if I'm going to mention God in any way. It's not an issue of who I'm going to offend or not, because the people who would really get offended at it, they would never be good customers for me anyway.

BEN SETTLE: And you may actually get more customers because those who are looking for someone who's a Christian – I mean, people like to buy from people like them, and more Christians are going to be attracted to that most likely.

TERRY DEAN: Yeah, and by that connection you'll have more connection with each other. They'll stay longer, they'll be better customers, and they'd be people that you'd have fun talking to anyway. We always talk about having fun in your business. I know some business people who hate their customers. That's not where you want to be.

BEN SETTLE: One of the things that you're really good at is joint ventures. I've learned a lot from you about joint ventures. First of all, what is a joint venture and how do you approach doing them, specifically as being a Christian. I know that some people may wonder, "Should I work with this type of person or that type of person?"

TERRY DEAN: Basically a joint venture means that you have an asset of some type. We'll say that you have a list. It's an easy way to explain it. Then somebody else has an asset. Maybe they have a really good product for your list, and you team up to offer it together. You take their product and you offer it to your list and you split the money. That's what we call a simple joint venture. A joint venture I've done a lot of before is getting with someone who has information that I know my audience wants, and you put a product together. Maybe it's me interviewing them, maybe it's some type of joint venture with a teleseminar or webinar together – the reason being is I have a really good skill of making things simple. That's what I do. If you want something complicated, don't come to me because I probably won't even understand what it is. I make things simple. I'm really good at interviewing people and making things simple as we discuss them, and that's what I'll do. That would be a joint venture. I take that skill that I have to make their process simple, we take their information, and we put it together to create a product. That's another type of joint venture. There's a lot of different variations to what joint ventures could be, and we could talk about it for hours, but we're not going to. As a Christian, when I start thinking about joint ventures, the #1 thing to me is does this person have integrity that I would feel okay inviting them – as you said, and this is probably a really good example; would you send this letter to your mother – would I feel okay introducing this person to my mother? Now think in the internet marketing field, who all would you feel okay introducing to your mother? Sometimes that cuts out a lot of people. In our market, I don't have to say it, it probably cuts out 80–90% of our market. That's people who could be joint venture partners. Would you trust them in going over to your mother's? I have a friend who says he picks his partners by who he would trust with the keys to his house.

BEN SETTLE: That's a good standard. That's even a better standard I think.

TERRY DEAN: "Here's the keys to my house," because that's what you're really giving them. You're giving them the keys to your business, because whatever they do, it reflects back on your business when you're a partner with them. If they mistreat your customer, then you're the one who gets in trouble. I'll say this, I've been in joint ventures before where something broke down. It wasn't the partner's fault. Something broke down, lots of orders came in, maybe his support went down – and you know where all the customers go if they can't reach the other partner? They go to you. It's up to you to also handle it. If they let something go in integrity, you're the one fulfilling it. For example, let's say that you sell a product to your list. There's been a couple times when I sold a product to my list – one of those mistakes I've made, where I partnered with someone I shouldn't – and the product had a refund guarantee and the person did not honor it. I gave the refund out of my pocket. You think I ever did business with those people again? No way! You're still the one who's responsible for it, because you still have to do good even if they did not. More than anything else it's the integrity.

Then the second thing after they have integrity is do they have something that really is going to be a winning deal for your customer, for their customer, for them – can everyone be profitable, and is it the right image that you want to portray. We're looking for deals where everybody benefits and everybody makes money. There's that money issue again. I'm not going to do a joint venture that doesn't in some way profit my business and profit my customers. I'm not going to give anybody charity. I'm not promoting your product just because you need help. I've actually gotten a lot of those emails. That's one of the disadvantages of people knowing that you're a Christian, is I've gotten tons of emails that people send me saying, "I really need help. If I don't make money by next week

I'm going to go broke. Will you promote my 'How to make a million dollars online' course?" You laugh because you know the set-up there, and you've probably seen it too. There's a lot of people selling courses on how to make money when they've never made any money. The other deal with joint ventures – and here's a big tip – is the more money the person promises you to make when they first contact you, the less likely it's going to work. It's less likely they're a person of integrity if they're promising you to make a ton of money on their first contact.

BEN SETTLE: They don't know anything about your list. How could they even promise that anyway?

TERRY DEAN: They don't know anything about your list, they don't know how big your list is, they don't know what they buy. I know what my list buys and I know what they don't buy, and I can tell you that if I sell something, they buy ten times as much of it as even if I sold your stuff. It's kind of a sad thing. If I were to endorse your stuff to my list, Ben, I would make 1/10 the sales as if I sold my own stuff.

BEN SETTLE: That's so true. People don't understand that until they've actually sold their own product to their own list. They'll say, "Why am I selling someone else's stuff?"

TERRY DEAN: I still do it. If I think it's going to benefit my audience – so in other words it's that win/win/win deal – I'll do it, because the truth is I don't come out with enough products for my list to buy. They'll buy more than I can come out with, so I can offer other people's offers to my list. The same thing with other people. They can offer my offer to their list. Here's the other deal that comes up. It doesn't happen in all markets, but it happens a lot in our business–to–business market because people know about joint ventures, and that is there's a reciprocity. If somebody promotes your product to their list, they immediately expect you to promote theirs to your list, even if you never said anything about it. That made me a few enemies over time, but remember me saying that I have no feelings of guilt? If I did not promise to promote your product, even if you and I were doing a joint venture, if you called me and said, "Hey, I want to promote your product to my list," I'd say, "Okay, I'll give you this much money," and it's a great deal and everything else and you do it. If the next week you call me back and you expect me to promote your product, I might do it, I might not, but there will be no feelings of guilt that cause me to do it.

BEN SETTLE: The worst case of that – and this one seems not to be as often, but it was a for awhile, and I think Michel Fortin even ranted about this once – is I will interview you for this, and then I'm expecting you to promote this interview to your whole list, which will drive people to my site and build my list for me, just because I interviewed you and 100 other people. They think everybody's just going to automatically mail their list about it.

TERRY DEAN: Here's the thing. You don't assume anything from it. Most of the people I do joint ventures with, we don't have a written contract. Most of them we don't. I trust the people, we do the deal, and again, I deal with people I could give my keys to. We trust each other. It's kind of funny, the kind of people I run with, we all know this, and that is whatever deal we make, we keep whatever promises we made. Don't assume anything else out of it. If I agree to do an interview with you, that means I will show up for the interview. I will be on time. I will do what I promised. I will do my best at whatever I promised to do, but don't assume anything else. I'll do what I said I was going to do.

BEN SETTLE: It's funny because that just have happened recently where the person said, "When are you going to mail it out?" Did I say I was going to mail it out or did I miss something? It's that entitlement mentality again.

TERRY DEAN: It is. I do what I promised I'm going to do. I don't have to do anything else. Just because somebody else did it for you doesn't mean anything to me. If you're trying to lay a guilt trip on me, that immediately just lost you a ton of points. It doesn't work here. That's one issue with joint ventures. You've also got to think is that going to bug you. If this person promotes my product to their list, do I love their product enough that I would promote it to my list? Then when they come back to me and ask me to, am I going to feel like I have to do it, even if I didn't say so? That's something you've got to think about here also, is a lot of people are going to immediately expect you to do the exact same thing, no matter what else is agreed to. I will promote your product only if I feel it's the right match for my list, and even then there's the possibility I might think you have a really good product and I still don't want to promote it because I've promoted three products like that and nobody ever bought anything and I don't want to waste our time. That's a possibility too. You've got to keep that in mind when doing joint ventures also, that whatever we say we're going to commit to, but the person who you're doing the partnership with, they might not always have that same attitude. They might be assuming something else into the deal. How are you going to stand with that? Are you going to still stand strong? With some people's products, I would see that as a negative, promoting their product, because their product isn't very good. There's a lot of products in our market that sell for $2,000 that don't have any more content than a $20 book. They're putting a bunch of fluff into the $20 book and just making it bigger. I'd rather just have the book. That's another tip that I think is funny in this market, that people say, "Well, you know, if you buy a $2,000 product and you learn one thing in there that earns you $10,000, then it was a great deal." They forgot the time I had to spend to go through the 80 hours of the course to find the one thing, when I could have found three other tips in those books sitting on my shelf.

BEN SETTLE: Not to mention the 17 DVDs and the five workbooks that often come with those big products, it's crazy.

TERRY DEAN: I even think about that. Is it a fair price for my list? Is this what they want? Somebody else's attitude of what a fair price is and mine might be different from what I think it should be. I always say with everything we do, there's a balance of what we need to do. That's where somebody could have a totally different aspect of it. Somebody else might think that a price for a product is fair, and they could be right. I might think it's different and we could have a disagreement. You and I could have an honest disagreement on something where we think something's right or something's not right, especially like in price issues, because that's not really an ethical issue, unless it's the fact that you're cheating someone. We could have a different issue there. One of us could have a product that the other one thought was over-priced and you don't want to promote that. That doesn't mean that the other person is bad or the other person is good. Your ethics for your business are your ethics between you and God. Again, remember we can't judge anybody for it, so that's an issue that comes in here as well when you're doing a joint venture. Are you comfortable with every point of the joint venture? Is it right for you? Is it right for the partner? Is it right for all of your customers who are involved in it?

BEN SETTLE: In what I'll call your struggling days, when you were doing the small house church and doing the pizza job and everything, let's say someone's in that same position. Maybe they're trying to do a church or maybe they're just trying to start a business online or offline. It doesn't matter, but they're in that same spot. What would you do if you could go back in time and maybe give some advice to yourself, knowing what you know now?

TERRY DEAN: At that point in time, once I actually bought the computer and started moving, I don't think I would have really done much different. The best advice I could have given was probably focus on some specific issues to help me move along better, but a lot of the same processes I would have done back then. When I first got started I worked like an insane person. I delivered pizza and I worked after delivering pizza, which meant some 12-hour days when you add the two together. I did whatever it took in testing and doing everything else, and I'm really happy about those days of learning. All I really would have done is give myself advice on a few of the specific things that I could have avoided, or maybe some of the specific things that I wasn't doing accurately. One of the things I would have told myself is start building the stinking list on day 1 instead of six months into it, because that's where the money came from anyway. That still is my advice today, so everybody who's listening, start now. The money is still in the list. It's not in social media, it's not in the blog, it's in the list. The purpose of the social media, the purpose of the blog, the purpose of the search engine traffic is to get the list. That's where the money's at, and it's easy to be distracted from that. That's one thing with all my coaching clients. I make them put it on a little card and put it by the computer. "The money's still in the list." That's how we say that – the money's still in the list – because it's easy to be distracted from that today especially, with all the social media and everything else. If you're reading this, write that down. "The money is still in the list." Write it that way, because somebody's going to come to you and they're going to tell you, "Hey, if you build up 100,000 Twitter followers you're going to make a ton of money." Then you can read your card that says, "The money is still in the list." No matter what you hear, that's what you still say to yourself. That's what I would have told myself from day 1 that I didn't learn till like six months down the road.

BEN SETTLE: And even someone who's doing maybe an offline business, they might get caught up in thinking it's the product, when it's really the list they're trying to build first.

TERRY DEAN: Yup. Even most of the corporations have caught up on that. How many stores do you go to that they don't ask you for your email address and other stuff?

BEN SETTLE: I know, it's crazy. Every retail store, if all they did was that, they would double their business probably.

TERRY DEAN: A lot of them have started catching on to that. A lot of them are doing it now I've noticed. I was with my wife at a department store the other day and they said, "Can I have your email address so we can send you some coupons?" and she said, "No." They said, "But we need your email address to put into the computer." "No." [laughing] The lady like freaked out. I don't know if the computer wouldn't work if they didn't put an email address in there.

BEN SETTLE: That's funny. You're right. I was just thinking Radio Shack is really good at this.

TERRY DEAN: They are very good at it. People don't have to give you their information, but you want that list to build a relationship with the customers. Online that's really all we have is our list. In person or in a brick and mortar store you have that personal relationship that comes in. You have an email list, you can build a direct mail list, you can build all these different pieces and they're all a part of your list, and that's still where the money is, is in that list. It's not in the product, because your product can be copied. Just ask Wal–Mart. Your product can be copied.

BEN SETTLE: Yeah, and price can always be beat.

TERRY DEAN: They can beat your price badly. People always complain about that and I don't understand that complaint. Wal–Mart comes into an area and all these small businesses go out of business. All Wal–Mart did was get rid of all the people who didn't know how to build customers. That's all they did. I always think it's funny. I shop at Wal–Mart because I live in a suburban/country type area and don't have a lot of other choices in some of the minor things, but that doesn't mean that we don't also shop at all the small businesses, the ones who have better service, the ones with other features. They still get your business if they build that relationship. It's not based on the product. People get mad at Wal–Mart because they think it's all about the product and it's not. Some things are all about the product. Basically if it's a little commodity product that can be bought anywhere, Wal–Mart's going to win, but with everything else there's an emotional connection with people we're doing business with. There's an emotional connection to stay with the people who provide better service, who provide the better customer service, who work with them on the issue. Something that people don't need to complain about is the big competition coming in and crushing them if they're building that list and building the relationship with the list. That's another advantage we have as small businesses. We already talked about the fact that I don't need everybody to be my customer. You know how many customers Wal-Mart needs? You know the overhead that they have? They have a ton! I don't need all those people. I need a much smaller portion of customers to live a very happy life, have a very good business, so I can have those that identify with me that want to build a relationship with me. It's so funny that we hear all about the recession going on, yet you look at it and a lot of companies are still profitable. I deal with clients who are in all different industries. When the government first announced we were in a recession, most of the sales dropped for about two or three months, but the majority of them were back at normal sales after that little two-to three-month scare period, and it's like it hasn't existed. My clients have not noticed the recession except during that point when the government first announced it. I don't even know what's going on with that. That's another reason we should all ignore the news.

BEN SETTLE: Let's talk about that, because I think that's extremely good advice. Just turning off the news can clear your mind in so many ways. Is that something you recommend all your clients do?

TERRY DEAN: I don't have cable TV. People are shocked by that too. I don't have cable TV at all. I have a big TV. I get Netflix because I watch movies. Netflix has a nice instant download you can watch on your TV. I watch it on my Xbox that goes onto my TV, so I can watch movies whenever I want and I get those DVDs in the mail. I don't have TV or cable, so you know what that means? I never get the news. I don't even know what's on the news. I've got a local newspaper here that I paid for the whole year. After reading it for about two weeks – we just moved to this area so we were like, "Hey, let's learn about this area" – I got the paper for about two weeks and I said, "This sucks." I called them to quit delivery and said they didn't need to refund me anything. I just said, "I'm tired of going out and picking it up, so don't send it to me anymore. You can keep my money for the year. I just don't want it." They were shocked about that. I told them, "Just keep my money but don't send me any more papers because I have to walk out, bend over, and pick it up. It's not worth it to pick it up."

Online I do glance at Google news when I log into my Google account, so I do see the basic news. I know what's going on in the world. I know what movies are out and things like that. I know basic things like that of what's going on. If there was actually a war started I'd probably see it on my Google News when I went in, big news like that. If Washington DC got a nuclear bomb attack I'd probably see that on my news when I logged in. The way I actually live with my news, if Washington DC was actually bombed with a nuclear bomb, I wouldn't know about it until tomorrow. I don't see any other news except when I log into Google accounts because I see the news on the side of the page, and I'm sure I would notice that headline. That's how much I basically turn off the outside news and everything else, because people think that the news is there to tell you what's going on. No, the news is actually entertainment. Like people will say, "Fox News is biased." Then the conservatives will tell you that the other news media is biased. You know what? They're all right, because all the news media is run by people who are marketing to a specific group of customers, and you're not going to hear them give news that disagrees with their sub-set of customers.

BEN SETTLE: That's true, and it's funny because the Fox News people never want to admit that the owner campaigned for Hilary Clinton.

TERRY DEAN: They would never admit that.

BEN SETTLE: They're serving their market. That's all they're doing.

TERRY DEAN: All the news media are serving their market. They're all biased because they're human. Even if they tried not to be biased they couldn't, because we all have opinions. Unbiased reporting is impossible. It's just totally impossible.

BEN SETTLE: They can't even do it with the weather anymore – they slip in something about so-called manmade climate change, global warming or whatever instead of just saying it's going to be hot or cold, rain, snow, etc.

TERRY DEAN: The weather's biased! I live in Florida, though. We don't have to look at the weather. It's going to be hot, it's going to be sunny, and it's probably going to rain somewhat, so I don't even need to look at the news for the weather. That's a running joke at our house. She'll say, "Hey, what's the weather today, since you're on the computer?" I'll say, "It's going to be hot and sunny and it's going to rain this afternoon." I don't even look at it. That's just what happens here. That's the same thing if you like to look at the news. You know what's going to happen if you watch the news? You're going to find out about how the bottom's falling out on something, there were three car wrecks, and something else happened. That's what you're going to find out about. It's going to be like that every day, because what's that old saying? The media says "If it bleeds, it leads." Then they're going to tease you with what's coming. That's another one. I don't know how anybody watches the news anymore compared to YouTube or something. They'll tease you about what they're going to show you 30 minutes later. "Hey, you want to hear about how these 15 people lost 475 pounds? We'll be back in a minute." Then for 30 minutes you've got to watch crap, when you could have just gone on YouTube and looked it up.

BEN SETTLE: Yeah, it's almost obsolete at this point.

TERRY DEAN: I could have watched three minutes of that section, so that's another issue. I don't watch the news and I recommend people stay away from the news totally. Even on the Christian side, I recommend that people take time – and don't do this all the time – but take time where you don't read any Christian books, you don't really listen to any Christian minister, but take a month or so and just read your Bible.

BEN SETTLE: It's amazing what'll happen when you do that. You don't have that biased opinion to any certain doctrine or anything. It's just you and God.

TERRY DEAN: You'll sometimes find some really shocking things and some scriptures that don't make any sense compared to what you used to believe. Then you'll ask somebody about that and they'll give you some little simple answer that again does not make sense to what it says in context in this passage. Again, I think a lot of people have the attitude that God is crazy or something. He talks about 15 different subjects in the same passage or the same little section. If you go to some of the shorter books like Ephesians, Galatians and the others, the entire book is all the same subject. It's all writing about the same subject, because it leads from one step to the next. As writers we know that if you want to write sales copy or write an article or write anything else, we're leading from one section to the next. We're not just randomly inserting facts about totally unrelated subjects, yet that's the way people look at the Bible. Like God just randomly inserted something that doesn't make any sense here, when it really has to do with whatever subject is being talked about.

BEN SETTLE: There was a guy I interviewed for this book named Matt Gillogly, and we were talking about the Apostle Paul and how he was actually a very good copywriter, the first multi-step direct mail marketer. He was very persuasive in that sense and very structured.

TERRY DEAN: Yes he was. The one I think is the best example of his persuasion skills is the "statue of the unknown God" speech, which anybody can go and read that passage. He goes in and he preaches about the "unknown God." He doesn't come in and say, "Hey, you're all wrong. All these gods are fake." He comes in and preaches about the one statue they had up for the unknown God, because they were afraid they weren't worshiping all of them, and he just told them about the unknown God. He came in on their wavelength.

BEN SETTLE: Which is really cool. That kind of stuff, that's the whole point is getting into someone's mindset when you're selling them. It's not just coming out with guns blazing out of context with things.

TERRY DEAN: It's kind of funny. The pastor that I originally learned from on how important context was and how important it was to keep all scripture in context, just as a side thing a couple times he wrote sales copy letters for a couple businesses in his church and he was getting nice big royalty checks from them. He was an extremely good copywriter who had never read a single book on copywriting. All he had done was read the Bible. He just read his Bible and he knew the context issue. He drilled constantly, "It has to be in context. It has to be in context," and he basically drilled us all on this thing that everybody believed, because it wasn't in context to what everything else around it was. That's the thing that I do like from the Bible college I originally dropped out of, was the fact that they drilled heavy on knowing the background of different passages and who it was being written to. We understand as copywriters that Paul is writing to a specific church that had specific problems, that you can say you know what was going on in the city at the time, so everything in that book makes a whole lot more sense when you know what's going on there and why he's writing that way.

BEN SETTLE: Just like the figures of speech and symbolism and all that. When I interviewed Ray Edwards for this book, he talked about the meaning of "turn the other cheek." In Greek society, when somebody kind of slapped you on the cheek it was the most degrading thing you could do to someone. It was basically calling them the worst possible name. It wasn't necessarily physically assaulting them like a bully or whatever. All the sudden that scripture makes a lot more sense to someone who thinks, "So I'm just supposed to let somebody attack me if they pull a knife on me or something? I'm not supposed to defend myself?" That's an example of that.

TERRY DEAN: When you go through the scriptures, some of the things you might understand might have to do with that. You go and get background information. Everybody should get a basic Bible study program. It's so nice we have these different software programs. I don't even know which one I have installed on my computer because I've had it for years and years, but it has tons of books included in it and it has tons of different stuff that you can look up really fast. That's a tool that we didn't have years ago that makes things so nice. If you want a copy of scripture to throw it somewhere, you just copy and paste it out of there.

BEN SETTLE: Imagine that. They used to have to hand write all this stuff, and they had to do it very carefully one stroke of the pen at a time when they were copying it. Now we just copy and paste it.

TERRY DEAN: We just copy and paste, and if you want to find out what the passage is, you put your little section into the concordance and it finds it for you. Then you copy and paste the passage out. You can click another couple little links and it shows you all the background information on the passage. That's some big advantages that we have today, yet it seems that people know less about the Bible than they used to.

BEN SETTLE: It's less work now. It's more passive. I'm sure when you were in school, and when I was in school, we didn't even have the internet until my last year in high school. When you did a research paper you had to get the note cards and you had to go through books and you had to look up the things you were going to write about and write each note separately on the note cards. You had to actually learn something.

TERRY DEAN: Right, and we have other things. I have a Kindle and I have a Bible on my little Kindle. Now if you want to know what a Kindle's for, you put a Bible on it with all your study books, and now you know what purpose a Kindle has. Bible study books are huge. Study Bibles are huge. The Kindle's this little tiny thing and you can carry everything with you. You really see the purpose of a Kindle with the Bible.

BEN SETTLE: You don't have to bring a Strong's concordance and three study Bibles and the Bible dictionary. Just your little Kindle.

TERRY DEAN: You just type in the passage you want. You can go to it and do all your stuff on it. That's a great tool. I think my study Bible on the Kindle cost me like $5. We're talking very cheap, very easy to do to use a study Bible. As believers in business, I want people to think about that you are a minister, wherever God's put you, even if you don't tell people about Jesus, even if that's not something that you do all the time. You're still going to live your life, you're still going to be an example, you're still going to be a light that shines, so you need to spend time in the Word for yourself and you need to pray about your business. I have days that I do phone coaching with clients. Those mornings I always start out praying for my clients and that God would give me wisdom in speaking to my clients. If you have that attitude with God, He's going to share it with you. You basically lead your business by what God would want. That's something that we all grow in, we all learn in, and it's a real purpose to have.

The big thing that we already talked about is that people are afraid of loving money or they're afraid of being successful and of business, like it's a bad thing or something along that nature. Just have the attitude that God wants you to be a blessing. He wants you to be blessed so that you can be a blessing to others, that you can affect others, that you can really reach others, and think of your business that way also. Here's something that's kind of hard for me to say, but I've had at least a dozen emails like this, with people saying that they wanted to do something online or they wanted to help their business and they were praying about it. Then they went and searched on the web and they found me. I've had at least a dozen emails like that over the past few years. If you take that kind of attitude and believe, it puts a responsibility in your business also. It gives you a feeling of responsibility that this isn't just a business. This isn't just a way to provide for my family. This is a ministry and I need to treat this business like a ministry. I care about my customers, I care about my clients, I care about their welfare and what they get out of this, because no matter what service or product I provide, am I a business that God could recommend?

BEN SETTLE: There's a good question.

TERRY DEAN: That's a good question to think about. Are you a business that God could recommend? We all talk about referrals. That's the ultimate referral. And with that even, are you a business that treats your customers in a way that other Christians should be referring their friends to you, because that's how He's going to do it. God's going to refer people to your business through others. Are you the kind of business that God would refer because of the way you take care of your customers, the way you treat customers, and the answer there for most of us is, "I don't know," and that's where it comes into the ethical dilemma of are we doing everything we can? That's something I believe that we should never lose. We should never lose the attitude, "Am I doing everything I should as a Christian?" That's kind of a note that we could come near the end of as Christian business people. We should never lose that attitude.

BEN SETTLE: That's really good. How does spiritual warfare affect Christian business owners, from what you've seen and what you've studied and experienced?

TERRY DEAN: First of all, let me give you my take on spiritual warfare. Paul only told us to fight one fight. He told us to fight the good fight of faith. That's the only fight he ever told us to fight. He never told us to fight principalities or powers or any of the powers of the air. He mentions them and talks about putting on the whole armor of God, and the whole armor of God is all stuff that revolves around faith also. It talks about peace. It talks about our righteousness. It talks about the Word in the armor of God. Our real fight is a fight of faith, nothing else. I know some Christians have an attitude that they're fighting something "out there." They're fighting the devil or they're fighting demons or they're fighting something that's trying to stop them, whatever they're fighting. But the truth is no matter what would want to stop you out there, Jesus already beat it. We are more than conquerors because He already took care of all those problems, all the powers in this world that would be against you. He already took care of them at the cross. He beat them. They've lost. They've failed. So since nothing else in this world has power over you because of what Jesus did at the cross, nothing has power over us. God could have power to make us do whatever He wants, but part of His love for us is giving us the free choice to do what we want. He doesn't make us do things. He leads us, He guides us, but He doesn't force us. If something is forcing you, then you have an addiction in you. It isn't God. That's something to keep in mind.

With the fight of faith, that means that since there's nothing out there that can control us or beat us, if we fail, that means there's only one side that's responsible. It's us. It might be because we should have never gone that direction in the first place. I told you I've had lots of failures, but they never stopped me. It might be because God never led us that direction. It might be because we didn't take a stand of faith, because no matter what we do, no matter what we're called to do, there's going to be obstacles. There's going to be something that gets in the way. It's never like an easy path. "Hey, if I'm on God's path it'll all be easy and there will never be anything in the way." Look at Paul's life and you'll see that was not true. "I was shipwrecked and I was in the ocean…and then I was in prison." You take Paul's daily routine and it wasn't always easy. Following God isn't always easy, but the fight of faith means that you keep on going anyway. You keep on having faith.

When I first started out, I started praying that God would give me wisdom and I believed that if I prayed for wisdom that would bring the money. That doesn't mean the money came the next day. It didn't show up as a check. It took time. It took me going through failures. It means that when you hit those failures, those mistakes, the things that don't work, you still have faith in what God is doing. I'll tell you this, this is a huge factor in whether people succeed online or not, and that is whether they have confidence and the desire to keep moving, even when failure gets in their way. That's a big key aspect of faith also. When you talk about spiritual warfare, that's where I move into first, is there's nothing out there that can stop me. There's nothing out there that can get in my way. There's things out there that can influence me, but there's nothing out there that can stop me. It's all on whether I stand on faith, I stand on God's Word, and I move forward in whatever He's led me to do. That's really how I see spiritual warfare more than anything else, is on that aspect of standing strong in the faith that God has for His business people. That's where it's at.

Your business is going to come under trial. Your business is going to have problems. As I mentioned earlier, Job had tons of trials at one point, and he had a business there, since he was the richest man. He had a business and he went through tons of trials through this and eventually gained it back. It doesn't mean that your business is always going to be successful. You might have a point that you go through with a whole bunch of trials. Maybe you're losing more money than you're making for a period of time, but you're still going in God's direction. That will take a strong stand of faith for you to get through and move through. Just expect at some point in time you're going to have those types of situations. That's where I really see the spiritual warfare going on. There's whole different groups when you talk about things like spiritual warfare. I think Christians can almost run themselves in circles because they're trying to fight demons or something else that's out there, instead of taking a stand in faith and stand on what God's doing and just moving forward.

Again, take a look at where Jesus went. Wherever Jesus was, He had authority. Wherever Jesus went, He was in control. You'll notice that when they put Him on the cross, the one thing He did was it said He spoke not a word. You'll notice that's the only time that Jesus was not in control was when He took our place. For the rest of His life He was in control. For Him not to be in control in that circumstance, He had to keep His mouth shut. That's how much wisdom was in Him. That's how much He had control over whatever situation He was in. He had to purposely basically keep His mouth shut and keep Himself out of the situation for Him to take our place. It's the same thing if you look at Paul going through his life. A passage that really sticks out to me with Paul is when Paul's sitting there in prison and he's discussing what's going to happen to him. As you read through it he's saying, "Should I go home to be with the Lord, which is better to me, or should I stay with you?" I want people to go and read that passage and read it with the mentality, "Why is Paul asking whether it's better for him to go or to stay when he's sitting in prison and they're saying they're going to hang him? Who's in control of that situation?" Paul's discussing this in his mind about whether it's better for him to go home or to stay. He's like, "I don't know which one's better," and then he decides, "I'm going to stay." He ended up getting out of that prison. He ended up not being put to death, and I fully believe that if he would have made the other decision, "It's better for me to go home," that would have been the end right there for him. Even in prison with them saying they're going to kill him, he was still the one in control of the circumstances, and that changes your attitude about a lot of things. No matter what circumstances we're in, we still, with God's help, control the ending. Go read that passage sometime. I can't remember which book it is. He's saying, "Is it more needful for you that I stay, or should I go home?" and think about that from the spiritual warfare side. Think about everything around saying, "I'm going to kill you tomorrow," and Paul's sitting there going, "Should I let them or not?" That's basically what he's doing there. "I don't know. Should I give up and go home?"

How many of us have had that situation when something's hard. "Should I give up or not?" But there was nothing in Paul's attitude about him having any chance of not being in control there, of God not being in control of his circumstance. I wouldn't even say it's that decision for him, because at that point in time he actually said, "It's better for me to go," so it's not him deciding if he's going to heaven or not. It's almost like God gave him the decision. I think in a lot of cases God does give us the choice in our life of what we really want. We have a choice of whether we follow the ministry He has for us or not, and I don't think that affects even our deepest relationship with Him. It does affect our results. It does affect our reward, I'm sure, when we get to heaven, but I'm sure He gives us a choice. At that point in time I think it was more Paul making the decision. "It's just been really hard, and should I just go to heaven now? Should I just let them win right now for the moment, let them finish this ministry right now, or should I continue on?" He decides, "I'm going to continue on." I think Paul has that kind of personality that he just would not quit, and that's an attitude we all need to get. We will not quit! I would say for running our business we have to have that attitude too. We just will not quit. That's a stand of faith that we have in God, that we have in God's plan for us, and that these mistakes won't hold us back and stop us. You'll never find anybody who has a straight path to success. It's always a zig-zagged path.

BEN SETTLE: Terry, where can people go to find out more about you?

TERRY DEAN: People can go over to www.MyMarketingCoach.com, where they can find out more about my online training business. You can find my free list that I invite you to sign up for. You'll find my blog, where I give constant free content several times a week, and you can find out about the different products and services I offer and the coaching that I offer for different clients. You'll find all that again at www.MyMarketingCoach.com. If you're interested just in the Christian financial side, I have a Christian financial product at www.NewChristianFinance.com that really has a focus on when I went and started praying for wisdom instead of finances, and goes along with that whole path. It's almost like the other side of the story that I talk about on the internet business side that you'll find at MyMarketingCoach.com, about how I came online and the different things I went through and how I learned to succeed online. NewChristianFinance.com gives you the financial side of that and gives you the Christian side of that and what was going on in my Christian faith during that time. It's like the other part of the story and it really talks a lot about how to get out of debt, how to walk in God's blessing, and how to find God's purpose for you.

BEN SETTLE: Finally, if somebody reading this is maybe not a Christian yet, maybe they were just reading this book and maybe this is their first exposure to it, or maybe they've been thinking about it – what would you tell them?

TERRY DEAN: They should pray right now. And here's the big thing about Christians. You know what we accept as Christians? We simply accept that Jesus paid the price for sin. We've all failed. We've all come short of being perfect. That's all you've got to say here, and everyone knows it to be true, that you're not perfect, I'm not perfect, none of us are perfect. We've all failed, yet God is perfect, so that sin separated us from God. Jesus came in the form of flesh. He came and He paid the price for that. He took our separation from God and basically He nailed it to the cross. When they killed Him, He took the death that we deserve. We all deserve death for what we've done, how we've treated people, how we've treated God and others. Jesus paid that price for you. I said early on that I'm delivered from guilt, and that's because He took that place for me. He paid it on the cross for us. As Christians, all we really do is we accept that He has done that for us, and that we could have never earned God's love. We could have never earned the position in God's family that has been given to us. It's just a free gift of grace that's given to us. Because of that, we accept the forgiveness of our sins. Pray to God and give Him your sin, give Him your life, in exchange for the life that Jesus had and that Jesus gave His life for you.

You'll see tons and tons of commands in the Bible, and you'll hear churches talk about all the rules, but God only gives us two commands – that we love God and that we love our neighbor as ourselves. Everything else hangs on those two laws. Those are the only two laws you have to remember – love God first, and then love your neighbor as yourself. When you pray, ask God to take your sins, take your life, and to help you do that, because that's not always easy and you can't do it without Him. Just like we said that the rich person couldn't go through the eye of a needle, it's impossible, loving God first and loving your neighbor as yourself. That's impossible also for us. We ask for God to do that. That's all that you have to do. Pray to God to come in and change your life, to make you a new person, a new creature, that you're going to follow after Him.

Then after you pray this prayer you're changed. Most people even feel guiltless when they make this prayer. You don't have to feel anything, but most people do feel that. As I said, you don't have to. Then at this point in time I really recommend that if you have any friends that you know are Christians, talk to them. Give them a call and let them know. If they're Christians they should be very happy about what you did, or if you have any family members. A lot of times you're going to find that people who come to the Lord this way, they've had family members praying for them. They'll be very happy for you to give them a call and let them know. You can know which ones have been praying for you, because they're the crazy people who talk about Jesus when you're around them. Give them a call and let them know!

Then I really recommend that you find a church in your area, not just so you can go sit in church, but a lot of times it's nice to find a bigger church because it helps you to change some of your friends that you hang out with, because sometimes the friends that you're hanging with, we all know from business also, that you often end up like the average of all your friends. That's true about your lifestyle also. It ends up the average of all your friends around you. Sometimes you need to change out some of those friends. I say the big churches, because usually the bigger churches have a bigger group of different people with different activities, and a lot of the bigger churches have tons of activities that likely have hobbies that would match up with you, and would likely have people whose interests would match up with you, and you can make some new friends to go along with the ones you already have. I'm not telling you to turn your back on anybody or anything of that nature, but do add other friends who'd be a good influence on you. That's the next thing that I would do.

BEN SETTLE: Terry, this has been a great call, man. I really appreciate you doing this.

TERRY DEAN: You're welcome. It's great to talk about the Lord. It's great to talk about business, and we had a good time.

Thank You For Reading!

For over 700 pages of <u>advanced</u> web marketing tips and secrets, please join our free mailing list at:

www.BenSettle.com